CONVERSION
TO JUDAISM

CONVERSION TO JUDAISM

LAWRENCE J. EPSTEIN

A JASON ARONSON BOOK

ROWMAN & LITTLEFIELD PUBLISHERS, INC.
Lanham • Boulder • New York • Toronto • Oxford

The author gratefully acknowledges permission to reprint the following:

"Divre Gerut: Guidelines Concerning Proselytism," prepared by the Committee on Gerut of the Central Conference of American Rabbis. Used by permission of the Central Conference of American Rabbis.

"Conversion Guidelines for the Rabbi," as drafted by the RCA Commission on Gerut. Used by permission of the Rabbinical Council of America.

"Guidelines on Conversion," as approved at the Annual Reconstructionist Convention on January 16, 1979. Used by permission of the Reconstructionist Rabbinical Association.

A JASON ARONSON BOOK

ROWMAN & LITTLEFIELD PUBLISHERS, INC.
Published in the United States of America
by Rowman & Littlefield Publishers, Inc.
A wholly owned subsidary of The Rowman & Littlefield Publishing Group, Inc.
4501 Forbes Boulevard, Suite 200, Lanham, Maryland 20706
www.rowmanlittlefield.com

PO Box 317
Oxford
OX2 9RU, UK

British Library Cataloguing in Publication Information Available

Library of Congress Cataloging-in-Publication Data

Epstein, Lawrence J. (Lawrence Jeffrey)
    Conversion to Judaism : a guidebook / Lawrence J. Epstein.
        p. cm.
    Includes bibliographical references and index.
    ISBN 1-56821-128-7
    1. Proselytes and proselyting, Jewish. 2. Judaism. 3. Jewish way of life. I. Title.
BM729.P7E66   1994
296.7'1—dc20   94-25

Printed in the United States of America

⊖™ The paper used in this publication meets the minimum requirements of American National Standard for Information Sciences—Permanence of Paper for Printed Library Materials, ANSI/NISO Z39.48-1992.

This book is dedicated to those
who have chosen to join the Jewish people
on its historic spiritual journey

Contents

Acknowledgments

It is with particular pleasure that I acknowledge all the help I received in writing this guidebook.

Arthur Kurzweil first gave the book its direction. Arthur knew of my interest in this subject and guided me to a way of presenting it for readers. No author can ask for more from an editor.

I have been researching the subject of conversion for a long while, so it is impossible to list all those people from whom I have learned. In addition, this volume includes material on basic Judaism, so proper acknowledgments would have to include all those who helped shape my understanding of Jewish life. Suffice it to say that this guidebook rests within Jewish tradition; it is a link in a very long chain.

There are many people I can identify as having made a specific contribution to this volume. Lena Romanoff, author of *Your People, My People*, is an inspiration in her dedication to the Jewish people. Every discussion I have had with her has yielded valuable insights for me. Egon Mayer, the foremost expert on intermarriage, sent an unpublished article and answered questions. I gathered important information in interviews with Dru Greenwood, Director of the Commission on Reform Jewish Outreach, Meryl Nadell, Director of Jewish Family Service of Metrowest, and Esther Perel, a couples and family therapist. Rabbi Stephen C. Lerner, as always, had much to offer in discussing conversion. I had an illumination conversation with Rabbi Neal Weinberg, director of the highly regarded Introduction to Judaism program at the University of Judaism in Los Angeles. Rabbi Robert A. Siegel provided valuable information, as did Rabbi Sylvin L. Wolf and Rabbi Bruce Kadden. I also received important information from Samantha Lindblad, who has written a column about conversion.

My rabbi, Howard Hoffman, is extremely supportive of my efforts in the area of welcoming converts, and his help is deeply appreciated.

Dr. Edward Hoffman provided encouragement and especially valuable advice.

Preparing a volume such as this one requires access to an extraordinary number of books and articles. The librarians at Suffolk Community College deserve special praise. Marge Olson, in particular, was indefatigable in tracking down the many hard-to-find books needed to write about conversion. Over the years, I have gotten material on conversion from a large number of libraries, including those at the American Jewish Historical Society, the American Jewish Archives, the Jewish Theological Seminary, the Asher Library of the Spertus College of Judaica, the Jewish Division of the New York Public Library, the Hebrew University of Jerusalem, the Hebrew Union College–Jewish Institute, Harvard University, and many others. Unfailingly, the professional staff at such institutions have been eager to help.

I would also like to thank the rabbinic groups within Judaism for providing their movement's guidelines about conversion. The professionals at the Central Conference of American Rabbis, the Rabbinical Council of America, the Reconstructionist Rabbinical Association, and the Rabbinical Assembly were extremely helpful.

This book could not have been written without the comments and suggestions from those who have converted. When I started this project, I sent out letters to various Jewish publications asking those who were considering or studying for conversion or who had converted to fill out a questionnaire. I was overwhelmed by the hundreds of responses. The stories told on those questionnaires were ones of courage and determination, of common sense and spiritual longing. These questionnaires provide eloquent testimony as to the sincerity and value of Jews by Choice. I have been able to include only a small fraction of the responses on the questionnaires, but I learned from all of them, and I thank those who took the time to write.

It is, of course, vital to have the support of family in order to write a book. My wife Sharon provides constant help and encouragement. Our children, Michael, Elana, Rachel, and Lisa provide evidence that the young enrich their parents in endless ways.

Despite the help that all these people gave, I bear responsibility for the material in this guidebook. In particular, the capsule version of Judaism in the latter parts of the book inevitably required making painful choices of exclusion. I daresay there is not one area where I could not have added more. The interpretative elements of the role of conversion in Jewish life are meant to be reportorial rather than controversial, but I am still sure there will be honest voices that disagree with what I have said about conversion in Jewish life. These are arguments for the sake of Heaven.

Introduction

This is a book for those who are studying to become Jewish, for those thinking about taking such a step, for those who have completed their conversion and are already Jewish, for the families and friends of all of these people, and for born Jews who wish to know more about those who choose Judaism. I will discuss why people have chosen to become Jewish and describe the conversion process. There is also a section on basic facts about Judaism and some suggestions to make the challenges of entering Jewish life seem exciting rather than overwhelming.

The subject of conversion is of special interest to me. I find it interesting that almost everyone I speak to assumes that if I am interested in this subject it must be because my wife or some close relative is a convert and my interest is an expression of support. In fact, my wife was born Jewish. I have no specific emotional reason to write about conversion. I have tried to think about why the subject is so important to me and have come up with several reasons. First, after an examination of Judaism's most fundamental beliefs, I have concluded that it is a religious obligation for Jews to welcome converts. Second, I was raised in a secular home so that when, in my early twenties, I reconnected to my Jewishness, I did so almost as an outsider; I had undergone a sort of conversion myself and so became sympathetic to those who literally convert. (In the literature, changing from one religion to another is designated as an *ecclesiastical conversion*, as opposed to my kind, a spiritual renewal in the religion of birth, which is designated as an *inner conversion*.) Finally, after meeting those who have become Jewish, I knew these were wonderful people and wanted to show my support of their choice.

Of course, most conversions take place in the context of marriage. That is, conversions to Judaism primarily occur among those romantically attached (as by engagement or marriage) to someone Jewish. In some sense, such a connection is misleading since so much that is interesting about conversion stands outside questions of marriage. Indeed, one of the most interesting results I found in questionnaires received from converts was that many of them emphasized that their choosing Judaism had absolutely nothing to do with a romantic relationship. Many of those attached to Jewish partners emphasized that their conversions were done not for convenience, but out of an honest search. There are important aspects of conversion (such as the conversion of minors who are adopted as well as individual religious quests) that need to be discussed in describing the phenomenon of conversion.

I also want to add a word about language here. Anyone who wants to write honestly about conversion is in a terrible ethical bind. First of all, there is the traditional dictum that once a conversion has occurred, the person is fully Jewish and should not be reminded of a prior status as a Gentile. However, in order to describe the emergence of conversion in contemporary Jewish life, and to discuss the post-conversion integration experiences and the fascinating stories of those who have converted, it is necessary to violate that dictum. However, this shall be done only with the expressed consent of the individual. All the people described in this book voluntarily agreed to have their stories told or made their stories publicly available elsewhere.

In addition, there is no clear language to describe people who have become Jewish. The word *proselyte* was used for a long while, but that is a Greek neologism, and is not widely used or understood. Many new designations have been born, such as "Jews by Choice,"

"New Jews," and "Choosing Jews," among others. Many of these are not linguistically felicitous. I have used the words *convert* and *conversion* to describe those who become Jewish. I have done so for several reasons. First, they are words that are widely understood to describe the phenomenon. Very few Gentiles understand what a "Jew by Choice" is. Second, their use provides for smoother reading and writing. I understand that some people find their use inappropriate, and I hope such readers will forgive me; I do not mean to offend but to help.

There is not much more exciting in life than establishing a religious identity. When completed, such an identity can serve as an organizing principle for the entirety of our lives, from our relationship to God, to our families and communities, to the values we live by, to how we measure the meaning of our lives. Such a search has the air of a cosmic mystery story, looking for the answer to life's riddles. I mean this book to provide an oasis on that sometimes lonely search, a place to find nourishment and support, a place to look for clues to help solve the mystery, a chance to see what Judaism has to say about life.

Sometimes after we read a great book or see a wonderful film or hear a moving piece of music we envy those who will read, or see, or hear it for the first time and learn of its beauty. Those of you new to Judaism are in such a position. You are going to be introduced to an exciting religious tradition. You are joining a people that has survived 4,000 years, been to every corner to the earth, had every experience available to a people, and has kept records of it all.

Some contemporary Jews have lost touch with their religious heritage and focused instead on their culture. That culture, too, is central to Judaism and so we will discuss it.

All Jews, whatever their beliefs, are proud of belonging to a people so rooted in history, so populated by interesting people, so fierce in its determination to survive and thrive.

Albert Einstein once startled an audience by announcing: "I'm sorry I was born a Jew." The audience was shocked until Einstein continued: "Because it deprived me of the privilege of choosing to be a Jew."

You who have that privilege are invited to read this book.

I
BECOMING JEWISH

1
First Thoughts

Some of you are considering becoming Jewish. Some of you have already considered the possibility and are studying formally or informally to join the Jewish people. Others of you have completed the process and are Jewish. Other readers care about you and are reading this book to find out about conversion.

Maybe the idea of conversion came to you one day while attending a religious function or maybe you were reading a book about Judaism and, with a shock of recognition, felt a sense of finding a spiritual home. Maybe you are engaged or married to someone Jewish and that person has asked you to consider conversion.

So now you sit, at an early or a late stage, thinking about what conversion means. The idea of conversion is an enormous one. In a crucial sense it is a reformulation of a personal identity. Such a step requires very careful consideration. That is where we must start. You are thinking about your past or future conversion to Judaism. Let's start with some stories, some reasons why people convert. There are a lot of different reasons to become Jewish. Before embarking on an investigation of conversion, let's take a look at some of the people who started where you are or once were and eventually became Jewish.

2
Why People Convert to Judaism: Some Stories

The woman across from me was laughing. She recalled her early days as someone new to Judaism. She told of the cascade of feelings, of joy at a new chance at life, a new self, and doubt about just how Jewish she really was. She described the residue of warmth she felt toward symbols from her past, especially a tree at Christmas, and her struggle to cherish the memories but not admit those feelings to the present.

The other people sat quietly in the room listening to her story. It was a meeting designed to begin a support group for those who have converted to Judaism. There were a lot of nods, some tears, and some smiles as shocks of recognition flashed across the faces of those who heard their experience, which they thought unique, being described by someone else. Others began telling their stories. As I listened, I realized that the stories of converts, romantic and heartbreaking, courageous and inspiring, finally speak to all people, not just to converts, not just to Jews. They are the stories of the search for meaning and love, stories at the center of all of our lives.

I knew that it was important for those considering or undergoing conversion as well as for those who have already completed the process to hear stories, to know their inner struggles are not signs of

weakness but of honesty. I also knew that it is important that those
of us who were born Jewish hear these stories as well.

I interviewed and received questionnaires from hundreds of converts in preparation for this book. I asked them, and many rabbis and
other professional experts in the field, numerous questions, but the
first one I usually asked—and the one they most frequently heard—
was the simple question: Why? This little question produced a lot of
stories of great human interest. I asked these people for advice, for
information about what they heard from a rabbi, about how they told
their parents about their conversion, about the particular challenges
of changing religious identity in contemporary America. Their responses inform all of this book. I have tried to include information
they told me new Jews most needed to know. I have tried to answer
the kinds of questions they faced.

I knew that, statistically, most people convert because they are
planning to marry, or are married to Jews, or they wish to have a unified religious atmosphere in which to raise children. But I found, first,
there were lots of stories from people other than these, and that, even
if a story did involve a romantic relationship, or a desire to raise children in a one-religion family, the stories beneath these precipitating
factors were more complicated. Still, it is important to note the basic
reasons for conversion before considering actual stories.

Here is a list, drawn from the research among various scholars
such as Egon Mayer in his many studies and Brenda Forster and
Joseph Tabachnik in their excellent study, *Jews By Choice: A Study
of Converts to Reform and Conservative Judaism*, of why people might
convert to Judaism.

SPIRITUAL REASONS

1. Judaism was seen to provide a religious worldview, or a set
   of values, or an ethic that was better than the religion or
   worldview previously held.
2. Judaism was considered important because Jesus was a Jew.

3. God was providing direction in some way to come to Judaism.
4. Judaism simply was coherent with common sense about what religion should be.
5. Jewish religious services were attractive.
6. Judaism's practices were very realistic.
7. Judaism provided good role models for a needed spiritual identity through biblical figures as well as contemporaries such as a romantic partner, friend, doctor, or employer.
8. There was a deep-seated sense of a religious void, and Judaism filled that void.
9. A specific personal event, such as a death, a divorce, or the breakup of a relationship, precipitated a religious crisis that resulted in a need to find a new religious self-definition.

ROMANTIC REASONS

1. It was desired that the children in a marriage have a Jewish religious identity.
2. There was a wish to be married in a Jewish ceremony.
3. There was a concern that children be raised in a unified spiritual home.
4. There was a desire to avoid inevitable fights over such questions as theology and religious observance.
5. There was a wish to please the Jewish in-laws.
6. The Jewish romantic partner would be pleased.
7. Conversion provided an opportunity to share the romantic partner's religion and thus bring the couple closer together.

COMMUNAL REASONS

1. Jews were admired for their survival in the face of adversity.
2. Jews were seen as forming a warm community, and it was seen as desirous to join such a community.

3. Judaism was seen as having a long, distinguished history and joining that tradition was seen as a worthy goal.
4. Jews were thought to lead better lives than Gentiles.
5. The convert had numerous Jewish friends.
6. The convert had a desire to identify with the Jewish people and become part of the fate of the Jews.
7. Jewish social life was seen as attractive.

PERSONAL REASONS

1. There was a belief that becoming Jewish would lead to gains in such things as status.
2. The idea of joining a new religion was seen as exciting.
3. Judaism had been a "forbidden fruit," so that becoming Jewish was exciting.
4. Becoming Jewish was a way of separation from birth parents.

STORIES BEHIND THE REASONS

With all these reasons, it is important not to forget that behind each reason lie many stories. Let me start by telling you some of the stories.

Sam and Cathy (their names have been changed to protect their privacy) were like any young couple in love; they simply wished to get married and be with each other. It seemed so easy, so simple a matter to declare their love publicly, until they told their parents. Sam's Jewish parents offered him $10,000 to forget Cathy. Sam refused to consider the possibility, and eventually his parents decided they could accept Cathy if Sam agreed to spend two years in Israel studying with a rabbi. At first, Sam refused this demand, but his parents persisted: "You are both young, and this will be a test of your love. If she waits for you and still wants to marry you, then you will have our blessing." Sam went to Cathy with the offer. They discussed it, and finally, reluctantly, they agreed.

Cathy's Protestant family was not happy either. Her father, a minister, joined the family in making threats. The possibility of Cathy's conversion to Judaism was raised, but it was made clear that such an option would not be accepted.

Both families met to discuss what they jointly called "the great problem." Cathy particularly noticed Sam's sister, "a sassy, spoiled little brat." No resolution emerged from the meeting, except that everyone thought the idea of Sam going to Israel was wonderful.

Cathy drove him to the airport on the day he was to leave. They embraced and swore eternal love. Sam sat on the plane and wrote Cathy a letter.

When he got to Israel, he continued to write every day. He never received a reply to those letters, and, so, desperate, Sam wrote to his family to investigate. They agreed to do so and wrote back saying Cathy was "out of town."

Unable to restrain himself after two months of hearing nothing, Sam returned to the United States to search for the woman he loved. He rushed to her house, only to be told by her parents that she was vacationing in Europe. They had told her such a trip would be helpful in getting her mind off her problem. They assured Sam that she would write him when she learned his address.

Sam left several of his letters for her. He journeyed back to Israel, awaiting word. It never came. Not a single letter from Cathy arrived.

Several months later, Sam got a letter from his parents. They told him very matter-of-factly that Cathy had married an old friend from school. Sam's mother suggested that Cathy was expecting a child.

Pained, uncertain about what to do, Sam finally flew back home again in search of Cathy. He went to see Cathy's parents. They told him to leave, but he refused to do so without learning where he could find Cathy. The parents called the police. Suddenly, Sam and Cathy's father began to fight. Thinking back, Sam reflects, "If the police had not arrived, I think I would have killed him with my bare hands. I was depressed, suicidal. Inside, I was like human driftwood."

Angry, unhappy, Sam did not know what to do except return to Israel. He found a cheap apartment in Jerusalem. The landlady, an older woman with three sons, was a widow whose husband had been killed by Arabs eight years earlier.

Sam worked hard all day. At night he drank himself to sleep. One evening he returned home and found the landlady waiting in his bed. He resisted her advances, but her campaign to seduce him continued. She would introduce him as her "husband." When Sam's parents came to visit, she embraced them warmly. His parents liked the woman. Sam says of those days, "I was not living; I was existing."

He yearned each moment to know what had happened to Cathy.

He would have been shocked had he learned the truth.

Cathy had returned home from the airport after dropping Sam off for his trip. Her parents greeted her with "a great idea." Why not go to Europe to get her mind off her "love-struck heart"? They promised to forward all of Sam's letters. Cathy loved museums and art, and so decided that as long as she could not see Sam anyway, the trip could be a way to pass the time.

Cathy went, and waited for the letters, which never came. Cathy wrote to her parents, but they told her that Sam had never bothered to write any letters. Cathy could not believe it. She wrote to all her friends, but no one knew where Sam was.

Cathy returned home, and her parents told her the news. Sam had gotten married in Israel and would not be returning. Cathy went to see Sam's parents and sister. The parents confirmed the marriage and told Cathy how happy Sam was. They refused to give her his address because they did not think it was proper.

It took a year of searching for Cathy to discover Sam's address. She wrote a letter, but did not mail it. "I was hurt and bleeding on the inside. My dreams had been shattered. I no longer believed in love."

Cathy changed jobs, but that did not help. Her parents tried to find someone for her to marry, but when she met those prospective love interests, she "made no effort to be nice or charming. In fact, I was rude and indifferent." However, Cathy's mother planned a marriage for her to the son of one of their family friends. Cathy never told her poor future husband that she loved him.

Cathy did get married. She and her husband slept in separate beds on their honeymoon. On her wedding night, repulsed by her husband, Cathy got physically sick.

The marriage lasted for four months before it was annulled.

Again adrift, Cathy rented a store and began selling hobby books. The time passed.

Four years after she had kissed Sam good-bye at the airport, Cathy was working in her store when the phone rang. It was Sam's sister. Cathy was shocked to hear from her because the two had never gotten along.

The truth came pouring out. Sam was coming back to the United States. He had written more than fifty letters, but the parents of both couples had joined together to destroy or hide the letters. Sam had never really married. Instead, he had been told that Cathy was married with two children and had moved to California.

Cathy sat down and cried. "The tears would not stop," she recalls. Sam's sister said she would bring her brother directly from the airport to see Cathy. On the trip, she would tell Sam the truth.

Cathy closed the store, barricading herself inside. She paced back and forth for four hours.

Then the knock came. Sam had arrived. For an hour they did nothing but hold each other and embrace, each refusing to let go of the other. Later, they began to talk, crying together "out of hurt and happiness."

The two, so in love, had never been intimate. They drove to a hotel, where they again declared their love for each other.

In the morning, Cathy awoke and quickly reached over to make sure Sam was still there. "The nightmare was over. The dream had begun," she says.

A mild breeze wafted through the open window, gently swaying the blue damask curtains.

Lying there in bed, Cathy decided that it was on that day that she would tell Sam her secret. Two weeks after he had left for Israel she had begun her secret conversion to Judaism.

There are few such dramatic stories involving love, although I received many stories about a conversion emerging from a romantic involvement. Yet, one conclusion that I drew after hearing stories was that, while it was the relationship that often led the Gentile partner in the relationship to look at Judaism, it was Judaism's values and beliefs, not the relationship, that was the impetus for conversion. That is, because no one has to convert in order to get married, in almost every case I examined, the conversion, while most frequently starting because of a relationship, did not proceed because of it. Joanne Stevens, for example says: "I found a religion with a fascinating, tragic, miraculous, amazing history, which fits the values, morals, and ethics that I hold. After putting my daughter Alexis in Hebrew Day School, I investigated the holidays the school observed. Reading Milton Steinberg's *Basic Judaism* late into the night one evening, I finished the book and said, 'My goodness, I'm a Jew.'"

Many people discovering Judaism for the first time are, in fact, shocked to discover that its beliefs and values are exactly the ones they hold. Sometimes the feeling of connectedness to Judaism is mysterious. I have a neighbor who once spoke at a meeting and called herself a "corrected cosmic error." That is, she felt she had really been intended to be Jewish, but somewhere along the way got born into another religion. Such a mystical feeling is more widespread than I realized. As Jodi Lewis put it, "I realized that I've always had a Jewish soul, and it wasn't until I discovered it that I really had a handle on who *I* am. I don't care for the term 'Jew by Choice.' I don't feel like I chose Judaism. If anything, it chose me." Judy Michelini once turned to a friend during intermission at a concert and announced: "I know this sounds bizarre, but sometimes I feel like a Jew trapped in a baptized body!" Carol Roth sums it up this way: "I truly believe I was genetically uprooted and born into the wrong family. Somehow in my past I came from Jewish ancestry and the act of conversion was really like going home to my roots." Often such a feeling emerges very early in life. Frances P. Molefsky says, "Don't ask me how, but even as a child, I had been drawn to Judaism. My ancestor, John Knox, the Scottish religious reformer, is probably still spinning in his grave."

This feeling of finally discovering one's true self was very liberating for these converts. Interestingly, sometimes it turns out that a convert has a Jewish ancestor, as Carol Roth suggests above. Sometimes, the ancestor is known, sometimes not. Julius Lester, the brilliant black writer, notes in his memoir *Lovesong* his Jewish ancestor, and that ancestor's effect.

One interesting story I heard involved a young woman who came to her parents to tell them of her desire to become Jewish and marry someone Jewish. Her parents were mildly upset, but warned her not to tell her grandmother who was deeply religious and would not accept the woman becoming Jewish. The young woman, who loved her grandmother, decided that she had to be honest about her life, so one day she told the grandmother. After hearing the news, the grandmother leaped out of her chair and went into her bedroom. Loud crying could be heard through the door. Upset, the young woman gently knocked at the door, went inside, and told her grandmother of her love and saying she had not wished to upset someone she loved so much. The grandmother drew her closer and said to her, "You do not understand. I was born a Jew. I have hidden this fact almost my whole life, ever since I married your grandfather. I never told your parents. Nothing could make me happier than you becoming Jewish."

Not all encounters with loved ones or others in the culture end so well. Dislike and even hatred of Jews exist. Yet, this very hatred, the very existence of anti-Semitism, even its most virulent forms has, almost ironically, led some people to become Jewish. Shoshana Stubin remembers a difficult past.

My father is Jewish; his family came to America in the 1840s to the 1860s and has almost completely assimilated. Knowing and caring little about Judaism, he married my mother, a devout Catholic. As he had nothing religiously to pass on to his children, he agreed to her desire to raise us as Catholics. I encountered frequent anti-Semitic slurs in parochial school from other children who knew my father was a Jew, and this made me very defensive, as well as curious to know more about Judaism.

Haviva Strugazow converted, in part, because she felt close to her father, a Jewish survivor of the Holocaust. She says, "I wanted very badly to perpetuate the fragile link to the past, and that is why I chose Judaism."

Her story is not the only one involving a relationship between the Holocaust and the decision to convert. Allyson D. Nesseler, for example, notes that "My father had been in the division which liberated Auschwitz. The Holocaust was a very real part of my childhood as a result of the books my parents had and my mother's frequent references to it."

Dr. Gilya Gerda Schmidt speaks very personally about why she decided to convert. "To me, the only meaningful way to respond to the crimes committed by my parents' and grandparents' generations was to help replenish the Jewish people. At first, I wanted to help educate non-Jews about Judaism, but I soon realized that there were many Jews who could use a hand. As a Jew, I have been working in both capacities."

Robert Frey, born in 1955, has written in his book *The Imperative of Response* about how his study of the Holocaust led him to convert.

Not all who come to Judaism because of anti-Semitism come as moral witnesses or victims. Some were anti-Semites themselves.

Take the case of Larry Trapp, at one time the Grand Dragon of Nebraska's Ku Klux Klan. Trapp started his spiritual journey in a most peculiar fashion. In June 1991 he made a threatening phone call to Michael Weisser, the cantor and spiritual leader of a Reform temple in Lincoln. According to published accounts of the incident, when Weisser picked up the phone, Trapp said, "You'll be sorry you ever moved into ——— Street, Jew boy."

Weisser immediately phoned the police. A tap was installed. For the first time, Weisser began to lock his doors.

The package came a few days later. It was filled with hate pamphlets from the Klan, Aryan Nations, and the American Nazi Party. Weisser looked at the material, and suddenly he began to think of Lincoln's most infamous racist, Larry Trapp. Trapp was widely known for sending such hate material. Trapp, in his early forties, was blind and confined to a wheelchair because of diabetes. His afflictions had increased the pace of his anti-Semitic activities.

Weisser discussed the situation with his wife. She made the startling suggestion that he talk to Trapp, but to do so in an unexpectedly pleasant fashion. Weisser got Larry Trapp's phone number. The answering machine included a tirade against blacks and Jews. Michael Weisser left his message: "Larry, you're going to be sorry for all this hatred, you're going to have to answer to God someday. Larry, you better think about what you're doing."

Weisser made his next phone call a week later. "Larry, you would have been among the first to be executed by the Nazis, because their first laws were against people with physical handicaps. You'd better think about how much you love those Nazis."

Frequent calls followed. Weisser would not quit. Finally, in October, Trapp picked up the phone and said, "Why are you calling me? If you're trying to harass me, I'll have you arrested."

Weisser was prepared with a response. "I'm not trying to harass you. You don't get around very easily, and I thought you might need a lift to the grocery store."

Trapp didn't accept the ride, but thanked him and asked him not to call.

Two weeks later, Weisser noticed an article in the paper. Larry Trapp had pulled an anti-Semitic program he sponsored from a local cable station, and was reportedly reconsidering his views.

Weisser called him, wanting to know if the article was accurate, offering to discuss the changes Trapp was going through. Trapp said he was doing all right by himself. There were other incidents, but finally Trapp called Michael Weisser. "I really want to get out of what I'm doing, and I don't know how."

Weisser and his wife went to visit Trapp. Weisser shook his hand. Trapp began to cry. He removed two rings with swastikas on them and handed them to Weisser. "I want you to take these away." The Weissers spoke to Trapp for several hours and left, dragging with them many cartons of hate literature, Nazi flags, and Trapp's robes from the Ku Klux Klan.

Trapp slowly began to apologize for his actions. By early 1992, Larry Trapp announced that he was studying Judaism. Eventually, unable to take care of himself, Trapp moved into the Weisser's home. Mrs. Weisser gave up her job as a nurse to care for Trapp. Larry Trapp completed his conversion to Judaism in June 1992, shortly before he died at age forty-three in September 1992 of diabetes. He was buried in a Jewish cemetery.

Such a case is, of course, rare, but not unique. For example, George Caudill served as area organizer for the Klan in Portland, Oregon. He had converted from his Baptist faith to Mormonism, and it was the Mormon leader, Dr. Ezra Taft Benson, who directly confronted Caudill and made him see that anti-Semitism was foreign to Mormon beliefs. Caudill eventually began to study Judaism, until he decided to convert.

Sometimes converts find in Judaism the answer to a personal need. Much of the psychological research on conversion (that is, about conversion in general; there is insufficient psychological research specifically on conversion to Judaism, although some recent doctoral dissertations contain fascinating material) points out the existence of personal turmoil prior to a conversion, and the promise of relief in the conversion. Some researchers believe a convert is on a quest for a perfect father (because the real father was absent, withdrawn, or aggressive). I did not find this sort of turmoil in the questionnaires I received, but many people facing a personal crisis found a new chance through Judaism.

Take the case of Carolyn. As in so many cases, the original reason Carolyn read about Judaism was a romantic relationship with someone Jewish. She says after that relationship began, "I started to read a lot of books. The more I read, the more interested I became in the possibility of converting."

Carolyn delayed until a personal crisis occurred. "Two years ago, I endured an extremely painful breakup of a relationship and, in order to avoid suicide, entered therapy. My therapist recommended two courses of action: attend meetings of Adult Children of Alcoholics and take instruction from a rabbi that might lead to formal conversion." She did and eventually became Jewish.

Ann also faced a crisis after the breakup of a relationship:

> After my divorce, which was very traumatic, I decided to take a path of discovery to uncover my spiritual roots and to get in touch with my authentic self. I spent about 5 years exploring other religions and teachings by study and experiences only to learn that they did not satisfy me completely. Then I "just happened" upon Judaism through a psychology workshop. I decided to study Judaism on my own. After 6 months of self-study, I was convinced that this was where I found my home, my religion, my spiritual self. I then met with a rabbi and studied for about 14 months.

Sometimes, converts struggled with their sexual identity. James, for example, says, "I decided to explore Reform Judaism because of its enlightened approach to homosexuality (along with other equally important issues). In Columbus's Gay and Lesbian Jewish *Chavurah*, there are three other Jews by Choice."

Lee Brannen is currently a prisoner in California, as is Brian Holbrook. Lee has completed a conversion while Brian is currently studying to become Jewish. Lee notes that he "needed something more out of life" and found, through a rabbi's guidance, the moral rules he sought in order to live an ethical life.

There were endless other reasons for becoming Jewish among those I have heard from. Susan Weisberger, for example, says:

> I found Judaism's rituals relating to death and mourning to be very comforting. Over the years I read a lot of Jewish books and gradually moved toward choosing Judaism. The catalyst for making the decision came after the hijacking of a TWA jet in the Middle East in 1985. When I heard the flight attendant's account of sorting Jewish-sounding names on passports from the

others, I found myself asking where I would be in that situation. I decided I wanted to be counted with my husband and son as a Jew.

Some people were initially attracted because of a Jewish friend or acquaintance. Sharon Sleeper, for instance, still recalls a patient she had as a nurse in the late 1960s:

I became very attached to a young patient with severe hepatitis. One day I came to work after having picked peonies for him. He was very ill, and I thought the flowers would make him feel better. At work I was told he had died during the night. I was crushed—we had worked so hard trying to save him. Two days later, I called his mother to express my condolences and asked when the funeral would be. His mother said, "We're Jewish, and David was buried yesterday."

Jean Lund also remembers how Jewish friends affected her:

At age 4 I had a "best friend" whose name I still remember. She was Diane Halperin, Jewish, and the child of a dentist in Pontiac, Michigan, where my father was a physician.

Nathan Rosenthal was my music teacher and one of the finest people I ever knew. His gentle guidance of the young, his marked sense of ethics in all his relationships, his honesty and true love for his pupils made him a most beloved teacher.

During this same time, a boy named Howard Weinberg was in our "gang." We literally roamed the countryside, riding our bikes to nearby farm ponds to swim and ice skate, exploring everything within five miles, hitching rides home on hay wagons and farm trucks.

Howard was a reserved, quiet boy, well-liked for his tact and grit. He would stop at my house to join me in the walk to school and we would hold hands completely unselfconsciously until we overheard our mothers giggling about it.

I knew that Howard went to Lorain, a distance of about 30 miles, for religious service, and I was mildly curious about it. All of us did notice a "peculiar" (for us) morality about Howard: he refused to cheat. When we blatantly cheated at marbles, when we passed around the answers to our algebra and geometry homework problems, when we swiped material to make our club houses and forts, Howard somehow managed to abstain without arousing our ire or ostracizing him. I remember his explaining that math was difficult for him and he had to work hard at it.

When I was 17 and Howard barely 18, he was killed. He had been drafted and went willingly into the Army after our graduation in May, 1943. In November he was in North Africa. Howard was among those taken prisoner, but he and two other soldiers were murdered.

The death of this gentle, most unwarlike boy, frightened of any violence but bravely facing it caused me to ponder about the maturity and morality in so young a person. I was ever after deeply curious about and respectful of his religion. I still miss him. I say kaddish for him. Our class will have its 50th reunion next year, and we plan special recognition for the memory of Howard and the three others who died in World War II.

While many people at the time of their conversion have a Jewish romantic attachment and therefore someone close who is Jewish, others recall having a Jewish acquaintance at the time of conversion who was also important. Frances Mann notes:

At the time I converted, I worked for a boss who was Jewish, and he told me a number of times how terrific he thought it was that I was converting. Over and over again my non-observant Jewish friends have said that they admire my persistence and knowledge. My conversion has made non-observant Jews think that maybe Judaism is worth checking out.

Many converts report moving spiritual experiences. Carol Pisetzky, for example, remembers

my first visit to a synagogue. It was summertime. Across the aisle
sat an older woman. She wore a sleeveless yellow print dress. I
saw the tattoo on her arm from the concentration camp. Sitting
there watching the Torah being carried through the congregation as people kissed it and touched it and seemed to receive
great joy from it, sitting there knowing that that tattoo was across
the aisle gave me an array of images. That day I caught a glimpse
of what Judaism is.

Rachel Garber says:

I fell in love with *Shabbat* and wanted to have that and all the
rest as part of my life. I was a mother's helper for a Jewish family
at a summer camp. The husband was a doctor, and he stayed in
Philly during the week. Every Friday he would come up to the
camp with challah and other baked goodies. The wife would
have a special dinner and they would light the *Shabbos* candles,
and I fell in love with that. I started taking books out of the
library. Nine years later I converted.

Books have played a central role in teaching potential converts
about Judaism. Sometimes specific books are remembered. Alexandra
Heath says:

I read *Exodus* not once but several times marvelling with admiration at the courage, defiant, tenacious bravery of Jewish men
and women who, with their backs to the sea, planted their feet
in the soil of Israel and wrote "Jewish Homeland" with their
blood and their sweat in the sand. Harry Kemelman's Rabbi
Small series of murder mysteries delighted me. Not only was the
protagonist a rabbi, but he solved the mysteries with Talmudic
logic, and I was granted a peek into the world of Jewish thought.
With Chaim Potok, I explored the world of two Jewish boys torn
by their inner callings and the religion that formed their beings.

The intellectual search for religious truth is summed up by Samantha Lindblad, who has written a column about conversion. She says: "To me, only in Judaism does one see true purpose and meaning to life. Only in Judaism does life and human existence make sense. As a Jew, I know where I stand. As a Jew, I believe in God."

These, then, are some of the stories, some of the myriad of reasons why people become Jewish.

Let us now look at how those of you at the beginning of your search can learn about Judaism and conversion and see if it is the right choice for you.

3

Getting Information and Advice about Conversion to Judaism

The idea of converting can seem simple and obvious to one person and overwhelming to another.

Almost every convert I spoke to and heard from expressed the view that the more learning prior to a decision to convert, the better-informed the decision.

If you are thinking about becoming Jewish, if your romantic partner (for example, someone whom you plan to marry) has asked you to consider conversion, or if someone else has, there are several important steps to take.

First, learn about Judaism. The second and third parts of this book are a very basic introduction to Judaism's basic beliefs and practices. Read some of the recommended books. Participate in some typical Jewish practices, such as lighting Hanukkah candles, or going to a seder on Passover. Talk to actual or potential family members, or friends, or others about being Jewish. If possible talk to those who have converted. Getting basic information is a first step to determine how you feel about Judaism. Most of those I spoke to were pleasantly surprised to find Judaism immensely more attractive than they thought it would be; they simply had never learned about it.

If, after reading, talking to Jews, and participating at some level in Jewish customs of the sort you wish to engage in, you should, according to those with whom I spoke, examine yourself. Dr. Holly Barrett emphasized the need to express fear and doubt. She said such an expression "makes the choice more solid, and finally more deeply carried." This is an important point. Unexpressed doubts are dangerous and can explode at a later date. Such a significant step as adopting a new religion and a new people requires careful consideration.

The single most common piece of advice I received from converts was that a person should not convert solely for marital reasons. Dru Greenwood, Director of the Commission on Reform Jewish Outreach, notes that marriage is a catalyst to learning about conversion. This is a crucial point because while there are a lot of reasons to learn about Judaism, including a romantic attachment to someone Jewish, the conversion should not take place without learning and without a real commitment to Judaism. Esther Perel, a therapist noted for her work with intermarried couples, distinguishes between a commitment to the relationship and a commitment to Judaism. As DeWitt Clinton, a convert, put it bluntly: "Half of all marriages dissolve, so a decision to become a Jew simply because of marriage should be taken very seriously, for if a divorce should occur, the convert cannot, in good faith, return to the religion she or he was born into." Ann Mudgett Hyatt expressed the views of almost all who contacted me in giving some advice for those considering conversion: "I would urge them to convert because it's right for *them*, *not* because their spouse or spouse's family insists on it. And, because my positive experience had so much to do with the uniquely wonderful congregation I found, I'd encourage them to find a congregation that fits them before they convert."

If you are romantically attached, your partner may belong to a house of worship in one particular denomination. If not, you should consider which of the denominations is appropriate for you. They are explained in detail in Part Two of this book.

At some point, you should consider meeting a rabbi. The rabbi is the religious leader of the faith community and can provide authoritative answers to your questions. To find a rabbi, check with a local board of rabbis, a local Jewish Family Services, your Jewish friends, or, if necessary, the phone book. While I will discuss the role of the rabbi at some length later, in this initial discussion, you should realize several things. First, rabbis, being human, vary in their attitudes toward converts. If possible, you should speak to several rabbis, unless you are lucky and immediately find a sympathetic one with whom you feel comfortable. Rabbis are very used to receiving calls from potential converts. They have heard all the questions and all the problems, and so, in most cases, can provide quick responses.

It is definitely worthwhile, as part of the consideration stage, to take an Introduction to Judaism course. Even if there is ultimately no conversion, learning about Judaism is simply interesting.

There are also various possible support groups to join, depending on the community where you live. Check with local synagogues and Jewish community centers. Dru Greenwood says such groups are not really therapy groups, but instead provide a useful opportunity during which to think about decisions.

Here are some questions for you to consider. You may want to write out your answers and discuss them with your romantic partner, friends, family, and other interested people.

1. How much do I know about Judaism? How can I learn more? Do I really want to learn more?
2. For whom am I converting? If it is for others as well, such as current or future children, a current or future spouse, is it also for myself? Is it just for them?
3. How will my family react to my decision?
4. Why do I want to become Jewish? What are the beliefs and values that Judaism offers that I find appealing?
5. In what ways does Judaism differ from the religion of my birth? Why is Judaism more appropriate for me than my birth religion?
6. What Jewish practices do I plan to keep? Is my romantic partner willing to keep these practices as well?

Without question, the initial probing of conversion can be confusing, with no set maps to serve as a guide. If after reading about Judaism and thinking about your own desires and motives you think you wish to keep going, you will be more prepared to do so.

To assist you as you begin your investigation, let's discuss conversion in Jewish history, conversion in Jewish life today—including the controversies, and the process you will have to go through if you decide to convert. After that, we can consider parents, partners, and in-laws; finding a rabbi; studying to be Jewish; and special challenges.

4

Conversion to Judaism in Jewish Thought and History

Conversion to Judaism has always been a part of Jewish life. It is a matter of some importance that the Jewish people begins not with the first human, Adam, but with a man and a woman, Abraham and Sarah, who were born as followers of other views. Although technically the word *conversion* is not correct, still when Abraham and Sarah became the ancestors of the Jewish people, they underwent an experience analogous to what we understand as a conversion. Indeed, the idea that Abraham and Sarah "gathered souls" as mentioned in the Bible was understood by later rabbis to refer to welcoming strangers into the religious family of Hebrews.

BIBLICAL TIMES

In biblical times, if people wanted to join the Hebrew people, they could do so simply by accepting the various practices of the community and giving up pagan beliefs. People often joined the Hebrews through marriage. There was not yet a full religion called Judaism, and therefore no official process by which the religion could be joined.

27

At this stage of Jewish history, "conversion" meant joining a people that had a distinctive religious view.

The Hebrew people developed their religion, as the Bible records, after their enslavement in Egypt, their escape under the great leader Moses, and their acceptance of a divine agreement made with God at Mount Sinai. Armed with the revelation from God to Moses and the entire people, the Jewish people came back to their promised land. Some people living in the land, the *nachri*, joined the Jewish people, while other foreigners, the *gerim*, became permanent residents, allowed to live in the land. Jews were enjoined to be especially kind to these *gerim*.

As Jewish history evolved, the meaning of God's revelation became crystallized. The Jews realized that God was not just the God of the Israelites, but of all humans. This idea became especially important when the Jews were sent into exile. (For a more complete understanding of Jewish history, see Part Two of this book.) Cut off from their national home, the Jews realized that God, being universal, could be worshiped everywhere. They also realized that if people wished to join them, those people did not need to live in the land of Israel, but could live anywhere so long as they followed Jewish beliefs and customs. Those who joined were called *nilvim*, that is, those who attached themselves to God, or *nivdalim*, people who had given up paganism.

The prophets, especially Isaiah, believed that Jewish views would in the future be held by all people, that Jewish morality would be applicable to all people. Jews were to follow their ritual and ethical teachings and simultaneously confront paganism, challenging its ethical shortcomings and misleading beliefs. Judaism, that is, was and remains a mixture of particular practices and a universal moral message. Judaism was supposed to be offered to the pagans, but it was not mandatory that they accept it. Indeed, there is in Jewish tradition the notion of a special covenant, or agreement, between God and Noah that lists the moral obligations for Gentiles, which is that they refrain from idolatry, incest, adultery, bloodshed, profaning the name of God, injustice (by the positive act of setting up law courts), robbery, and cruel acts such as tearing a limb from a living animal.

Judaism did not think that only those who were Jewish could achieve salvation; that was available to all those Gentiles who followed the commandments given to Noah. Jews believed that "The righteous of all nations shall have a portion in the world to come." Because of this view that no one has to be Jewish to be saved, there was no special need to form a mission to "save" pagans, or other nonbelievers. On the contrary, Judaism looked for the good in other worldviews, looked for ethical content and right behavior to praise it. Still, Judaism was to be available to those who wished it.

Of course, the most famous convert in the Bible is Ruth. Ruth was from Moab (an area east of the Dead Sea) and married Mahlon, a Jewish man originally from Bethlehem. Mahlon, his father Elimelech, his mother Naomi, and his brother Chilian had come to Moab to escape famine. Unfortunately, Mahlon, his father, and his brother died. Naomi, although old and tired, desired to return to the land of Israel. Her other daughter-in-law left her to return to her own mother, but Ruth would not abandon Naomi. In stirring words that have become an anthem for converts, Ruth said: "Do not try to persuade me to leave you, to turn back and not go with you. Wherever you go, I will go too. Wherever you stay, I will stay. Your people shall be my people, and your God my God." Ruth is especially important in Jewish history because she was the great-grandmother of King David, from whose line the Messiah is supposed to arise.

BEFORE THE COMMON ERA

There were evidently many converts during the years 323 B.C.E. until 70 C.E. (As you will see, Judaism dates history differently from other religions. B.C.E., equivalent to B.C., stands for Before the Common Era, and C.E., equivalent to A.D., stands for the Common Era.) In a very few limited cases there were forced conversion to Judaism. The Idumeans, for example, were converted by John Hyrcanus in 125 B.C.E. Such forced conversions were outside Jewish tradition, and the results of such types of conversion, bringing people into the religion who did not wish to join, had serious consequences in Jewish history.

Most converts, however, came on their own. Many had read some literature specifically aimed at winning over converts. This literature included such works as *Against Apion* and the *Syballine Oracles*. Other converts came to synagogue services and were attracted to the beauty of the liturgy and the morality of the monotheistic views presented. The idea of a universal, good, single God over all was a novel and attractive idea to many. Others came in contact with Jews, fell in love, and got married. Then, as now, many conversions came about because of a romantic involvement.

It is unclear whether there were ever any official Jewish "missionaries" in the sense that we use the word today. There were numerous Jewish travelers and merchants who, as they went, would meet strangers and explain their religion. At any rate, during this era very large numbers of Gentiles joined the Jewish people.

COMMON ERA

The Jews lost their second Temple in the year 70 C.E., and would not have their own nation for almost two thousand years. Without a nation and political power, the Jews had to devise a way to survive outside their land. They did so, as you will read in the next part, by writing down very specific religious laws in a body of work called the Talmud. (All religious texts are explained in detail in Part Two.)

The Rabbis who edited the Talmud generally had very positive attitudes toward converts. The most famous positive comment in the Talmud about converts was made by Rabbi Johanan (*Pesachim* 87b), a passage in which it is asserted that God exiled Jews from their homeland for only one reason, to increase the number of converts. It is a striking notion that so horrible an event as exile should be seen as having a divine use. That use—seeking converts—had to have been considered so valuable that it justified exile from the sacred, promised land.

The word *gerim* came to be understood as specifically referring to a convert. A conversion process and ceremony was established so that those who wished to join the Jewish people could do so.

There are some negative comments in the Talmud about converts. The most well-known one by Rabbi Helbo (*Yevamot* 109b) is that converts are as troublesome as a sore. However, even this most negative comment has been interpreted in various ways, such as that Rabbi Helbo was simply making an historical statement since Christian authorities punished both the convert and the Jewish community when a conversion took place.

Probably the most famous of all conversion stories in the Talmud involves two famous scholars, Shammai and Hillel. A pagan came to Shammai and, wishing to have some fun, asked the great scholar if he could learn all the first five books of the Bible (called the Torah) while standing on one foot. Shammai yelled at the man, telling him to go away. Still wishing to have some fun, the man then went to Hillel and made the same request. Hillel also saw the man was joking, but instead of turning him away, Hillel said, "That which is hateful to you, do not do to anyone else." The stranger, interested in this ethical idea, asked if that was the whole Torah. Hillel answered by saying, "That is the foundation. All the rest is commentary. Go and study." That is exactly what the man did. Hillel had taught a pagan about Judaism in order for the man to study the Torah and become a Jew.

There are some famous stories about conversion from this era. One involves King Bulan (786–809 C.E.), who ruled a people called the Khazars. According to one story, the king had a debate with representatives from all religions arguing their case. The king, according to this story, chose Judaism, and his entire kingdom converted to Judaism and followed their new religion until they were conquered in the eleventh century.

While the talmudic attitude toward conversion was generally extremely positive, and while the Jews absorbed relatively large numbers of converts, there were changes occurring in Jewish attitudes. Over a long period of time, Jews began to change their welcoming views. They eventually came to view converts with suspicion and did their best to discourage conversions.

The reasons for this transformed view are many, but mostly have to do with anti-Semitism. Roman, Christian, and eventually Muslim political and religious authorities passed very strict laws against Jews seeking or welcoming converts. A convert's property could be seized and the convert put to death. The entire community could be punished. Eventually, the community saw the dangers in accepting converts and did not do so publicly.

Another reason for the changing attitude was that Christianity and later Islam changed the notion of welcoming converts from the Jewish one of making the religion available, but not mandating it for salvation. Both Christianity and Islam taught that their religion was the sole path to salvation, so that conversion changed from being a voluntary act to one forced on people, whether they wanted it or not, in the name of saving them. Jews were repulsed by such activity and by the very idea of offering a religion.

As Jews became more isolated, frequently forced by their host rulers to live in squalid quarters, mocked, injured, even killed for their religious beliefs, Jews came to see Christians as an enemy and so came, over time, to think of Christians less and less as people to whom it was possible to teach the Torah. Additionally, to justify their separate existence, it was natural that Jewish thinkers emphasized the particularistic elements of their religion and let the universal elements wither.

As Jewish law evolved, the codes of Jewish law changed from a very pro-conversionary attitude to a more mixed view in the authoritative code, the *Shulchan Aruch*, which was written in the sixteenth century.

The idea of welcoming converts, once so powerful an idea in Judaism, once so widely practiced in Jewish life, lay more or less dormant for hundreds of years. There were, throughout Jewish history, individual conversions, but not in very large numbers.

NINETEENTH CENTURY

The idea of Jews being a light unto the nations, having a particular purpose to reach out to non-Jews, came back to Jewish life in the nineteenth century, introduced by some Reform Jewish thinkers. (The branches of Judaism will be discussed briefly in the next section and more fully in Part Two.) The early reformers wanted to make ethical monotheism known to all the world. The Conservative movement, while officially remaining open to the idea of welcoming converts, did not feel about a Jewish mission the way the Reform movement did. The Orthodox movement was split in the nineteenth century between those who were lenient when it came to conversion candidates and those who were more strict.

The most famous convert to Judaism in nineteenth century America was a man named Warder Cresson (1798–1860). Cresson, using a political connection, became the first American consul to Jerusalem. He went to the land of Israel in the nineteenth century, before there was a Jewish nation, to do missionary work among the Jews. He worked in this capacity from 1844 until 1847 until, overcome by the attractiveness of Judaism, he decided that he himself would become Jewish. He went back to his home in Philadelphia thinking his wife and children would be pleased by his religious choice. Instead, shocked at his views, his family charged Cresson with insanity and put him on trial. The sensational trial was reported around the country. In May 1851 Cresson was declared sane. Cresson divorced his wife, returned to the land of Israel, and remarried, this time to a Jewish woman.

TWENTIETH CENTURY

In the twentieth century, there developed, starting after the Second World War, small groups in American Jewish life that favored letting Gentiles know about Judaism and welcoming converts. However, such groups had little power because they were outside the structure of the large religious movements.

In our own time, however, conversion has become a very important part of Jewish life, as we shall now see.

5

Conversion to Judaism in Jewish Life Today

The importance of conversion in Jewish life came about directly because of the rise in interdating and intermarriage among Jews.

The Jewish community, forced into ghettos and other areas, separated from many of their neighbors across the centuries by religion, culture, and much else, faced a new situation in the modern world. Starting in Europe after the French Revolution, various countries began to give freedoms to all their citizens, including Jewish citizens. Such new rights were revolutionary for Jews. For the first time, they could, in varying circumstances, live where they wished, provide a general education for their children, obtain employment, vote, and meet their Gentile neighbors as civil equals. Nowhere was this revolutionary change in Jewish life more evident than in the United States.

Especially after the Second World War, American Jews emerged from their immigrant households, fought still-lingering anti-Semitism in universities and employment, and went in large numbers to prestigious Ivy League schools and to state universities. They moved to once-restricted neighborhoods in the suburbs of America. Their children went to school with Gentile children. They, themselves, worked with their Gentile neighbors and found much in common with the American character of hard work, desire for education, and a concern for family and faith.

INTERMARRIAGE

Inevitably, as Jews and Gentiles met, they became curious about each other's beliefs and practices and about each other as potential romantic partners. By the early 1960s, the very low rate of intermarriage had increased to about 9 percent, meaning 9 percent of Jews marrying married someone not Jewish. As high as this number was compared to the past (for a long time there had been virtually no intermarriages), it still was not seen as threatening.

Jews inevitably were concerned about their numbers. As a small people, making up considerably less than 1 percent of the world's population, Jews knew that each new baby, each Jew, was a vital resource for survival. Jews intermarrying were thought to be abandoning Judaism, so that intermarriage was seen as a loss of a Jew and therefore a demographic danger. In large numbers, intermarriage was seen as a real threat to Jewish survival.

Those large numbers, that demographic nightmare, began to emerge from the mid-1960s to the mid-1970s. From 1965 to 1974, 25 percent of Jews intermarried. Still higher numbers were yet to come. Between 1975 and 1984, the intermarriage rate was 44 percent. The most startling figure is that since 1985, the intermarriage rate is 52 percent; more than half the Jews marrying are marrying someone not Jewish.

These figures emerged in a population survey conducted by the Council of Jewish Federations. Their 1990 National Jewish Population Survey confirmed all the fears brought by earlier studies and anecdotal evidence.

Jewish visions of disappearance began to fill newspaper stories about the intermarriage rate. A loss of Jews would mean, it was asserted, a loss of political power, losses of a population to consume Jewish culture, to support Jewish institutions in the United States, Israel, and around the world, the shrinking of importance of Jews in American life, and much else.

Often overlooked in the intermarriage rates, however, were at least two crucial factors. First, many Jews who intermarried did not do so with the intention of abandoning the Jewish community, as had been the usual case involving intermarriage, but instead had simply fallen in love with and chosen to marry someone not Jewish. Thus, hundreds of thousands of Jews wished to remain as synagogue members, or participate in additional ways in American Jewish life, as through philanthropy, volunteer work, attendance at Jewish cultural events, or in other ways. The American Jewish community was not quite sure what to do with these people, and in many ways is still uncertain over how much participation by Gentiles is appropriate in Jewish life even when the marital partner is Jewish.

The second factor is that accompanying the romantic involvement of Jews to non-Jews was the rise of conversion to Judaism by the non-Jewish partner. Again, it is important to note here that conversions to Judaism for entirely nonromantic reasons also increased. For example, the very interaction between Jews and Gentiles that led to romance also led in some cases to intellectual curiosity on the part of Gentiles about Judaism. This intellectual and spiritual adventure has led thousands of Gentiles to convert to Judaism without any romantic attachments involved. Additionally, Jewish families have adopted non-Jewish babies and converted the infants.

Nevertheless, the large increase in conversions starting in the 1970s was precipitated, in about 90 percent of conversions, by the non-Jewish partner in a romantic relationship wishing to become Jewish in order to marry the Jewish partner, or, if the marriage had already taken place, to have a unified religious household in which, for example, there would be no religious confusion for children.

JEWS BY CHOICE

The Jewish community was simply confused by all this. First, Jews intermarried and still wanted to be Jews. Then, Gentiles, who for millennia had rejected Judaism, now wanted to become Jewish. Many Jews had been brought up to think there was something fundamentally un-Jewish about a convert, or that conversion itself was outside

Jewish tradition. Rabbis, trained to discourage those who came to convert with a stern discussion of the legacy of hatred of the Jews, of the difficulty of leading a Jewish life, were frequently surprised at the pure numbers of people coming for conversion.

In 1978, sensing the big changes in Jewish life brought about by the intermarriage rate and other factors, Rabbi Alexander Schindler, president of the Union of American Hebrew Congregations, a Reform group, suggested Jews actively welcome those he called "unchurched," that is, spiritual seekers not part of another religion. Rabbi Schindler thought it natural that non-Jews married to Jews would form a sympathetic audience for these efforts. Eventually, the Reform movement formed an outreach commission to oversee its efforts. Conservatives, seeing the increase in conversion, came to see the increase in converts as a positive new aspect in Jewish life. The Orthodox, however, were more cautious. Indeed, as the Orthodox more and more came to see significant distinctions between themselves and the non-Orthodox, they saw problems with conversion, problems that have led to serious confrontation.

Part of the problem was the sheer numbers of converts. The 1990 survey made by the Council of Jewish Federations estimates that there are 185,000 Jews by Choice in the United States. The term *Jews by Choice* is used by those who designed the survey to include both those who have formally converted to Judaism (about 70 percent of the 185,000) and those who have not formally converted but who follow Jewish practices and, for practical purposes, consider themselves Jewish. Many scholars put the number higher. I would say, using conservative estimates, that today there are probably more than 200,000 converts to Judaism in America. Put another way, it is probable that 1 in every 37 American Jews was born a Gentile.

This increase in conversions for a while resulted in a paradox. As conversions increased, it looked as though the soaring intermarriage rates would not result in the loss of Jews because of a high conversion rate. As it has turned out, however, the conversion rates have fallen, so that conversions, which were once estimated to have occurred in as many as 40 percent of the cases in which someone born Gentile married someone born Jewish, today occur in probably only about 6 percent of the cases. The reasons for this drop are varied, but most experts believe the major reasons are the increased acceptance of intermarriage in American culture, including among American Jews, the increased willingness of some rabbis to perform an intermarriage without requiring a conversion, and other factors, including the accusation by some that a change in defining Jewish status by the Reform movement contributed to the decline in conversion. This change of Jewish status will be discussed later.

EFFECTS OF CONVERSION

While conversion never turned into the weapon against intermarriage it was once thought to be, it has nonetheless profoundly affected American Jewish life in many significant ways.

The first important effect is that it has brought in hundreds of thousands of dedicated new Jews. It is no longer surprising to hear rabbis reporting that their temple's president is a Jew by Choice, that the leader in a United Jewish Appeal (UJA) campaign or the president of a Hadassah chapter or the rabbi of a congregation was born a Gentile. This tremendous burst of new talent has immeasurably enriched American Jewish life and given it new vitality.

The second effect is on those people born Jewish. Although some born Jews remain ignorant about the place of conversion in Jewish thought and history and, for instance, incorrectly believe that Judaism believes someone born Jewish is somehow more authentically Jewish than someone who chooses Judaism, most born Jews have changed their attitudes about conversion. Converts are much more widely acceptable as Jews, as marriage partners, as religious leaders, in every role in Jewish life. There is an interesting psychological phenomenon in such a born-Jewish appreciation of converts.

American Jewish life, because it is so free, is at its heart a voluntary enterprise. That is, American Jews have the freedom to abandon Jewish life. There is no formal system to prevent their assimilation. American Jews voluntarily choose to retain their Jewish identity when they could choose not to do so. Such a decision makes all American Jews truly Jews by choice. The decision to remain Jewish, to remain a minority in an attractive non-Jewish culture, is often painful. American Jews need as much validation of their choice as possible. Ironically, one of the principal sources of such validation comes from Gentiles who voluntarily choose to become Jewish. After all, the decision to choose Judaism, to alter one's identity, perhaps to confront one's family and friends, makes the decision to keep a Jewish identity seem easier. It also makes such a decision seem sensible. Seeing Gentiles wanting to become Jewish makes Jews see Judaism as more attractive, as a religious "product" that consumers are choosing to "purchase." Born Jews are seeing the value of a religion that many of them took for granted. The Bible speaks of the Jews being "a light unto the nations," showing them the way to a godly life. Rabbi Neal Weinberg, of the University of Judaism, once told me that he thought that converts were so valuable that they were "a light unto the Jews," showing all of us who were born Jewish how much we should appreciate the beauty of the religion we were born into.

Converts have affected organized Jewish life as well. Rabbis, perhaps more than the Jewish laity, recognize the contributions that converts are making and the sincerity of those undertaking the difficult task of becoming Jewish. Conversions were suddenly being widely praised, especially as it became apparent that in an intermarriage (that is, marriage between a Jew and unconverted non-Jew), there was a 75 percent likelihood that the children of such a marriage would be raised as non-Jews or without a religion, whereas in conversionary marriages (that is, marriage between a born Jew and a partner born non-Jewish but who converted) there was just the reverse: a 75 percent chance that the children would be raised as Jews. Scholars were at first, in fact, amazed to note that conversionary households were more likely to observe Jewish rituals than households headed by two born Jews.

CONVERSION AND THE DENOMINATIONS
OF JUDAISM

The increase in the number of conversions, then, has had an enormously positive effect on Jewish life. Unfortunately, however, there are difficulties as well brought about by the divisions within organized Jewish religious life. Those divisions have resulted in friction concerning conversion, among many other religious issues.

Although the divisions will be explained in detail later in this book as Judaism is explained, it is important for someone considering or undergoing conversion to understand this dispute early in the process.

In Israel and in most countries of the world, there is only one officially recognized denomination or branch of Judaism, which strictly follows the traditional Jewish law, the *halachah*. In the United States, however, Jewish life is more fragmented. There are various denominations. The three major ones are Orthodox Judaism, which is strictly traditional, Conservative Judaism, which follows the *halachah* but believes it is inherently susceptible to change according to current conditions, and Reform Judaism, which focuses not on traditional Jewish law but on the moral autonomy of the individual worshiper. A fourth denomination, small but intellectually influential, is Reconstructionist Judaism, which focuses on Judaism as an evolving religious civilization and does not subscribe to a belief in a supernatural deity.

In general, the conversion dispute centers around the acceptance of converts in one denomination by the other denominations. In practice, Reconstructionist and Reform Jews recognize all conversions; Conservatives, while wishing to ensure that the conversions were carried on using halachic processes, examine each case individually and are generally accepting of conversions by all other denominations. Orthodox Judaism, however, does not accept conversions performed by non-Orthodox branches (or even by an Orthodox rabbi if it is deemed the conversion was not conducted according to *halachah*).

Most conversions in the United States are performed by Reform and Conservative rabbis. That is, there are about 200,000 people in the United States who have converted to Judaism, think of themselves as officially Jewish, and are thought Jewish by their movements and by most American Jews but not by Orthodox Jews. The potential for friction in such a situation is obvious. If converts are not recognized as genuine Jews by the Orthodox, then, for example, Orthodox rabbis will not see converts as acceptable marriage partners, will not perform Jewish ceremonies with converts, and so on. The Orthodox maintain their position, citing the necessity of performing all Jewish practices according to *halachah*. Because Reform and Reconstructionist Jews do not view the *halachah* as binding, their conversions are deemed not valid. Because, according to the Orthodox, Conservative Judaism has veered away from such traditional Jewish beliefs as that the entire Torah was given by God at Mount Sinai, Conservative rabbis are seen as not fit to perform conversions. Additionally, the Orthodox require converts to accept all religious commandments (such as keeping kosher, keeping the Sabbath, and so on) and do not find a desire to marry someone Jewish as an acceptable motive for studying Judaism.

Of course, the non-Orthodox branches of American Judaism do not agree with this Orthodox understanding. In general, Conservative Jews argue that the Orthodox are debating religious policy rather than religious law and that Conservative conversions follow the *halachah*. Reform and Reconstructionist Jews believe that their converts are sincere and dedicated Jews and that the Orthodox position is more a matter of politics and power than anything else.

The dispute widened in 1983 when the Reform movement (specifically, the Central Conference of American Rabbis, a Reform group) adopted a Resolution on Patrilineal Descent. The resolution declared "that the child of one Jewish parent is under the presumption of Jewish descent." That is, the Reform, joining the Reconstructionists, said that if a child had a Jewish father and non-Jewish mother, under certain circumstances the child would be considered Jewish. According to traditional Jewish law, a person is Jewish if that person had a Jewish mother or converted to Judaism. The patrilineal resolution, then, effectively extended the definition of who was a Jew. The child of a Jewish father and non-Jewish mother was not considered automatically Jewish under the resolution. That child had to make public acts of identification with the Jewish people in order to have a Jewish identity. Such acts might, for instance, include a ritual circumcision, acquiring a Hebrew name, studying the Torah, and having a *bar* or *bat mitzvah*. There are thousands of patrilineal Jews, people considered Jewish by the Reform and Reconstructionist movements who are not accepted as legitimately Jewish by either the Conservative or Orthodox movements.

Another related source of interdenominational friction has to do with converts who move to Israel. Although the number of such converts is extremely small, a large dispute has arisen. Under the Law of Return, Israel grants automatic citizenship to any Jew who wishes it when immigrating to the country. Such automatic citizenship has been given to American Jews who were converted to Judaism by non-Orthodox rabbis in the United States. The Orthodox religious establishment in Israel has sought to amend the Law of Return so that it is understood that conversions must be "according to *halachah*," which, for practical purposes, would mean performed by an Orthodox rabbi. As of this writing, the law has not been amended. American Jews have forcefully resisted attempts to amend the law, citing the effect it would have on their legitimacy.

There have been many efforts to solve these interrelated problems. Conversion is just one of many problems separating the groups within Judaism, but it has received prominence as the number of converts has grown.

There have been attempts to form joint religious courts, so that conversions would be approved by all groups. There have been suggestions that all children of non-Orthodox converts be converted at birth by an Orthodox rabbi. Other ideas have emerged as well.

It is important for those becoming Jewish to understand the consequences of their various choices. More than one convert has told me they wish they had known of these disputes before they con-

verted. Not that such knowledge would have prevented their conversions, but they would have been more informed about what they
faced. Indeed, I think as the number of converts grow, as their self-
confidence to assert their rightful place in Jewish life increases, there
will be more efforts to find solutions to these problems. It has been
widely noted that the dilemmas are internal to the Jewish community. We do not have to face great anti-Semitic powers. We simply
need creativity and cooperation to find a solution.

This is the Jewish world into which those considering conversion must come. Knowing the dilemmas, they also need to know how
much they are needed, how much the overwhelming number of Jews
welcome them.

As they start out on their journey to Judaism, learning about
the religion and the people, knowing why people like themselves have
come to choose to be Jewish, knowing the dilemmas they face in the
Jewish community, they must then turn to those around them—to
their partners, their parents, their in-laws, and their friends—as they
search for answers.

6

Roles of the Partner, Parents, In-Laws, and Friends

THE PARTNER

Some born Jews with a Gentile partner very much want their partner to convert, and, subtly or overtly make known their wishes. Many other born Jews may wish their partner to convert but are unwilling to raise the subject. One rabbi told me a story about this reluctance to ask. A woman rose in the audience and said she had been married for many years to a non-Jewish man and had not asked him to convert because she knew he would be resistant to the idea. The rabbi asked if she were certain of that. She said she was and if the rabbi wanted to know for sure he could ask her husband who was sitting next to her. The rabbi did ask, and, to his wife's surprise, the man said he found Judaism attractive but had not considered conversion because no one had ever asked him!

Dru Greenwood emphasizes the sensitivity of the issue of raising conversion. She notes that there are certain occasions when the issue can fittingly be discussed, such as marriage or childbirth, but that an open invitation should be extended. Meryl Nadell notes that the ability to discuss sensitive issues—such as conversion—openly is a sign of good communication in a marriage. She also notes the importance of the Jewish partner expressing the idea that the partner is valued as a Jew and as a non-Jew.

One reason that some born Jews are reluctant to discuss conversion is that they do not think it is fair to do so because they themselves would not convert for their partner. Also, many born Jews are secular and feel uneasy about asking their partner to learn about and practice religious ideas and rituals that they have abandoned. These are some of the reasons the conversion rate has dropped so much.

Yet, both points should be considered. It is possible, for example, for many Gentiles to find nothing foreign in Judaism and much attractive about it. If they are not currently involved with another religion, Judaism, indeed, may meet a real need. It is startling to look at the percentages of those who intermarried but were never asked to think about conversion who eventually did become Jewish.

It is not at all uncommon for the born Jew to follow the learning of the converting partner, become interested, and begin to learn more about Judaism. Gloria, a psychologist, tells of her Jewish romantic partner who had abandoned his faith completely, going so far as to join another religion. One day the two attended a *bar mitzvah* and liked the young rabbi. Cautiously, they attended services again. Eventually, the partner came back to Judaism and Gloria converted.

The role of the partner does not stop at raising the issue of conversion. It is vital to discuss its ramifications for raising children, celebrating holidays, making life-style choices, joining religious and other institutions, and other issues. These issues, which are part of counseling, are important to discuss in defining the nature of a relationship.

Perhaps the most important role of the born-Jewish partner is to support a conversion candidate. I remember hearing one woman say to a group, in a mournful voice, that she had started to study Judaism but that her husband had shown no interest. She asked pointedly why if he were uninterested should she go through with the process?

The most frequent piece of advice on this issue that I heard was that the Jewish partner should attend a support group or an Introduction to Judaism class with the person considering or undergoing conversion.

In general, then, the question of conversion is a useful barometer of the entire relationship. Can the two partners discuss it openly, freely expressing their feelings, even if they think their own feelings are unfair? Will the Jewish partner support the Gentile partner through a conversion process? Can the two discuss the Jewish content of their relationship?

A partner is also vital is finding the harmonious blending of backgrounds within a Jewish context. It is vital for the partners to know about each other's backgrounds, to understand why and how they react to certain emotional triggers, and to discuss how each holiday is to be celebrated and what cultural contributions each side can bring to the relationship.

For the couple contemplating the prospect of conversion, discussing these issues or taking a course is a vital part of the decision-making and conversion process. Here are some guidelines:

1. Discuss the issue of conversion as early as possible in a serious relationship.
2. Use the discussion to evaluate the relationship and decide how important Jewish issues are to the relationship. Many people discover as they discuss their relationship (often their impending or current marriage) that their religious or ethnic heritage was far more important to them than they themselves had ever realized. There is a videotape available entitled, "Intermarriage: When Love Meets Tradition," produced by the Union of American Hebrew Congregations, a Reform group, that shows couples undergoing such a realization.
3. The Jewish partner needs, if necessary, to learn about Judaism along with the Gentile partner and to show constant support.
4. Attend a support group, discuss the issue with a rabbi, and engage in other activities to think about religious identity issues in the relationship.

It bears repeating that conversion should not be done for the sake of someone else, including a partner. One convert, now a rabbi, offers this advice:

If you are contemplating conversion for marriage, ask yourself how you will feel if the marriage later breaks up. For that matter, find out if your conversion will be a cause of marital discord, either because of your own ambivalence about the decision when faced with Christmas and Easter, or because your spouse chose you as a partner at least partly because you were *not* Jewish. Both of these are potential problems.

Ask yourself how you are going to feel when confronted with major Christian holidays. Can you dump the Christmas tree? Can you contend with a born-Jewish spouse who *wants* a tree, without realizing that no former Christian can successfully divorce the tree from its religious symbolism?

These are important questions, many of which vary depending on the individuals involved. The general point is that a partner may invite a person to convert, and the relationship may be the cause for studying Judaism, but the conversion cannot be for the partner; it can only be for oneself. There have been many cases, of course, when a halfhearted conversion took place that was followed in time by a more warmhearted embrace of Judaism. However, it is a good general rule to make sure the conversion is not just to please a partner, or anyone else but yourself.

THE PARENTS

Sometimes, in hushed tones, a convert tells the story that the parents have not been told of the conversion. Many converts fear telling their parents or other family members and friends.

Meryl Nadell points out that choosing to become Jewish is not tantamount to discarding the religious values that a person was brought up with. She counsels people, when appropriate, to tell their parents that they learned the value of a spiritual identity from the parents, that they learned that it is important for a family to be cohesive. They are, Nadell notes, simply choosing a different way to express those same values.

This continuity is important for many converts to see. Still, it is difficult sometimes to raise the issue in person. Same people prefer to make a phone call or write a letter, using phrases like "I have things to say that are hard to say in person." George Murray sent a very long, introspective letter to his mother. He first summarized his religious history and the evolution of his thought, and then wrote:

> All this does not mean that I am not going to be the same peculiar son you have always had. . . . For me to be Jewish means many things. It is good for the kids. It is also good for me. I like Judaism. One thing is that, ideally, one tries to imbue spiritual observance into every aspect of one's life. This is something that I have strived to do for the last twenty years.

Conversions to Judaism are not always easy on the parent–child relationship. Parents need to be reassured that they are not being abandoned. Still, a conversion can cause great pain among the family members of the convert.

Devorah Wigoder experienced such pain and wrote about it in one of the most moving books about conversion, *Hope is My House*. Born Jane McDwyer, educated in a convent, sister of both a priest and a nun, Devorah faced a pained parent. It was long after her conversion. Devorah was living in Israel with her husband, a well-known scholar and editor named Geoffrey Wigoder. One day in 1956, she received a telegram from her brother, the priest. He told her that their mother was dying in a New York hospital. Her brother pleaded with Devorah not only to visit but also to convert back to Catholicism. Such a move, her brother suggested, would ease their mother's deathbed pain. She wished to stay in Israel because of the difficult times there, but her husband urged her to visit her mother and told her the conversion issue was hers to decide.

Devorah knew she was being asked to choose between her dying mother's most profound feelings and Judaism, the religion Devorah cherished. She flew through the night, constantly praying for a way out of her dilemma. She arrived at the airport. Her brother was there, waiting to help her through a reconversion ceremony. Instead, Devorah went directly to see her mother. She walked into the room, tiptoed to the bed. Her mother was sleeping as Devorah looked down at the kind face. Somehow her mother felt a presence and woke up.

"Jane! Jane! My child! Jane, what is this radiance that glows around you?"

"It is the Jewishness in me, Mother."

"If that is so, then God bless you, my saintly child!"

Devorah and her mother clung to each other and wept. Her mother died the next day and then Devorah began to write her book.

Here are some suggestions for discussing the issue with parents: Decide on the best way to tell a parent. Most converts report that telling a parent in person is best if possible, but, as I have suggested, many people find alternatives to be easier on everyone. Each person must make the decision. Involving a parent as early as possible is a good idea. For example, if it is done before a wedding is planned, the parents can be active participants in the planning, and although they may never have even attended a Jewish wedding, they can provide insight and advice on various matters such as the reception. In that way they are given concrete proof of the ongoing closeness of the relationship with their child and their child's new family. It is vital that parents not hear about the conversion from someone else, so that telling them as soon as the final decision has been made helps the relationship. There is no special time to tell. Most people suggest avoiding days of obvious religious significance such as Christmas or Easter or obvious personal significance such as a birthday or anniversary. A neutral holiday might be appropriate. If there are two parents involved, both should be told, preferably together. The convert should tell each parent and not ask one parent to tell the other. There is a difference of opinion among the converts I spoke to about whether or not to bring the Jewish partner to the discussion. Most of the converts thought it better to speak to the parents alone, while others needed support and help during such an occasion.

It is valuable for converts to rehearse what they wish to say. They should consider the obvious questions they may be asked and some of the feelings, positive and negative, that may be expressed. They should consider their own reaction if their parents are very negative about the conversion. Most converts found their greatest success in simply explaining what they found attractive about Judaism, how it met a need, how it helped a relationship, how they feel closer to their parents, not further away, because of Judaism's emphasis on family, how their decision is a sober, serious, mature one, how their decision was personal, not subject to any pressure from their partner or their partner's parents. Such a statement needs to be supported by an expression of continuing love of the family, of a desire to maintain the relationship as it has always been.

The vast majority of converts I spoke to reported support from their parents, or some initial resistance and then support. There were cases, however, of continuing resistance. Such considerations have to be taken into account when considering conversion.

JEWISH IN-LAWS

There are sometimes problems for a convert in dealing with in-laws, although frequently the relationship is warm. Indeed, John David Scalamonti, a former priest, credits his conversion to the parents of a Jewish woman he was seeing. He writes about his experiences in his book *Ordained to Be a Jew*. However, problems do arise. Lisa (not her real name) writes about her partner's parents:

> [They] are pleased I converted, but are still embarrassed by my inadequate background. We are on speaking terms, because I realize I will have to deal with this for the rest of my life. However, because of their narrow-mindedness, I do believe that they caused irreparable damage to any "normal" relationship they could ever have with me.

Lisa says of her mother-in-law to be that she "has told me she considers me to be Jewish, but she hesitates in her reply just enough that the 'yes' sounds like a lie, trying to save face."

The lesson of all this is that Jewish families differ as much as other families. Some are warm, caring, and knowledgeable about Judaism. Some are kind, but do not know Jewish customs. Some are observant, but unwelcoming toward converts. Some are ignorant about Judaism and hostile to a convert. The luckiest convert is the one who can use an in-law as a role model, asking questions, and receiving support and help. Such cases do exist. Finding a common interest helps. If, for example, a convert and her mother-in-law both enjoy baking, looking for some particularly Jewish recipes can bring them together.

Be prepared for a variety of reactions, including odd ones. The Jewish identity for many American Jews is ethnic rather than religious, so you may see in your partner or in-laws an ignorance, even a hostility toward Jewish religious beliefs and practices accompanied by a fierce attachment to Judaism, sometimes of an ethnocentric nature, such as the view that converts are not really Jewish, that only someone born Jewish could truly understand how a Jew feels.

Learning that Judaism is religion plus ethnicity is helpful for the convert in understanding such a view, but problems remain because conversion is a religious process. It is an embarrassing situation, for example, for a convert, having learned about Judaism, to be lectured to by an uninformed Jewish family member and being given incorrect information about Judaism. Many converts, by virtue of their education and drive, know more about Judaism than some born Jews, sometimes including their partner or in-laws. A simple suggestion that a disputed issue be resolved by referring to an authoritative text or consulting a rabbi is preferable to a confrontation when a convert realizes that the born Jew is incorrect.

The relationship between people and their in-laws is often a difficult one. Questions of conversion and religious identity can add to that difficulty.

Many Jewish parents are fundamentally pleased that there will be a conversion. Most Jews are concerned with Jewish continuity. They may not know a lot about conversion in Jewish thought and history, but the idea of having Jewish grandchildren is very appealing. Telling them about the conversion process and educating them about the role of converts in Jewish life are important in helping them understand conversion's legitimacy within Judaism.

In-laws need to accept the convert as a genuine Jew. For many of these in-laws, raised to think there was something vaguely un-Jewish about conversion, such an acceptance is at least initially difficult. Although information or discussion with a rabbi may provide an answer for their minds, they still need one for their hearts. I think in-laws who see sincere, loving converts inevitably come to accept them as full Jews.

FRIENDS

Many of the problems converts face with their own family and their Jewish in-laws they also face with friends: how to tell them, how to keep their friendship, how to keep the relationship stable.

One problem that several converts mentioned to me was the difficulty in dealing with the anti-Semitism of their friends (or family). Jim said he felt guilty when some of his friends, knowing of his conversion, made jokes about Jews, including several particularly crude ones. Jim's guilt arose because he was reluctant to confront them, fearing the loss or diminution of their friendship. Eventually, Jim did say that the jokes made him feel uneasy.

Most friends are friends because they are supportive and understanding, like most parents. The same rules apply to friends as apply to parents: tell them early; ask for their help, advice, and support; and reassure them that your relationship with them will continue as it has always been.

7

The Conversion Process

You have thought long and hard about conversion, but you still need to know the exact process that you will be going through if you do convert. Here is a description. Please note that different movements, and different rabbis, will emphasize, and include or exclude, various parts of the process described; in addition the order of events may vary due to circumstances. I have tried to be inclusive, so there will not be any surprises, and have tried to describe which steps different movements are likely to require. Still, be prepared for variations.

So, if you do go ahead with the conversion, here are the steps in the process.

THE FIRST STEP: FINDING YOUR RABBI

After thinking about conversion and deciding to pursue your interest, it is vital at the very earliest time possible to consult with a rabbi. As suggested, meeting with different rabbis and considering which movement within Judaism to join (given the disputes within Judaism) are part of this decision. There are converts with whom I spoke who underwent conversion by one denomination and, after leading a Jewish life for a while, decided to undergo conversion by another group. One person had undergone three conversions. Thinking about the issues beforehand, and most especially discussing them with a rabbi, are very helpful. Many considering conversions attend services at different temples to get a feel for the kinds of people who attend, the warmth and comfortability of the service, the qualities of the rabbi and cantor, and for other important factors. As discussed, contacting a local board of rabbis or other Jewish group, or just looking in a telephone directory will help you find Jewish houses of worship if you or your partner do not know of any. Synagogues welcome visitors, so you need not feel like an intruder.

What happens when you see a rabbi? What will the rabbi ask? First, the rabbi will want to be sure that you are sincere. Here are some possible questions the rabbi will ask:

1. Why do you want to convert?
2. What is your religious background?
3. What is your personal background, such as marital status?
4. What do you already know about Judaism?
5. Can you truly accept the basic differences between Judaism and Christianity?
6. What experiences with Jews have you had?
7. Was it your decision, without being pressured, to become Jewish?
8. Are you willing to spend the necessary time studying in class and at home to become Jewish?
9. Have you discussed this decision with your family?
10. Are you willing to raise your children as Jews?
11. Do you have any questions about Judaism or conversion?

One woman describes her interaction with the famous Zalman Schachter-Shalomi, of the Aleph Alliance for Jewish Renewal in Philadelphia:

He asked about my childhood religion and my ancestor's religion and suggested I look there. I refused. He asked how my mother felt about my conversion. She is supportive because she sees I am happy and being nourished spiritually. Zalman said he already considered me Jewish in 3 of the 4 worlds—did I have to make it so in the 4th? His hesitation was that I had no man in my life, and what if I fell in love with a Gentile? I restricted my dating to Jewish men, and am currently in a relationship with a lovely Jewish man.

He asked me if I had questions for him before the conversion. I didn't.

One typical aspect of this dialogue is that many rabbis feel it useful and necessary to try to dissuade the convert from becoming Jewish. This is in keeping with Jewish tradition and is part of a test of sincerity. Some rabbis try to balance this tradition with a more modern sense of welcoming. Do not think an attempt at discouragement is particular to you or a sign that you are not welcome. Think of it simply as a chance for you to reconsider your decision, to ponder again before continuing on with your spiritual journey.

If you and the rabbi agree to continue with the conversion, your next step is deciding how to learn Judaism.

LEARNING JUDAISM

As part of your process of considering conversion, perhaps you read books, visited places, and talked to people. Depending on the movement and the rabbi with whom you are working, there are a variety of ways to study Judaism.

Some rabbis will work directly with you, giving you reading and other assignments and meeting with you on a regular basis to discuss what you have learned. It is common in such circumstances for a rabbi to ask that you attend services and specific Jewish events, such as a seder at Passover. Some converts feel intimidated by having to deal with so learned a person so soon.

One alternative available for some converts is participation in an Introduction to Judaism class. Typically, the class will be made up of people considering conversion, some single, some with their partners, and perhaps a sprinkling of born Jews who, honest in their understanding that they lack knowledge about their religion, have chosen to learn as well. Classes are valuable in that you can hear the experiences of others and feel part of a group.

What material is covered in a class? Much of the material in Part Two of this book is the basis for what will be studied. There will be variations, such as, for example, additional information about the particular movement you are joining. A typical course might meet once a week for several hours over the time span of a year from September to May, about thirty sessions. Some courses are shorter. Most classes will cover the same basic material: basic Jewish beliefs, Jewish practices, the nature and history of Jewish people, holy days, the Jewish home, the Jewish life cycle, the Holocaust, Zionism and Israel, and similar topics. An overview of all of these is available in the next section of this book.

The complaint I most frequently heard was that the classes were too intellectual and not experiential enough. Many converts did not just want to study the Sabbath, but to learn how to do it. Finding a role model or someone in the synagogue willing to answer these kinds of questions will be extremely helpful.

The period of study for conversion varies greatly, depending on the convert's prior knowledge, available time, requirements of the rabbi, and other factors. In general, the range is from six months to a year, but many converts told me they studied for several years before they felt ready. Taking this time into account is important if you are planning to convert prior to a marriage. (Remember, if conversion takes place prior to marriage, there is no intermarriage, just a Jewish marriage. You, your partner, and your in-laws may need to take this into consideration, especially if you choose a rabbi who will not perform an intermarriage.)

During this period of study, it is especially useful to practice Judaism at the level you prefer as much as possible. Many converts try out ceremonies they have never done (or heard of) before, and sometimes are surprised to find they like them. Even, for example, if you and your family are not planning to keep kosher, it is an interesting experience to sample what it feels like. Even if you will not keep the Sabbath every week, the learning period should be used to sample it. These customs have not survived for thousands of years for no reason. For many centuries, they provided an emotional and spiritual anchor to everyday experiences. While reading the second part of this book, it would be useful to keep a list of worthwhile experiences to test out.

Here is a story, written by Lena Romanoff, herself a convert, and author of the wonderful, highly recommended book *Your People, My People: Finding Acceptance and Fulfillment as a Jew by Choice*. Lena is also director of the Jewish Converts and Interfaith Network. She has lectured internationally on conversion and is one of the most insightful experts on the subject. This story is a memoir of one way that she learned Judaism, and its meaning.

It may be helpful to provide some guidance about some of the religious vocabulary in the memoir. *Pirke Avos* is a tractate in the Talmud and includes many rabbinic ethical maxims. *Kashrut* refers to keeping the kosher dietary laws. A *chillul Hashem*, as explained in the piece, is a profanation of God's name, that is a violation of one of God's laws. An *eruv* is a partition used for Sabbath observance by traditional Jews. Finally, a *goyishe kup* means to think like a Gentile, rather than a Jew; this is not meant to be a compliment.

FLOWERS FOR SHABBOS

by Lena Romanoff

The late summer air was heavy with the humid sweet fragrance of honeysuckle. Mrs. Reuben and I sat on the creaky and splintered wicker porch chairs. We sipped pale, tasteless iced tea made from worn out tea bags that had given up their essence days ago. Mrs. Reuben read aloud to me from *Pirke Avos* in her thick Hungarian-accented English: "In *Pirke Avos* we find that

Envy, Desire, and the need for Honor drive a person from this world." I listened intently and tried to incorporate as much Judaism as possible into my whole being. Mrs. Reuben and I feasted on Torah together and I basked in the glow of her wisdom every Friday afternoon as we awaited Mr. Reuben's return from work. Friday and Saturday were the two days that the Hospital of the University of Pennsylvania could not claim my medical nursing skills.

I spent the entire year with the Reubens, my adopted surrogate family. My rabbi, in his great wisdom, had chosen the Reubens because they were pious and humble ambassadors for Judaism, and because they could use the money that I paid them for my room and board in exchange for living Judaism. At the time I did not know how much they really needed the extra income that I provided. They lived modestly—frugally and simply. I was, however, keenly mindful of how desperately I needed them, my Jewish family.

The Reubens provided me with Jewish memories and a personal Jewish past history. My Jewish past is just as memorable and poignant as the Jewish past of a born Jew. It just begins a little later.

Mrs. Reuben and I also diligently studied the laws pertaining to *kashrut* and the ritual laws of purity. The transformation that had started out at the *mikveh* was almost complete as I experienced my Judaism one day at a time.

At exactly 5 P.M. we heard Mr. Reuben's familiar dragging footsteps on the rickety wooden porch. Soon *Shabbos* would begin.

Inside the modest house, the tiny kitchen always commanded center stage, but the whole house was redolent with the distinctive aromas of *Shabbos*. It was my privilege to set the table. I carefully spread Mrs. Reuben's vintage crewel and lace tablecloth on the shaky maple table. The cloth was frayed at the edges and had faded wine stains that refused to be washed away with soap or tincture of time. The fanciful birds and flowers had been stitched by

Mrs. Reuben when she was a young girl in Hungary. It was remarkably still cheerful and folksy after all these years. Mrs. Reuben gingerly removed four candles from the discolored box and fingered them reverently before handing them to me. The *Shabbos* candles were bent, dusty, and brittle. She had bought an entire case of them years before when the local Jewish grocer, Mr. Levine, went out of business. A good buy it was! Indeed, their pale shade of anemia matched the tablecloth perfectly.

Cookbooks and food fads came and went but *Shabbos* dinner with the Reubens was always the same without variation on the theme. We began each and every *Shabbos* meal with fish served whole—fins, bones, and all. Mr. Reuben was especially fond of fish heads. The roast chicken came to the table with neck and feet intact, but without one pin feather. It was my least favorite task to sear off the pin feathers with a candle. I washed my hands twice to remove the smell of burnt dead flesh. Thick homemade egg noodles received a flavorful lacing of chicken pan gravy to keep them from sticking together and overcooked carrots rounded out the meal. Everything was sprinkled liberally with salt, pepper, and paprika. I forced myself to nibble on a piece of chicken breast and some carrots. Not only did I miss my mother's light and elegant North Italian cuisine, I was also *skilfu*, a dialectical Italian word that is difficult to define but roughly means that one is overly fastidious about food.

By far the most delectable part of the dinner for me was the freshly baked and braided *challah* loaves. Mrs. Reuben and I baked *challah* every Thursday. My Italian kitchen upbringing made me a natural at this pleasant task. We made four loaves of bread for the Sabbath. The others were sprinkled with caraway seeds (my idea) and frozen for use for the remainder of the week. As I write these words, my mind is permeated with the haunting fragrant aroma, and it hovers there every time I bake *challah* to this day.

I clearly remember Mr. Reuben's pounding footsteps as he stalked into the kitchen to inspect the "ladies' goings on." We coyly pretended to chase him away from our domain, but not before he had jabbed a thin finger at the pliant dough while making his usual pronouncement: "It smells mighty good in here. I can't wait till *Shabbos*. Did you remember to take *challah?*"

We feigned surprise and insult at the question and then in unison we replied: "Yes, yes; now leave us be." Of course Mr. Reuben knew that his saintly and pious wife had remembered to take *challah*. The question was really meant as a reminder to me, the fledgling Jew.

Mr. Reuben never spoke directly to me, often deliberately averting his eyes from mine. He addressed me by speaking to his wife about me in my presence. It was a strange habit, and yet at the same time a comfort, because he seemed less formidable to me when he looked away.

Shabbos with my adopted family, the Reubens, never ceased to be wondrous and joyous. Our humble abode was transformed into a magical place filled with songs, stories, and serene happiness that seemed to be captured in the flickering *Shabbos* candlelight. *Shabbos* made me feel special. It gave me a true sense of Jewish ownership, an anchor for my new identity. It became embracingly familiar and excitingly magical at the same time.

I would not have wanted to change a thing, except for the hideous green plastic bowl with the dusty, bright orange plastic roses that made their appearance on the *Shabbos* table every Friday. The fake flowers assaulted my aesthetic sense.

One Friday afternoon I brought home a bouquet of clove-scented pink carnations for the *Shabbos* table. I hoped to surprise and please Mrs. Reuben. She was surprised, but she was not pleased. She coolly chastised me for being so extravagant. "A real *goyishe kup* you are. You must not be so frivolous."

Mr. Reuben eyed the carnations with apoplectic consternation. "What are these?" he demanded. Obviously he knew *what* they were. He really wanted to know *why* they were! As usual, he talked past me, sparing me the full brunt of his displeasure. "Miriam, it is not the child's fault. She has been taken in by all these fanciful pictures in your cookbook. Tell her that if it cannot be eaten, worn, or put to use, it is a waste of money." He shook his head and mumbled something in Hungarian to his wife.

Thereafter, I brought home a bag of fresh fruit for *Shabbos*, which immediately won their approval. The plastic flowers continued to make their debut every Friday because Mrs. Reuben insisted that we have flowers for *Shabbos*. With each week that passed, the roses became increasingly odious to me.

One shiny, cloud-flecked *Shabbos* in July, I ventured out into the Reubens' overgrown and much neglected garden. I had wanted to weed the garden for months, but my combined full-time nursing and full-time graduate student work did not provide me the stretch of daylight necessary for gardening.

To my delight, I found the garden awash with mint, honeysuckle, and southernwood. Sprinkled here and there were some white daisies struggling in the tangled weeds. In the middle of the garden was a huge honeysuckle bush that threatened to choke anything in its path. I could almost feel its roots moving beneath my feet.

Armed with a rusty trowel and dull scissors, I tamed a small area of the garden. In the process, I made a sprightly bouquet of honeysuckle mint, southernwood, and daisies. Why not avail myself of God's beautiful bounty? These were gifts from the garden. *Shabbos* was almost coming to a close, but the bouquet would look delightful during our *Havdalah* service. So I thought.

As I absentmindedly arranged my *Shabbos* flowers, I caught sight of Mr. and Mrs. Reuben glaring at me from the foot of the garden gate. Mr. Reuben's rheumy eyes dilated to their fullest. "No, no, no!" he raged. "This is a *Chillul Hashem*; you are violating the Sabbath! You must not cut flowers! You must not do work in the garden! Did you forget that you are a Jew?!"

His words fell like a knife plunging into my heart. I wanted to respond, "Yes, yes, of course. I know what is forbidden. I am a good Jew. I do not have an excuse, except that the sun was warm and the garden beckoned. I simply forgot that something as pleasurable as gardening is really work. I did not forget that I was a Jew." These words were never uttered. They froze in transit when I was suddenly numbed by the additional thought that my transgression would surely be made known to my beloved rabbi. Surely he would be terribly disappointed, but certainly not surprised. I had transgressed before. He would recall the time that this *goyishe kup* hung her bathing suit on the *eruv* during a visit to the Catskills. Converts can be so trying!

I retreated to my room, which seemed to reflect my mood by being stifling hot and oppressive. I soon fell into a deep sleep and dreamt that an evil dybbuk had possessed me. It was leading me into a flower-filled garden. I struggled to escape the dybbuk's grasp and mercifully awoke with a start. It was time for *Havdalah*.

I tentatively approached the kitchen and immediately noticed that my *Shabbos* bouquet had been placed in an old mason jar. The pungent smell of mint, southernwood, and honeysuckle permeated the tiny kitchen and made the air more breathable.

The *Shabbos* flowers remained fresh and fragrant in the jar for the entire week. Every time Mr. Reuben sat at the table he absentmindedly fingered the mint leaves, releasing their volatile oils into the stale, damp kitchen. We also started to add mint to the tea.

The following Thursday we baked our *challah* as usual. As usual, Mr. Reuben came in to inspect the "ladies' goings on." "You didn't forget to take *challah*, did you?" With a gleam in his eyes he looked directly at me and added, "Don't forget to gather some flowers for *Shabbos*."

I eventually married and moved to New York. Written correspondence with Mrs. Reuben became increasingly difficult as arthritis gnarled her once busy fingers. They hardly answered the one phone that they owned, partially because of increasing deafness and partially because the phone was located in the bedroom hallway—a flight of steps away. I visited them every time I visited my own family in Philadelphia. My beloved Mrs. Reuben died five years after my move to New York. Mr. Reuben began to spend more time with his son in Canada.

One day I received a cryptic letter from my avuncular rabbi informing me that Mr. Reuben was back home and quite sick. My rabbi warned me that since Mrs. Reuben's death, Mr. Reuben had become "a shadow of himself. He is weak and old," cautioned my rabbi. "A surprise visit on a hot summer day may not be wise. Don't be disappointed if he is not himself."

I found the screen door on the front porch slightly ajar, and the flies were entering and exiting with abandon. I shuddered when I entered the shabby interior. The plaster and wallpaper were hanging in huge pieces from the sides of the walls. The kitchen was dingy and unkempt. My heart limped between two emotions—shock and anger. Why had the Reubens steadfastly refused to cash my checks or accept my cash gifts? Instead, they'd stubbornly insisted that I give the money to the *shul* in their names. Reluctantly I had complied. How stupid I had been to listen to them, to be so blindly dutiful!

My eyes had hardly adjusted to the dimness when I spied Mr. Reuben hunched over the old maple table poring over the Talmud. In front of him was a glass of pale-colored water, a mere excuse for tea.

For a fleeting moment I feared that this humble and erudite man would not recognize me. Then I saw his eyes begin to swim. Tears rolled down his wrinkled cheeks and splashed onto the maple table. We embraced in a clumsy sort of bear hug. I had valiantly fought back my own tears until I smelled a faintly familiar fragrance. Was it the power of memories wanting to recall smells and sights of the mind's past?

My eyes were so blurred with tears that I had not caught sight of an old mason jar in the middle of the table. It was filled with gifts from God's garden—flowers for *Shabbos*: honeysuckle, mint, southernwood, and daisies.

THE *BET DIN*

A *Bet Din* is a religious court most often consisting of three people, one or more of whom is most often a rabbi. Most rabbis in all denominations want a candidate to appear at some point in the process before a *Bet Din*. More traditional rabbis may want the conversion candidate to appear at the *Bet Din* after the learning period has occurred and have an appearance at a *Bet Din* at the conversion ceremony itself. Other rabbis may want other ceremonies done first, or have a *Bet Din* and a ceremony later, or may bypass a *Bet Din* altogether.

In many cases, especially among Reform and Conservative Jews, the candidate's partner may be in attendance at the *Bet Din*. Because the *Bet Din* takes place after learning about Judaism, one substantive part of the process will be to determine the Jewish learning of the conversion candidate. For example, there might be a question about the meaning of the Sabbath, or on the Jewish belief in one God. These questions are not meant to be traps, and a little (or more than a little) nervousness is expected and understood. In general, the candidate knows the rabbi asking the question and, during the course of study, has learned the material very well. Of course, there will also be an effort to insure that the conversion is entered into freely, so the candidate might be asked if there was any pressure to convert. Candidates might be formally asked if they are ready to cast their lot with the Jewish people, to identify their fate and the fate of their family with a people who has suffered persecution. Often an oath of allegiance to the Jewish people is officially signed.

CIRCUMCISION

Both Conservative and Orthodox rabbis require a male candidate for conversion to undergo circumcision (a *brit milah*, an entering into the covenant as God required Abraham to do in the Bible) prior to the conversion. Circumcision is not a requirement in Reform Judaism.

There are male candidates who were born without a foreskin or who have already had a circumcision, typically as an infant for health reasons. In such circumstances, Conservative and Orthodox Judaism require that a drop of blood be drawn as a symbolic circumcision. This ceremony is called *Hatafat Dam Brit*.

People with special medical and psychological problems should consult a rabbi.

IMMERSION

Orthodox and Conservative Judaism also require both male and female candidates for conversion to immerse themselves in a ritual bath called a *mikveh*. This ceremony is called *tevillah*. While Reform Judaism does not require use of a *mikveh*, more Reform rabbis are recommending it. Immersion, which makes the candidate ritually clean to enter Judaism, symbolizes the total commitment to the new religion and the rebirth of the person.

The *mikveh*, technically, can be any body of natural water. An ocean, a lake, and other natural waters are acceptable. Conservative Judaism also allows, when necessary, a swimming pool to function as a *mikveh*. The term *mikveh* also refers to a specific pool that is built for the purposes of ritual purification. A *mikveh* that is built has enough water so that an adult can be immersed in the water. A *mikveh* might be located in a house of worship, or a YM-YMHA, or in a separate building, or elsewhere. Many modern ritual baths come with such equipment as hair dryers.

Depending on the *mikveh* used, the equipment may vary. The immersion ceremony typically includes making sure the body is thoroughly cleaned (as by a shower). There is a covering over the candidate that is removed as the candidate enters the warm water, which is usually about four feet deep. (When the immersion ceremony is not done in a private *mikveh*, but in a public place such as a lake, the conversion candidate is allowed to wear a garment that fits loosely.) One common method of immersion is to stand, legs separated, arms loose, bent over until all the body has been immersed in the water. While immersing yourself, say this blessing:

בָּרוּךְ אַתָּה יְיָ, אֱלֹהֵינוּ מֶלֶךְ הָעוֹלָם, אֲשֶׁר קִדְּשָׁנוּ בְּמִצְוֹתָיו, וְצִוָּנוּ עַל הַטְּבִילָה.

Baruch attah Adonai, Eloheinu melech ha-olam, asher kideshanu be-mitzvotav, vitzivanu al ha-tevillah.

(Blessed are You, Lord our God, Ruler of the universe, who sancti-fied us through Your teachings and taught us concerning immersion.)

This blessing is followed by the *Shehecheyanu* blessing:

בָּרוּךְ אַתָּה יְיָ, אֱלֹהֵינוּ מֶלֶךְ הָעוֹלָם, שֶׁהֶחֱיָנוּ, וְקִיְּמָנוּ, וְהִגִּיעָנוּ לַזְּמַן הַזֶּה.

Baruch attah Adonai, Eloheinu melech ha-olam, shehecheyanu, vikiye-manu, vehigiyanu la-z'man ha-zeh.

(Blessed are You, Lord our God, Ruler of the universe, who has kept us alive, and sustained us, and allowed us to reach this day.)

By Jewish religious law, there must be three male witnesses to the immersion. In the interest of modesty, when the candidate is a woman the witnesses remain outside the *mikveh* room and are told by the female attendant that the ritual immersion has been performed and that the ritual blessings have been recited. Frequently, this rule is reinterpreted so that Jewish females are allowed to be witnesses.

OFFERING

A traditional part of converting to Judaism in ancient times was bring-ing a sacrifice or offering to the Temple. After the Temple was destroyed in 70 C.E., this ceremony disappeared. Some traditional scholars argued that converts had to set an offering aside that would be offered when the Temple is rebuilt, but Jewish law does not require such an act.

The idea of an offering is, however, an attractive one. A few rabbis are incorporating this idea by having conversion candidates donate money to the poor, or engage in some other act of charity, as a symbolic way of sacrificing something. In ancient times the sacrifice allowed a person to enter the Temple sanctuary. The symbolic entering of an inner Jewish sanctuary through a good deed can voluntarily be added to the conversion process.

CHOOSING A NAME

Again, particular conversion processes will vary in the order of all these steps. Sometimes, after a *Bet Din* and a signing of the oath a Hebrew name is chosen, and this is followed by a visit to the *mikveh*.

At some point in the process you will be asked to choose a Hebrew name, which will be used for future religious ceremonies, such as a marriage. A new name, in part, is also meant to symbolize a new life, indeed a new birth.

By tradition, male converts are given the Hebrew name Avraham as their new Hebrew first name, and female candidates are traditionally named Sarah or Ruth. Abraham and Sarah were, of course, not only the first Hebrew couple but also actively engaged in the act of "gathering souls," bringing Gentiles to their religion. However, the convert may choose any legitimate Hebrew name.

Among traditional Jews, a person is called in Hebrew by their Hebrew first name and then by a parental name, such as Shimon ben Yitzhak, or Shimon the son of Yitzhak. Because the convert has no Hebrew-named parent, traditionalists add "ben Avraham Avinu," meaning "son of Abraham, our Father," after the Hebrew name. Thus, if a convert chooses the name "Avraham," the full Hebrew name would be "Avraham ben Avraham Avinu." For women, the addition is "bat Sarah Imenu," daughter of Sarah, our Mother.

The naming ceremony typically includes the convert reciting a set blessing.

THE CEREMONY: SOME POSSIBILITIES

In certain circumstances, this conversion process is completed by a public ceremony. In some cases, there is a graduation ceremony. In other cases, the convert stands in front of the congregation and gives a speech.

Many converts are reluctant to have such a public ceremony; some are simply shy while others say that such a ceremony unfairly marks off one group of Jews (Jews by choice) from another (Jews by birth). This is a valid criticism, but most converts I spoke to who had a public ceremony recommended it highly for several reasons. First, the act of explanation for the conversion provided an opportunity for the convert to thank publicly those who deserved it and an opportunity to ponder the entire experience in a way that often led to greater self-understanding. In addition, many born Jews are fascinated to hear conversionary stories. Such stories inevitably sensitize born Jews to the needs of converts, but can do even more. Hearing how attached new Jews are to their religion, born Jews often come to appreciate their heritage in a new way.

THE CONVERSION OF MINORS

Minors can be converted for various reasons. Perhaps a parent converts to Judaism and wants the children to convert as well, or a Gentile child is adopted by Jewish parents, and they want to raise the child as Jewish.

In traditional ceremonies, a female child (that is, by Jewish law, under age twelve) is immersed in a *mikveh* and follows those ceremonies while a male child (that is, by Jewish law, under age thirteen) is circumcised (or, as with an adult male, if that is not possible, a drop of blood is drawn). Several weeks later, the male goes to the *mikveh*. An adopted child can be adopted in the presence of a *Bet Din*. These ceremonies differ, especially among Reform rabbis, who may have simply a naming ceremony.

QUESTIONS AND ANSWERS ABOUT THE CONVERSION PROCESS

Q. How can I honor my natural, non-Jewish parents? I'm especially concerned about what to do when they die.

A. First, in all instances, you should consult with your rabbi. In general, the biblical commandment to honor your father and your mother applies to all children and all parents, so they should be accorded full respect in all the ways you did prior to your conversion. If you are familiar with Jewish rituals surrounding death, you may wonder if you can sit *Shivah* and say *Kaddish*. Reform and Conservative Judaism, in general, allow such acts as signs of piety. Orthodox Judaism is split on the issue. (These rituals are explained in Part Two.)

Q. I'm a woman who converted in the Conservative movement. I already had very young children, so they had to be converted as well since they were not considered Jewish by Conservative Jews. My question is, what if, when they grow up, they decide they don't want to be Jewish. Can they change?

A. Jewish law allows a person who has achieved religious maturity to renounce a conversion and revert back to the original faith. It is important to discuss the issue early. Of course, without an explicit renunciation, the Jewish community considers the child legally and officially Jewish forever. It is especially important in such cases to provide the child with a good Jewish education and a sense from the parents of the importance of being a Jew.

Q. My mother-in-law said something about my fiancé being a *kohen*, so that he isn't supposed to marry me even though I have converted. Is this true?

A. Traditional Jews divided the Jewish people into three classes: the *kohanim* (plural of *kohen*), the levites, and the Israelites (see Part Two). A *kohen* was a priest. Reform Judaism does not recognize these distinctions, and so a Reform Jew who has been told he is a *kohen* can marry a convert. Conservative Judaism, in general, says that it is not historically possible to determine who exactly is or is not a genuine *kohen*, so that Conservative rabbis allow a marriage between a man whose family believes he is a *kohen* and a convert. Orthodox Judaism recognizes these distinctions and does not sanction a marriage between a *kohen* and a convert.

Q. What happens to a convert who goes back to a previous religion?

A. Judaism takes conversion extremely seriously. After a formal conversion, the person remains a Jew forever. If the person leaves Judaism, that person is considered an apostate, a defector, but still a Jew. Incidentally, the child of such a woman apostate is considered to have been born Jewish.

Q. I'm pregnant and going through a conversion ceremony. Does the baby have to be converted after it is born?

A. No, if the baby is born after your conversion ceremony, the baby is Jewish, and need not go through a separate conversion.

Q. Both my husband and I are Gentiles. I want to convert to Judaism, but he does not? Am I allowed to?

A. You are allowed to, but many rabbis will be especially reluctant because once you convert you will automatically be part of an intermarriage.

Q. Is it worthwhile to go through this whole process just to become Jewish? Why can't they just say a prayer over me and I'll be Jewish?

A. Sometimes the length of time it takes to study is frustrating especially if there is a planned marriage or an upcoming birth involved. Still, Judaism is a very morally serious religion. Judaism does not want you to convert under pressure, or without understanding exactly what it is you are converting to. The time is not just for adequate study, but also to allow for a period of introspection and reflection.

Conversion carries with it special joys, but also special challenges. The next chapter discusses some of those particular challenges.

8
Feelings, Holidays, Children: The Challenges of Conversion

As the swirl of activity surrounding conversion begins to gather force, those undergoing it often are surprised at their own feelings or the questions that arise in their mind. While people go through very different experiences in different ways at different paces, there are some widely reported reactions that warrant mention.

There are many feelings concerning conversion. They often are initially aroused when the issue of conversion is first raised. If the conversion occurs because of an intellectual search, the idea of conversion is most frequently a logical conclusion drawn from the intellectual growth attendant on studying Judaism. More typically, however, conversion is an unexpected subject in the context of a romantic relationship. In the most statistically typical case, a Jewish man involved with or engaged or married to a Gentile woman asks her to consider conversion. Sometimes the question is asked by the man's father or mother or a rabbi, or someone else. While these relationships will be explored in the next section, it is this initial question that arouses feelings.

It is common for a person to examine Judaism, decide for any one of a variety of reasons to convert, commence conversion classes, even finish the conversion process, and then face questions that were not even considered when the conversion option was first considered.

The following sections discuss the main challenges as reported by the hundreds of converts with whom I was in contact.

A SENSE OF THE LOSS OF A PREVIOUS IDENTITY

Bob had been raised as an Italian Catholic but had drifted away. It was only while studying to become Jewish that he thought about the heritage of his birth. He felt guilt at leaving it and a loss of his own background. This feeling precipitated a series of conflicts about converting in the first place. Finally, Bob realized that his Jewish identity was the one that represented how he truly felt. A counselor led Bob through a "mourning process," by which he gradually came to terms with his sense of loss through a self-examination of who he was, what he wanted out of life, why he was converting. As in all stages, Bob's support group and a model—someone whose conversion has been successful—were also of great help.

Bob's loss was analogous to a death, the death of part of one's past. That is why Judaism sees conversion as a sort of rebirth, a chance to begin life again. Seen as a new opportunity and fresh start, his conversion gave hope to Bob.

A SENSE OF BEING OVERWHELMED

Frequently reported, this sense of being overwhelmed is on the one hand emotional and on the other hand intellectual. Emotionally, the change of identity is so unsettling that it is common to feel that the entire experience is beyond one's ability to handle. Intellectually, Judaism is filled with history and customs, some or much of which is foreign and difficult for those coming to it for the first time. Many born Jews do not know a lot about Judaism, but conversion candidates often express concern that they do not really know enough to be Jewish.

A FEELING OF MARGINALITY

One common feeling is of marginality, of being uncertain about one's real religious identity. This often happens soon after the conversion process has been complete and is sensed as not really feeling Jewish, or feeling neither Jewish nor Christian. In the former case, the person may legally be Jewish, but internally there is a sense that the person's root reactions, instincts, and sensibilities—one's central identity—are not yet Jewish. This feeling of belonging frequently just takes time. It comes with performing Jewish tasks, raising Jewish children, thinking Jewishly. One woman told me she knew she was really Jewish when she found herself rushing to the television to hear a news report about Israel, something she never would have done prior to her conversion.

The usual antidote suggested for these feelings is joining Jewish life.

HOLIDAYS

The holidays are frequently a time of special tension. The infamous "December dilemma," in which Hanukkah "competes" against Christmas, is a problem of particular significance. For intermarried couples holidays form one of the crucial areas of argument (along with raising children). For the convert, the problem is not so much how to celebrate the holiday, as it is what to do with pleasant Christmas memories. It is common, for example, for converts to recall with particular fondness decorating a Christmas tree or waking up early on Christmas morning to rush down to look at presents. The pervasiveness of Christmas in American culture only makes such memories more poignant. There are some converts who continue to keep a tree, but most, recognizing that such a tree is outside Jewish tradition, have stopped. Some decorate a tree at a charitable institution or through Girl Scouts as a reminder or simply as a good deed. Born Jews can do such a deed as well out of a sense of kindness to those who enjoy looking at a tree.

Christmas is not the only difficult holiday for converts. Many recall Easter egg hunts, visits to churches on Easter Sunday, and may have special memories of other religious holidays.

As in the case of other feelings, attitudes of attachment to the past should not be repressed. There is nothing odd or unusual about remembering cherished experiences in our lives.

Meryl Nadell notes that holidays are particularly difficult because that is the time when families get together and such a reunion reignites early memories. She says it is naturally difficult to let go of imagery that has defined family love and closeness, such as tree. Because of this, Ms. Nadell suggests getting family together on Thanksgiving or Fourth of July, or some other religiously neutral holiday.

As in most cases, discussion of these issues in a support group for conversion candidates or converts is particularly helpful. Hearing the experiences and suggestions of peers provides not only information and advice but an incentive to act as well.

RAISING CHILDREN

While the practical questions of raising Jewish children are discussed in Part Three of this book, the emotional questions arise very early. In particular, there is frequently a concern about adequacy. Some converts feel unsure about whether or not they can raise Jewish children adequately.

There are clear steps to take to overcome such a feeling. First, make sure your own sense of Jewish identity is clear. Sit with your spouse and discuss the nature of the Jewish identity you want your children to have, what kind of education, family experiences, and home environment can foster that identity, and the methods to get that education and home environment and have those experiences.

Put your ideas into practice. Plan to celebrate holidays in your own ways or according to tradition. There are many suggestions for each holiday in Part Two of this book. Add Jewish experiences, small or large, to your life. For example, many parents start a baby album for a newborn. Include Jewish subject matter in that album.

If possible, one of the best family experiences is to take the children to Israel. My family went to Israel for our daughter Elana's *bat mitzvah*. All the children (then 15, 13, 11, and 8) greatly enjoyed the experience, learned a tremendous amount, and got a good sense of what being Jewish means in the modern world. Our 15-year-old son, Michael, said that crawling through some caves while examining an archeological site was the best experience of his life. The two younger girls, Rachel and Lisa, were extremely comfortable trying out some Hebrew expressions and just entering into the life of the country.

One of the best ways to get closer to one's children is to learn with them. Many Jewish parents—Jews by birth as well as Jews by choice—had minimal childhood exposure to Jewish ideas. When children bring home texts, such parents can read the book with their children and learn right along with them. More than one parent has been taught some Hebrew letters, words, prayers, or blessings by a child. Used as a shared moment of joint learning, such an exchange can help the child feel important and add to self-esteem, and can show a child how important a parent considers Jewish learning.

Children are naturally curious. They will ask questions and when appropriate, often as early as three or four years of age, they can be told about the conversion. This is especially important if the Gentile grandparents live close by and frequently see the child. Many children in the United States do not fully understand religious identity, but in sorting out their rightful place they ask such questions as "Do we celebrate Hanukkah or Christmas?" rather than "Are we Jewish or Christian?" It is most helpful for children to be given clear and distinct responses, with explanations when necessary, such as "We celebrate Hanukkah. Mommy celebrated Christmas when she was a child, but then she became Jewish so now she celebrates Hanukkah not Christmas," or "Grandma and Grandpa celebrate Christmas, which is nice for them, but we don't. We celebrate Hanukkah."

It is very important to communicate with Gentile grandparents about the decisions you have made about your family's celebration of holidays and how your children are to be raised. It should be clear, for example, that the children won't be going to church, don't expect Christmas presents, don't want any presents with Christian themes, such as a cross, and so on, depending on your views. Harder questions include food choices. Some converts do not completely keep kosher, but, for example, refrain from eating pork products. Some do keep kosher in their homes but not outside. If these considerations enter your life, it is vital to tell Gentile grandparents about them.

These are just some of the major challenges a new convert might face.

A central part of conversion is learning about Judaism. The next part of the book considers Judaism's basic beliefs and practices.

II
JUDAISM:
A BASIC GUIDE

9

Jewish Beliefs

Sometimes it is falsely asserted that Judaism is made up simply of a series of specific religious acts, such as praying or keeping the Sabbath. These practices, so vital to Jewish life, are, however, only part of what it means to be Jewish. It is important to remember that the practices exemplify certain beliefs.

Writing about Jewish beliefs is difficult for several reasons. First, there is no set list of beliefs to which all Jews must subscribe. Several such lists have been attempted, the most famous of which was compiled by Moses Maimonides (1135–1204). Yet none of these lists was left unchallenged and none universally accepted. Unlike other religions that have official creeds, Judaism does not.

An additional source of difficulty in writing about beliefs is that, because there is no official creed, people with very different beliefs are considered Jewish according to Jewish law. For example, a person born of a Jewish mother who does not believe in the sacred nature of the Torah, indeed does not even believe in the existence of God, is still considered Jewish.

All this sometimes leads to confusion, both for born Jews and for those joining the Jewish people. The Jewish de-emphasis on beliefs was, in part, a reaction to Christianity, which focused on a specific dogma required of believers. It was also a profound psychological assertion that mere beliefs cannot substitute for real action, that right thinking was secondary to moral behavior. For Jews, the belief could follow the behavior.

Yet, Judaism does have a worldview, a belief system that is comprehensive, but from a specific point. In its formative stages, Judaism developed a set of beliefs about God, the world, and humanity. These beliefs can be deduced from the sacred literature of the Jews and can be put in summary form. In some respect, the Jewish practices that developed were meant to render beliefs into behavior so that the beliefs could be given life. As such, it is important to note that the Jewish worldview cannot be separated from the other aspects of Judaism. It is equally important to remember that Judaism does have beliefs, even though a Jew is not required to believe them to remain Jewish.

Here, then, is a summary of the basic beliefs of Judaism.

GOD

Moses Maimonides listed these Thirteen Principles of Faith that he claimed defined Judaism.

1. God created the entire cosmos.
2. God is one.
3. God is without form, without bodily existence.
4. God is everlasting, an eternal being.
5. God should be the sole object of human prayer.
6. God's word is revealed through prophets.
7. Moses is the greatest of all the prophets.
8. God gave the Torah to Moses.
9. The Torah is meant for all time.
10. God is omniscient, knowing all that people think and do.
11. God seeks justice, providing reward and punishment.
12. God will send the Messiah who will lead us to a better life.
13. God will revive those who have died.

A belief in God is the central idea of Judaism. God, as understood by Jews, is not an impersonal force but a personal Being accessible to humans, not a creator who has no interest in the fate of the
world created, but who instead is intimately involved with the ongoing history of the creation. The idea of God in Jewish thought developed over time, but several crucial elements in the understanding of
God were and remain central. It is important to note, however, as
Maimonides pointed out, that God is of such a different order of being
than we are, that in trying to grasp the infinite we may fail. Despite
the chasm of differences between us and God, however, Judaism provides some ways of understanding.

The Jewish view of God starts out with the basic premise of God's
existence. According to traditional Judaism, God is a Being separate
from the cosmos (the natural world) who really exists. That is, God
is not an invention of the human imagination or a projection of the
human mind. *God* is not a term used to refer to humanity's deepest
longings or ultimate concerns. Rather, God is a real Being. There are
movements in contemporary Jewish life, most especially Reconstructionism and Humanistic Judaism, that question the existence of a
supernatural God, but most Jewish movements continue to assert the
traditional position. The Reform movement, in particular, emphasizes
the individual autonomy of the members of its movement in defining God for themselves.

Who is this Being that traditional Judaism placed at its center?
God's most crucial characteristic is unity. Indeed, one of the central
prayers of Judaism, the *Shema*, includes the declaration: "Hear O
Israel, the Lord is Our God, the Lord is One." God's unity meant that
God is one Being.

This statement about unity is important on several levels. First,
in stating that God is one Being, Judaism claims that God is not other
than one. That is, God is not none. God is also not two beings. Such
a view was widespread at the time of Judaism's founding, with some
peoples believing there were two gods—one good, one evil—who
fought for control. God is not three; that is, God is not divisible in

the way Christianity has portrayed God. Finally, God is not many. The prevalent pagan belief at the time of Judaism's formation was that each natural manifestation was divine. The sun had one divinity, the trees another, and so on. In some religious systems, these divine beings acted very similarly to humans, loving each other, and, just as frequently, fighting each other. Judaism's summation of God as a single Being who ruled over all was, therefore, a direct assault on pagan beliefs. Judaism believed in one God (monotheism) rather than many (polytheism).

Unity means that God is the only divine being, unique in all creation, and, therefore the only Being to be worshiped. Unity also means God cannot be subdivided into smaller units. There is another crucial aspect to the unity. The oneness of God implies an order; God can create a single order out of all. This oneness provides us with a vision of meaning, of elegant simplicity, of order to the cosmos and so order to our world and our lives.

God is incorporeal, that is, without form and without substance as are found in the natural world. God does not have a body. While there are many references to God with a bodily form, the Rabbis noted that such terms were used to help us understand God, but were not to be understood literally. Many of the Rabbis compared the incorporeality of God with the part of humans with no substance—the soul.

God's presence is everywhere. God is universal, the Being that rules over all. This omnipresence indicates that God's spirit is not limited, as it would be in a body, but is all around. There is a moral point the Rabbis wished to make in emphasizing God's existence in all places: God's morality and kindness is everywhere available; God's observance of our moral actions extends to all places in our lives.

God is omnipotent, having all powers that are conceivable but not contradictory. The idea that God is all-powerful means that God can do all that can be done. It does not mean, for example, that God can create a square circle. God's power is not limited by the laws of nature or the other limitations faced by natural beings. God is capable of performing miracles and of entering the natural world, as was traditionally understood to be done at Sinai.

There is another important aspect to God's power. God can choose voluntarily not to use all potential available power. One well-known talmudic principle is that "Everything is in the power of Heaven except the awe of Heaven." That is, God has allowed humans to decide whether or not to obey God's laws. While God, being all-powerful, could have forced humans to obey, it is clear that God wanted morally independent beings and so voluntarily withheld that power in order to make humans free.

God is all-knowing, omniscient of every event that can be known. No knowledge is hidden from God. Knowledge here is understood not simply as a matter of understanding all about the natural world, but understanding the depths of the human heart as well. The ancient Rabbis were quite sure that God knows what will happen in the future. Some modern thinkers, however, believe that God has chosen not to use such knowledge. Still other thinkers assert that, if humans are free and must make moral choices, their freedom is dependent on it being unclear which moral choice they will, in fact, make. Under these circumstances, God cannot have foreknowledge.

Just as God is independent of space by having no form, so God is independent of time. God has existed and will exist for all eternity.

The Jewish conception of God emphasizes that God is good, just, and merciful. God is often seen in sacred literature in a parental role, or as a moral guide and judge. As such, God is a helper to humans through revelation (God revealed moral teachings to humans; God "spoke" to humans) and prayer (in which humans talk to God).

God is a personal, intimate God. The character Tevye in the play *Fiddler on the Roof* goes around all day talking to God as though talking to a friend, imploring, questioning, chatting. This closeness, so foreign, even embarrassing, in the twentieth century, was understood as normal for thousands of years before.

Finally, God is holy, separated from the world and deserving of worship. The Rabbis understood holiness to mean being apart from all else so that God could not be defiled or profaned by the world and that, as a Being apart, God remained a perfect Being. Indeed, the name "the Holy One" was the most common name applied to

God. God's perfection is, of course, not attainable by human beings. Its crucial aspect for Jews, however, lay in the moral effort not to taint that perfection by immoral behavior. Such immoral behavior on the part of God's greatest creation was seen as reflecting on the perfection of God. The Jewish people were the guardians of God's worldly reputation. Their moral behavior would determine how the peoples of the world reacted to God. So it was of the highest religious obligation not to profane God's name, but, by ethical behavior, by obeying God's laws, to sanctify God.

THE COSMOS

As an eternal Being, God existed before the creation of the cosmos. Indeed, God created the cosmos. All natural laws emanate from God. The creation of the cosmos poses an interesting question: since God is a perfect Being, not in need of a cosmos or companions, why was the cosmos created? The answer to this question must be that God had a purpose, and that purpose seems to involve human beings.

Whatever its purpose, the natural world makes many modern people question God's existence and others God's morality. The reason for this is the existence of so many natural disasters: the AIDS virus that kills an innocent child; the hurricane that rushes across a densely populated city; the earthquake that kills good and bad people alike. From such events, some people conclude that there is no God or that God does not care. These problems seemed to bother our ancestors less than they do us.

In the past, such events were seen as divine displeasure or punishment, and were accepted as such. For some, questioning God at all was irreligious, so the very notion of challenging God for creating natural "evil" did not arise. Modern Jewish thinkers, though, do consider this problem. Some thinkers have pointed out that what we call accidents only seem to be accidents because there is a natural order to begin with. It is still possible, however, to ask why God did not create our world without any accidents, or with fewer, or less dangerous ones, or with accidents that seem so random, so unconnected to the morality of the sufferers. Most modern thinkers who wish to affirm God's morality and goodness focus on the natural disasters as shaping humanity in a certain way and as giving us a specific task. A world with no natural laws would have made no sense to us and so values would be meaningless. A world without accident would have taught us that everything is permanent, that no dangers will befall us. Such a world would not have permitted us to make up a complex morality. For example, in a world without danger there would be no need to worry about people getting hurt or facing an accident. Human chances to be heroic or even just help others would be drastically reduced in such a world, reducing our chances to develop our morality and grow morally. Evidently, the nature of human morality God intended required us to have the peculiar natural structure we do, even with its morally disturbing disruptions.

While such an explanation, or some variation of it, does not satisfy some contemporary Jews, most Jews use an ancient or modern explanation and accept the continuing riddle of natural evil as they worship God.

HUMANITY

The Jewish notion of a universal God who created all and is Lord over all extends as well to God's greatest creation: human beings. It is significant, as mentioned earlier, that the Jewish Bible begins not with the origins of Judaism, but with the origins of all the cosmos and all humans.

Those humans, Judaism stresses, were created in the image of God. One crucial aspect of this kinship with God is that humans have a soul. In the classical Jewish sources, the soul was seen as that part of the human that allows us to reach out to God through prayer and right actions, to receive God's message, to inspire us, to prompt us to choose the good, to make us strive for spiritual rather than simply material ideals.

Judaism emphasizes the oneness of the human family by its insistence that God created the first human couple, Adam and Eve, and that all people come from this same couple. Judaism stresses that all humanity is ultimately part of one universal family. This notion of family is important for the obvious ethical reasons that such a relationship makes all people of equal spiritual worth and makes all of us have a family stake in the fate of all others. We as a family share a universal history and a universal destiny. God cares about all people, not just one nation or one people. God is not the God of one place or one group but of everywhere and everyone.

Such a family connection also provides the hope that people will unite and follow God's moral and religious teachings.

Humans, however, remain free to accept or reject those divine teachings. Humans, as the Rabbis understood it, had both a good inclination and an evil one. That is, in Jewish thinking, people were not born naturally good. Neither were they born with "Original Sin" that could be removed from them, a belief central, for example, to traditional Christianity. For Jews, each individual had the moral strength to resist evil within the confines of natural law. That is, a person biologically incapable of reasoning could not be expected to choose freely. But for the overwhelming majority of people there is a series of constant moral choices that must be made. Judaism insists that people have the ability to keep choosing the good, and provides through religious rituals ways that such choices can be made. This human free will is God's gamble that humans, given freedom, will choose good.

Such a free choice to choose good or evil sometimes results in a choice to do evil. Sometimes this choice is called a sin because it violates God's spiritual teachings. Maimonides, in his great book *A Guide for the Perplexed*, distinguished between natural evil, as discussed above, and two kinds of human evil, the kind caused by others to us (assault, for example) and the kind we bring on ourselves.

Jewish thinkers had to consider the implications of their view that God is the provider of our evil impulse. With such an impulse, it is inevitable that all of us will sin from time to time. Judaism provides for a way to overcome the sinful act. This is the way of repentance (in Hebrew, *teshuvah*) and atonement. Repentance means a returning to God after committing sin. There are several crucial aspects to the Jewish view of repentance. First, simply praying and confessing sins will not bring atonement for the sin, unless such verbal efforts are supplemented by real changes in ethical behavior. Such changes are the real test of sincerity. Judaism, of course, specifically provides Ten Days of Repentance, starting with Rosh Hashanah and ending in its holiest day, Yom Kippur. The fast on Yom Kippur is itself an act of penance. Judaism stresses that, even on Yom Kippur, God can forgive the sins we commit against God (such as insufficiently following divine teachings), but we must also seek forgiveness directly from those human beings we have hurt and not just from God. The sin must be corrected as much as possible. For example, if I stole a watch, I cannot receive forgiveness for the theft from God, but must return the watch and ask forgiveness from the watch's owner.

Some contemporary Jewish thinkers focus on the free choice humans have to do good or commit sin to explain moral evil. Just as natural evil prevents some in the modern world from accepting the existence of a moral God, so, too, does evil committed by people against each other. According to the view of free will, the existence of such human evils is the price we (and God) must pay for true spiritual freedom. As terrible as the price is, there does remain both the potential for change, for goodness.

Of course, some people do not find such an explanation satisfying and remain mystified about how a good God can allow such horrible human evil as the Holocaust.

THE JEWISH PEOPLE

According to Judaism's sacred tradition, God called Abraham to leave his native land and make a journey to a new land, one that God promises will belong to Abraham's descendants for all time. This agreement, this covenant, developed a special relationship between God and the Jewish people.

The Jewish people was elected by God to receive holy teachings. This election is the origin of the term *the chosen people* to refer to Jews. God's choice seemingly was made because the Jews were willing to accept God's moral standards without getting any special human privileges.

It is vital to stress that *the chosen people* concept does not mean that Jews are, or think they are, somehow genetically better than other people. They were chosen, rather, to receive a divine message. Judaism has always stressed that the divine message is available to all. Indeed, because Judaism allows converts to become full Jews, it is possible for anyone to choose to be chosen. All people can be God's chosen people if they accept the moral teachings given at Mount Sinai.

God's revelation of the holy teachings occurred as the Jews were escaping slavery in Egypt. Mount Sinai was in a desert, a place chosen because a desert belonged to no nation and no people. Therefore, the spot underscores the notion that such teachings are available to all people.

According to Jewish tradition, God made two divine manifestations at Mount Sinai, one to all the Jewish people and one to the great leader Moses, who had led the exodus to freedom from Egypt. The tradition is that God provided Moses with the Torah, the first five books of the Hebrew Bible (usually translated as Genesis, Exodus, Leviticus, Numbers, and Deuteronomy). This was known as the Written Torah. Traditionalists also believe that God revealed an Oral Torah, which Moses would pass down until eventually it was written down in the work known as the Talmud. (The term *Hebrew Bible* is used by Jews to designate the three sections of the traditional Jewish Bible: Torah, Prophets, and Writings. Jews do not use the term *Old Testament* because a testament is a covenant, and the Jews do not believe that the "old" covenant has been replaced by a "new" covenant.)

Many modern thinkers have difficulty accepting this traditional position. Modernists have very different views, but, in general, they see the Hebrew Bible as compiled over a long period of time by different people and the Talmud as its own historical document without the seamless connection to the Bible expressed by traditionalists. Some modernists believe biblical and talmudic writers were acting under divine guidance, or were inspired. Others believe the Bible and Talmud are simply valuable historical documents of Judaism's evolving religion.

Whatever their view of the divine origin of these books, however, all Jews are united in making study of them central to a religious understanding of Judaism. The sacred books are the indispensable basis for all later Jewish learning.

The Jews entered into a legal agreement at Sinai, a covenant (in Hebrew a *brit*). The children of Israel agreed to obey God and in return God would consider this people unique, "a kingdom of priests and a holy nation." There are various interpretations of the covenant and the purposes God meant for the Jewish people. One such interpretation is that God wished Jews to offer their religion and welcome new converts who voluntarily and without force or coercion chose to become Jewish. For an elaboration of this interpretation, see my book *The Theory and Practice of Welcoming Converts to Judaism: Jewish Universalism* (Edwin Mellen Press, 1992).

Obeying God meant obeying the legal rules of the divine law. This divine law is known in Hebrew as *halachah*. The *halachah* defines religious duties commanded by the Torah. Such a religious duty is called a *mitzvah* (the plural is *mitzvot*), although in ordinary language today *mitzvah* is also used to refer to any good deed, not necessarily to a specific commandment. By tradition, there are 613 *mitzvot*. The *mitzvot* include rules for prayer, for holy days, for various religious rituals, and for much else. Obeying the *mitzvot* is seen by traditional Jews as central to leading a Jewish life. One *mitzvah* is studying Judaism's sacred texts, especially the Hebrew Bible and the Talmud.

The behavioral obligations of Jewish law are supplemented in Jewish religious life by the ethical obligations, stressed in the law and by many of Israel's prophets, such as Isaiah and Micah. The prophets in ancient Israel did not have as a primary mission the foretelling of the future, but rather served as messengers from God, exhorting the people to lead better lives and to provide guidance about how to live. Micah, for example, records what God expects of us: "Only to do the right, to love goodness, and to walk humbly with your God" (Micah 6:8).

The ethical dimension in Jewish life continues to have a centrality, even for those who have departed from strict observance of the ritual obligations. Jewish ethics center on love, compassion, justice, benevolence, and holiness.

Love in the religious sense means to avoid vengeance, to avoid bearing grudges. Probably the most well-known biblical verse regarding love is from Leviticus 19:18: "Love thy neighbor as thyself."

Compassion (in Yiddish, *rachmones*) involves being able to feel the sufferings of others, and, in so doing, desire to alleviate that suffering. Compassion is a frequently cited characteristic of God, and so in feeling it ourselves we are trying to act in the image of God. Compassion extends not only to all people but to animals as well.

Justice means settling disputes between those with opposing views in a fair and impartial manner. The Jewish people set up courts of law and established elaborate legal systems to assure such fairness. The Talmud is, in some respects, an elaborate training manual to teach how principles of justice can be established. Jewish tradition emphasizes that God tempers justice with mercy, so much so that at one point in Jewish literature, God says the world cannot endure if justice were applied without mercy (*Genesis Rabbah* 34:6). It is sometimes claimed by Christian theologians that the Hebrew Bible shows God to be just but not merciful, a stern God, but one without sufficient love. Such an inaccurate characterization is used to provide the supposed alternative in the Christian testament of a Divine Being who embodies love. It is important to emphasize that such a view is simply incorrect. The Christian notions of love, compassion, and mercy are all present in, and derived from, Judaism.

Benevolence is the natural outgrowth of compassion, justice, and mercy. It is the behavior that comes from a compassionate feeling and a striving for justice tempered with mercy. There are, by tradition, two aspects of benevolence. One involves acts of kindness and the other involves direct charity (or *tzedakah*). Acts of kindness include such activities as visiting the sick, comforting those who are in mourning, praising those in need of emotional support, helping the aged or others in need, providing hospitality to visitors, lending money or goods to those in need, or just being friendly. Acts of *tzedakah* involve contributing money to the poor, who need such help to sustain themselves and their families.

AN ACT OF CHARITY

Rabbi Nachman Grodner (1811–1879) was well known in Lithuania for devoting his life to helping the poor. The people nicknamed him the Father of the Poor, and called him by the familiar name Reb Nochemke.

One day a man came to see Reb Nochemke. The man asked the Reb to be the godfather at the circumcision of his newborn son. Reb Nochemke knew the man had no money, not even enough to celebrate the birth of his new child.

Reb Nochemke went to see the man. "Tell me, are you going to visit Kovno?" the Reb asked.

"What if I were going to visit Kovno?" The man was curious about the question.

"If you were going to visit Kovno, I intended to ask a favor of you. You see, I owe twenty-five rubles to a man who lives there. I wanted you to return that money to him for me."

"I haven't been to Kovno for two years. I have no idea when I'll be going there."

"Really, there's no hurry. The man from whom I borrowed the money can wait." With this, Reb Nochemke then gave the man twenty-five rubles. "The next time you are in Kovno, I would appreciate it if you could return the money. Of course, should you need the money for some reason between now and when you go, you can certainly use it and then replace it later."

The man, delighted at this sudden, unexpected money, spent some of it on a joyous party for his son. As Reb Nochemke arrived at the circumcision, the man came up to him and said, "You did not give me the name and address of the man in Kovno to whom you owe the money."

Reb Nochemke pretended to be trying to remember. "I'm sorry. I don't seem to recall the name and address. I must have them at home. I'll tell you some other time. Come, let us enjoy this festive party."

Reb Nochemke eventually told the man that the name and address had been lost. In time, the man saved twenty-five rubles and proudly returned them to Reb Nochemke.

Holiness (*kedushah*) refers to acting in a sacred manner in the image of God. By our acts, by the feelings in our heart, we characterize ourselves. It is by being charitable, kind, compassionate, just, and loving that we have prepared ourselves to receive God. When we have reached such a state we are holy.

Each Jew is enjoined to struggle spiritually so as to embody these characteristics. The personal life of the Jew is filled with prayer, reaching out to God, and study, to learn and be guided through life, to probe life's meaning and find a purpose for our individual lives.

That meaning comes from the special relationship between God and the Jewish people and the Jewish belief in immortality. The purpose of creation for Jews is to glorify and sanctify God and God's creations through worship, observance, and proper conduct through the *mitzvot*, which encompass ethical behaviors. Judaism stresses that meaning occurs precisely because our lives matter to God, and the relationship is important for God as well as us. In several places humans are seen as the partners of God.

Some people use the word *goal* or *mission* for such a purpose, trying to locate how the aim of a particular life can supplement the aim of that individual as part of the Jewish people. Sometimes such a goal is seen through a vocation, or work. Judaism stresses the importance of our work believing such labor elevates people, provides an outlet for creativity, and helps build human society. Labor is the human assigned task in the world. Our work, however we understand it, and our observance of God's laws form the ethical foundation and meaning of our lives.

Judaism stresses both our individual and our communal selves. Social life and social roles are crucial to Judaism. Institutions of particular importance include the family, the synagogue, and communal organizations as well as the more secular understanding of a person as a citizen of a nation and as one member of all humanity.

Today, there are various religious movements within Judaism. Although it is very difficult to provide general observations about these groups, some differences are important to note. The Orthodox movement believes that God literally gave the Written and Oral Law to Moses at Mount Sinai, that all Jews are bound by the *halachah*, that the *halachah* is unchanging, that the fundamental religious obligations for Jews are to obey the *mitzvot*.

Conservative Judaism also accepts the religious authority of the *halachah*, but perceives it differently than do the Orthodox. According to Conservative views, the *halachah* provides within itself the possibility of change as historical developments make such changes warranted. For example, the Conservative movement now ordains women to be rabbis, whereas the Orthodox do not. Conservative Jews vary about how literally they interpret the revelation at Mount Sinai, but it is fair to say that all view the Torah as a fundamental, sacred document.

The Reform movement does not accept the legal authority of the *halachah*, tending to emphasize personal religious autonomy. Few Reform Jews believe in the literal revelation at Sinai. Reform Jews emphasize the adaptability of Judaism to meet the needs of the modern age and the ethical imperatives of Judaism, most beautifully expressed by the prophets, in calling upon Jews to work to repair the world.

The Reconstructionist movement does not subscribe to a belief in a supernatural personal God. Reconstructionists redefined Judaism, seeing it not just as a religion, but as an evolving religious civilization, with all the attributes of any civilization.

MARRIAGE AND FAMILY IN JEWISH LIFE

The institution of the family has been at the core of Jewish life since its inception. In biblical times, Jews were counted not by individuals but by families. It is a biblical metaphor to think of all humanity as one large family.

Marriage is itself a *mitzvah*. Indeed, the very first *mitzvah*, "to be fruitful and multiply," connotes a marriage and family.

A Jewish marriage is defined as one between two Jews. Even if a rabbi performs a marriage between a non-Jew and a Jew, that marriage is not considered by most rabbis to be legitimately Jewish. There is considerable argumentation within the Jewish community about whether a rabbi should perform, participate in, or even attend an interfaith marriage. Those who argue for some kind of participation suggest that the rabbi's presence will keep the Jewish member of the intermarriage, and perhaps both members, close to the Jewish community. Those who argue against such participation suggest that participation sanctions intermarriage.

Why is intermarriage considered such a threat to Jewish survival? One answer to this question relies on demographics. There are fewer than 13 million Jews in the world. Those Jews make up less than 1 percent of the world's population. Because the Jewish people is so small, each person is significant. If there were 100 million Jews, losses through assimilation or intermarriage would be much less noticeable.

There is an historical side to this question as well. The Jewish people has been in continuous existence for 4,000 years. A Jew today has many ancestors who suffered persecution to remain Jewish. Because of this longevity, and the pain endured to insure it, Jewish parents see in an intermarriage an end to a 4,000-year-old tradition and, although they might not use the term, a betrayal of all those Jews who suffered persecution and death so that Judaism might continue.

The threat of intermarriage is, in this sense, a threat to the continuity of raising the next generation. If the child is not considered Jewish by *halachah*, then the chain of tradition has been broken. Even if the child is legally Jewish, however, that child needs to learn about

Judaism so that as a parent the tradition might continue. Jewish education is not an enterprise left to the schools and the synagogues. Home and family play a crucial role, so that if one parent is not Jewish it is much more difficult to teach Jewish ideals, beliefs, and practices to children. Non-Jewish grandparents, with the best intentions, may confuse that educational process.

Some born Jews understand these considerations, but they claim individual autonomy should rule their lives, not claims by long-dead ancestors or even living parents. Such Jews argue that love should triumph over religious tradition.

Some born Jews claim that they have no attachment to specifically Jewish values, that they cherish the same values as their non-Jewish spouse, values at the heart of America. The problem with such a position is that the born-Jewish partner is rejecting a worldview and way of life that have not been tried. Many American Jews, in particular, identify Judaism with the unhappy experiences they had in Hebrew school. They think of Jewish practices as childish because they stopped learning about Judaism when they were children. In fact, it is a frequent situation for the Jewish partner in an intermarriage to study Judaism in adulthood, after the intermarriage has taken place, and discover the beauty of Judaism and the loss inherent in a non-Jewish marriage no matter how much in love the Jewish spouses might be with their partners. Judaism, believing in lifelong learning, stresses that we grow as we learn; we change as we mature. Such changes occur as well in our religious outlook. The twenty-two year old atheist or agnostic can, by thirty, feel deep spiritual yearnings. When Judaism is rediscovered after an intermarriage, or a non-Jewish religion by the non-Jewish partner, there is considerable pain brought to the marriage.

Other Jews argue that they believe themselves to belong to all humanity, not just to one people. However worthy the goal of a universal peoplehood might be, it is hard to see that the surrendering of Judaism achieves such a purported peoplehood. Rather than the vast human melting pot inherent in such an idea, it is more valuable to consider humanity as a mosaic, with each distinct people contributing to the overall beauty. Jews as Jews have an important contribution to make to humanity; Jews as nothing have no communal contribution to make.

There are many Jews in an intermarriage who do not wish to sever their relations with the Jewish community. They say that they simply fell in love with a non-Jew, but they consider themselves Jewish and wish to continue in the Jewish community. All Jews are welcomed by most institutions, and non-Jewish spouses are welcomed by many as well. However well-meaning such Jews are, they neglect the crucial facts of continuity, the effects of intermarriage on children.

Intermarriage has detrimental effects on children. Many people entering into an intermarriage find they can negotiate compromises (a Christmas tree and a menorah might both be present in the home), but such negotiations become infinitely more difficult when children rather than trees become the objects of the negotiation. Some parents raise the children in both religions, letting the child decide. This approach, so seemingly balanced, usually has the effect of confusing children at a young age and making children choose between their parents at an older age. It is unsurprising that many children choose no religion or a religion separate from either parent's; choosing one religion, many feel, would wound the parent of the other religion.

Other parents change religion, choosing a "neutral" religion. Still others try to bring up children without any mention of religion in the home.

The effect of these or other choices is to reduce the possibility that the children will be brought up Jewish. It is not surprising that most studies indicate that in an intermarriage less than 25 percent of the children are brought up as Jewish. The only factor that changes such a statistic is that when a conversion to Judaism takes place, the chances are greater than 75 percent that the children will be raised as Jews. This startling difference accounts, in part, for the increased Jewish interest in conversion.

Despite such an admiration for conversion, it is important to note that traditional Judaism favors marriage between two born Jews.

However, marriage between a born Jew and a validly converted non-Jew is legally a Jewish marriage.

Judaism does not see remaining single as somehow being more religious; marriage for life, with children (at least one boy and one girl, according to Hillel in the Talmud) is the ideal. There are many legitimate reasons why such an ideal cannot be reached. Judaism, for instance, permits divorce. It is possible that a couple may not be able to have children. A spouse may die; under such circumstances Judaism sanctions remarriage. But each of these is considered against the ideal. While divorce is permitted, all efforts need to be made to save a Jewish marriage. When no natural children are possible (and also when they are), adoption is a possibility. The talmudic view of the adopted child is that when an orphan is adopted, it is as though the adopting couple has given birth to the child. In a remarriage after a death, the Rabbis note that it is likely the survivor thinks kindly and frequently about the first spouse.

Romantic love, so powerful a force in our society, is not the sole criterion for picking a marriage partner in Jewish thought. Romantic feelings are, of course, important in picking a partner, but are not considered the sole basis, in part because feelings change over time. Judaism's stress on the family means that, beyond romantic satisfaction, a prospective mate should come from a good family, be a good person, and should be considered in nonsexual situations as well, such as how much respect does that person command, how well does the person deal with children, and other similar issues so vital to the creation not just of a sexual relationship but of a marriage and family. Judaism has important laws about the family and the nature of sexual relations. In general, Judaism sees the sexual urge as natural, best expressed through a marital relationship, and an indicator of moral character. That is why Judaism is so opposed to such dangers to the family as incest and adultery, seeing them as profoundly moral questions, threatening the family, that most central of Jewish institutions.

Parents have a central responsibility to raise their children, to teach them about Judaism, to provide opportunities for study so they may learn a vocation as well as learn to be good. The Jewish emphasis on education has often been noted. Some observers believe that because Jews were so frequently uprooted, forced to move from place to place, they focused on what could be carried with them anywhere— a faith in the universal God, and the learning that they carried in their minds and books. Whatever the reason, there is no doubt that Jewish tradition cherished those who learned, so much so that the family duty to educate is repeated in the central Jewish prayer, the *Shema*, which is recited several times every day.

THE COMMUNITY

Jewish obligations extend beyond the moral obligations to God, to ourselves, and to our family. We are also responsible for our community. Human beings are inherently seen as belonging to groups, not just existing as individuals.

One important Jewish view in this regard is that each society can be judged morally just as each individual can be judged. Judaism calls upon each Jew as a citizen to be responsible not just for personal inadequacies but for communal ones as well. Judaism, in particular, stresses that a just society must be free from oppression, treating all humans as equal before God. In real terms, such treatment needs to insure that those who cannot take care of themselves are provided for. That is why giving to the needy is so valued in Jewish tradition, with a particular emphasis on helping a person become independent. There is no one political party or philosophy that automatically creates such a just society. Indeed, different philosophies of social order may legitimately differ about how best to reach a common goal. Judaism emphasizes the moral nature of that goal.

It was Hillel who provided the injunction "Do not separate yourself from the community." We are not moral if we act morally as individuals and countenance immorality in our communities. Jews, as a rule, do not wish to, and have not, separated themselves from the world. Sometimes the world has not wished to hear the Jewish voice of conscience, but the voice remains strong.

REDEMPTION: THE MESSIANIC AGE

Redemption describes the time when God and humanity will be reconciled, a time when human moral behavior will render concrete the currently abstract promise of human moral potential. Such morality will justify God's original creation of humans and, at the same time, provide humans with the ultimate meaning of their existence. Redemption is often put in terms of a climax to world history, an emergence of the Kingdom of Heaven when the world will be as perfect as it can be, when humans will be freed from all their sins and willingly conform to God's moral teachings.

Such a vision is frequently tied to another idea in Jewish thought, that of the Messiah, a human anointed by God to rule over this Kingdom of Heaven. The Messiah will rebuild the Temple in Jerusalem, gather Jewish exiles to live in the land of Israel, restore the ancient religious practices associated with the Temple, and, in general, usher in such a great moment. Orthodox Jews believe that such a literal person will emerge one day from history; some Orthodox believe that day is soon to be.

Non-Orthodox versions of messianic thought have come in at least two varieties. Some Zionists who rebuilt the modern State of Israel see their efforts as a secular version of the messianic zeal, a desire for a perfected age, but a zeal forced to live in a world that could not believe in a literal personal messiah. Orthodox Jews reject such a notion, as do many Zionists themselves. Reform Judaism provided the other non-Orthodox version of messianic thought. Reform Judaism taught that a person known as the Messiah would not come, but that humans on earth, through their efforts at cooperation, could usher in a messianic age.

DEATH AND THE HEREAFTER

While the notion of a messiah or a messianic age focuses on the here and now, Judaism also considers the question of what happens after we die. Such concern is not, however, primary in Judaism, which, in general, focuses on life, preferring to work to improve this world and face the next one at the appropriate time. Judaism has stressed the natural fact of death and its crucial place in giving life meaning.

The normal human concerns about death deeply affect Jews. Jewish thinkers have long pondered the fear of death and our attachment to life, the pain and sense of loss we feel when someone we care for dies, the ethical concerns we have that life seems unfair, but God is just, so final justice must occur somewhere, the drive we have to continue our life's achievements, the desire not to be separated from those we love, and many other concerns.

Traditional Judaism did have an eschatology, a view of the chronology of the end of the world. The first step in such eschatological thinking involved the arrival of the Messiah. After some time, those who have died will be resurrected. Their bodies will somehow arise from the graves. This resurrection of the dead is the reason that many traditional Jews oppose cremation or other acts that destroy the body that God will resurrect. The souls of the resurrected, until then residing in Heaven, will cleave back to the resurrected bodies. God will then give the Last Judgment about our fates. Ultimately, all bodies will die, but the souls will continue on forever. (There were Jewish thinkers, such as Nachmanides, who believed that the newly refurbished bodies would remain forever alive as well.)

Traditionalists also considered how individuals would be rewarded or punished after their deaths. There are some grand descriptions of Heaven and Hell, but these are relatively rare. Immanuel ben Solomon of Rome (born 1720), for example, wrote *Tophet and Eden* (Hell and Paradise), which is filled with such descriptions. Immanuel was a contemporary of Dante's and probably fashioned his work after the *Divine Comedy*.

Traditionalists gave the name *Gehenna* to the place where souls were punished. Many Jewish thinkers noted that since, essentially, God is a Lord of mercy and love, punishment is not to be considered to be eternal or, even, real. There are, similarly, many varying conceptions of paradise (or *Gan Eden*). One thinker, Isaac Abrabanel

(1437–1508), commenting on a biblical passage (1 Samuel 25:29), suggests that Paradise is the place where we finally understand the true concept of God. It has also been suggested that there is no separate Heaven and Hell, only lesser or greater distance from God after death, with the good closer to God, and the evil more distant and waiting for the purification of their souls.

Modern Jewish thinkers have focused more on a belief in the soul's immortality rather than in the literal resurrection of the dead. Some have rejected a literal Heaven or Hell. Some thinkers note the perfectly natural ways in which we may understand immortality: through our children, through those who remember us, through our influence in doing good, through our efforts and achievements, and much else. Those modernists who affirm a soul and its existence after death frequently take the moral question raised above into consideration and consider the soul to be rewarded or punished on the basis of the person's ethical conduct while alive.

JUDAISM AND CHRISTIANITY: THE DIFFERENCES

There are substantive and crucial differences between Judaism and Christianity. There are also many similarities, in large part because Christianity grew out of Judaism. But Christianity officially separated itself, and it is misleading, however comfortable the thought might be, to consider the two religions essentially the same, or to see one as the natural continuation of the other.

Before discussing the differences, it is important to reiterate that Judaism believes that all people are the children of God. All people have God's love, justice, mercy, and help. Judaism does not require that someone be Jewish in order to achieve salvation, only to be ethical.

While Judaism accepts the worth of all people, it also allows anyone who is not Jewish and who voluntarily wishes to enter Judaism as a convert to do so. The traditionalist believes Judaism to be truer than other religions, while modernists tend to see all religions as providing their own special contribution to the world. However, both the traditionalist and the modernist believe that Judaism is a distinct religion, one not subsumed under another, one not replaced by any other, one so precious as to make its preservation a central religious obligation.

Just as it is virtually impossible to summarize Judaism fairly, so, too, is it impossible in a summary of differences to be entirely fair to Christianity. The beliefs described are mainstream Christian beliefs, but various Christian theologians, people, and movements have views that vary considerably from those described. In such cases, the differences between those views and Judaism need to be considered individually.

The basic differences between Judaism and Christianity are numerous. The differences begin with the Jewish insistence on a pure, undiluted monotheistic conception of God. The Christian notion is that God is made up of God the Father, God the Son, and the Holy Spirit. Such a view, even if called monotheistic because the three parts are, by divine mystery, only one God, is incompatible with the Jewish insistence that no such division of an indivisible God can be made. Judaism sees such an attempt as a partial throwback to a pagan conception of many gods.

As has already been mentioned, Judaism does not accept the notion of original sin, a belief vital to Christianity. The idea of an original sin that damns a soul before birth and requires salvation is entirely alien to Judaism. The Jewish alternative, to reiterate, is that the soul is not born in sin, but with both good and bad inclinations. Against original sin, Judaism posits a belief in a free moral will with which humans choose whether or not to commit a sin. Indeed, Judaism's entire ethical system presupposes human moral freedom.

Starting from its position of original sin, Christianity logically posits the required next step, atonement from that original sin. But atonement cannot come from simple human repentance and the desire to repair one's moral failures. Instead, Christianity believes that the saving act of grace provided by the vicarious atonement for human sins made by Jesus is all that can save people. Atonement for original sin can, according to Christianity, only come through an acceptance of Jesus. The whole idea of "vicarious atonement" leads to the role of Jesus as an intercessor between God and humans, a belief directly at odds with the Jewish view that no intercessor is necessary because all people have direct access to God. Judaism also emphasizes the ever-present possibility of repentance with a promise to mend one's moral failures. That, in the Jewish view, is how to counter sin.

Christianity pits the body against the soul and denigrates the body as inferior, that flesh is evil. Judaism believes the body to be good in that it is a gift from God. Our hope is not only for an afterlife for the soul, but for a good (meaning moral) life on earth for the body.

Christianity says the *mitzvot* are not binding, that ethical commandments have been replaced by a faith in Jesus, that the *halachah* is no longer binding. Judaism does not believe that faith alone is a sufficient religious response to life. Rather, a religious life requires a carefully considered ethical plan. Action, in Judaism, must supplement belief. In Judaism, there is not a distinction between "law" and "faith." Both are inextricably linked, and both are necessary.

One final difference between Christianity and Judaism is the way both religions consider Jesus.

To Christians, of course, Jesus is the Son of God, part of the trinitarian nature of the Godhead, the Savior of souls, who is the Messiah. He is God's revelation through flesh. Jesus was God incarnate, God in the flesh, not just in writings.

To Jews, whatever Jesus may have been, He was not the Son of God, because God does not have children, except in the metaphorical sense in which all people are equally God's children. God's nature is not trinitarian in Judaism, so that there could only be one being in the Godhead, God. Jesus cannot save souls; only God can, in conjunction with human efforts to repent and change their behavior. Jesus was not the Messiah; the Messiah has not yet arrived. Jesus was not God in the flesh.

Jews may vary about what they think about Jesus as a man. Some consider him an exemplary moral teacher, bound to *halachah*, not seeing himself as the Messiah at all, but someone who challenged the priestly leaders, as they had been challenged by many others. Jesus, by these accounts, created no new theological concepts, but was consistent with many of the mainstream movements of the Judaism of his time, an argument seemingly buttressed by the Dead Sea Scrolls. That is, the lessons Jesus taught, the parables He used, may not have been meant to create a new religion, but to revolutionize Judaism. Other Jews are more dismissive, arguing that, theologically, Jesus has as much impact on Judaism as Mohammed, that is, none.

Whatever the Jewish response is, however Jesus is conceived, one point is clear. No one who is Jewish, no born Jew and no convert, can believe in Jesus as the Son of God or as the Messiah. For the Jewish people, there is no God but God.

10
Jewish Texts

THE BIBLE

The word *bible* means "little books," so that the Jewish Bible should not be considered as one text, but as a sacred library of books. Not all ancient Jewish religious writings were put in the Bible. Traditionalists believe God provided the Torah and the Oral Law (which will be discussed later) to Moses at Mount Sinai. Modernists tend to believe that the Bible was a selection of sacred writings, writings done by humans perhaps under Godly influence. By tradition, there are twenty-four books of the Bible, but one of these, the Book of the Twelve Prophets, is sometimes subdivided, making for a total of thirty-nine books.

The Jewish Bible is divided into three parts: the Torah, the Prophets (*Nevi'im*), and the Writings (*Ketuvim*). The Jewish Bible is also called the *Tanach*, an abbreviation of the three parts.

Here is a list of the twenty-four books of the Bible:

Torah

1. Genesis
2. Exodus
3. Leviticus

4. Numbers
5. Deuteronomy

Nevi'im

6. Joshua
7. Judges
8. Samuel 1 and 2
9. Kings 1 and 2
10. Isaiah
11. Jeremiah
12. Ezekiel
13. The Book of the Twelve Prophets (Hosea, Joel, Amos, Oba-
    diah, Jonah, Micah, Nachum, Habakkuk, Zephaniah, Hag-
    gai, Zechariah, Malachi)

Ketuvim

14. Psalms
15. Proverbs
16. Job
17. The Song of Songs
18. Ruth
19. Lamentations
20. Ecclesiastes
21. Esther
22. Daniel
23. Ezra and Nehemiah
24. Chronicles 1 and 2

THE APOCRYPHA AND PSEUDEPIGRAPHA

There were a large number of books written by Jews that were not
included in the Bible, but were included as sacred and put into the
Old Testament by the Roman Catholic and Eastern Orthodox

churches. These books are known as the Apocrypha (or "hidden books"). They had no crucial influence on Jewish religious development, but are important historical documents and shed considerable light on Jewish life, including religious life. They include such works as Maccabees 1 and 2, Tobit, and Judith.

Other books were also written, but not included in Christian Bibles. These writings are called Pseudepigrapha. They include such works as The Testaments of the Twelve Patriarchs, the books of Enoch, and others.

THE TALMUD: MISHNAH AND GEMARA

The ancient Rabbis interpreted the Bible and the Oral Law, which, by tradition, had been passed down originally from Moses verbally, generation by generation. The interpretation of biblical verses became known as *midrash*. The writing down, study, and formulation of the Oral Law, done by scholars known as *tanna'im* (those who wrote from about 70 C.E. to about 200 C.E.), became known as *mishnah* (from a word meaning "to repeat"). Eventually the Oral Law was written down in edited form in about 200 C.E. under the guidance of Judah Ha-Nasi, Judah, the Prince. The Mishnah consists of six orders. Each of these six orders is divided into tractates (there are sixty-three tractates in all), and each of these tractates is divided into chapters. The chapters in turn are divided into paragraphs.

The Mishnah is the most vital, sacred Jewish text after the Bible itself. It focuses on and expands and explains the laws of the Bible. In that sense the Mishnah is in large part halachic. There are parts of the Mishnah that do not deal with the law, parts known as the *aggadah*. The Mishnah was a legal code book for judges and a textbook for teachers, summarizing Jewish law. For example, the Bible includes the commandment that Jews are not supposed to work on the Sabbath. Such a commandment requires an understanding of just what constitutes "work." In the years after the Bible, such discussions were frequently held, and the decisions passed on verbally until written down in the Mishnah.

Six Orders of the Mishnah

1. *Zera'im* (Seeds). This order first includes a discussion of blessings and daily prayers. Most of the order deals with agricultural laws.
2. *Moed* (Appointed Seasons). This order describes the laws concerning how Jews are to observe the Sabbath, various religious festivals, and fast days.
3. *Nashim* (Women). This order deals with marriage, divorce, and various other issues.
4. *Nezikin* (Damages). This order focuses on civil and criminal law, appropriate punishment, idolatry, and ethical teachings.
5. *Kodashim* (Holy Matters). This order describes ritual slaughter, sacrifices, and the Temple service.
6. *Tohorot* (Cleanliness). This order discusses the laws of ritual purity.

After the Mishnah was published, Rabbis continued to discuss the vital religious subjects raised in its tractates. These discussions, by rabbis and scholars known as *amora'im* (writing from about 200 C.E. until about 500 C.E.), were in turn collected and were known as the Gemara. Eventually the Mishnah and the Gemara were put together to form a body of work called the Talmud (a word that is derived from the Hebrew for both "teaching" and "learning"). There were, in fact, two different versions of the Talmud. The Jerusalem, or Palestinian, Talmud was completed about the year 400 C.E. It discusses 39 of the 63 tractates of the Mishnah. The second, much more well-known, Talmud, is the Babylonian Talmud (also known as the Bavli). It was completed some time after 500 C.E. and includes discussion on 36 of the tractates.

The Talmud is organized on the basis of the Mishnah, citing the particular portion of the Mishnah and then the Gemara, which examines the Mishnah's text, using arguments to be precise about the requirements of the law. The Talmud was the chief religious text of Jewish life, in some communities used with more frequency than the Bible, for more than one thousand years. Its vastness has often been compared to a sea, so filled with stories and learned arguments is it. The Talmud remains a source of study for traditional Jews, but even for modern Jews, the Talmud is an incomparable repository not only of Jewish history and religion, but also a valuable resource to develop logical and legal abilities. The Talmud's role in Jewish history is almost impossible to overstate. Anyone who wishes to understand Judaism must at the very least sample talmudic thinking, such as by reading the tractate *Avot* ("Fathers"), the ninth tractate of the order *Nezikin*. *Avot*, which is also known as *Pirke Avot* ("Chapters of the Fathers"), is, as Lena Romanoff learned in her story in the first part of this book, a collection of rabbinic maxims and wise sayings. Because the Talmud was written in Hebrew and Aramaic, and its language and structure of argument are difficult, many readers who have not been trained in traditional Judaism read the Talmud in English translation. There is an increasing number of such translations.

MIDRASH

As has been noted, *midrash* means an examination of a biblical text, an exposition concerning its meaning. Such commentary was meant to make *halachah* clear (Midrash Halachah) or to provide lessons using a variety of literary devices including parables and legends (Midrash Aggadah).

Midrash also refers to the literature that resulted from such an examination. Some famous *midrashim* (plural of *midrash*) include *Mechilta* (a discussion of the book of Exodus), *Sifra* (a discussion of Leviticus), and *Sifre* (a discussion of Numbers), and another *Sifre* (a discussion of Deuteronomy). There are many other collections of *midrashim*.

BIBLE COMMENTARIES

While the *midrashim* meant to provide expositions of biblical texts, in most cases they were too extensive to be put alongside the actual biblical text and studied along with it. Therefore, various Bible commentaries developed. The most popular of such biblical commentaries was written by Rashi (Solomon ben Isaac (1041–1105), who lived in Northern France. Rashi's commentaries about the Bible are still studied today. There have been many biblical commentaries. Among the most famous are those by Abraham ibn Ezra (1089–1164), the Rashbam (Samuel ben Meir, c. 1085–c. 1174), Radak (David Kimchi, 1160–1235), the Ramban (Moses ben Nachman, also known as Nachmanides, 1195–1270), the Ralbag (Levi ben Gershon, also known as Gersonides, 1288–1344), Don Isaac Abravanel (1437–1508), and Obadiah Sforno (c. 1470–c. 1550).

COMMENTARIES ON THE TALMUD

The Talmud is a particularly difficult text, filled with complex subject matter, dense argument, sometimes difficult language, historical allusions, and other impediments to clear understanding. As with the biblical text, commentaries appeared to make sailing the sea of Talmud a lot easier.

Maimonides, for example, wrote a famous commentary about the Mishnah, taking each paragraph and trying to render it sensible to his readers, at times going so far as to differ from the interpretation given in the Gemara. Other significant commentaries on the Mishnah include one made in 1548–9 by Obadiah Bertinoro, *Tosefot Yom Tov* by Yom Tov Lipmann Heller (1579–1654), and *Tiferet Yisrael* by Israel Lipschutz (1782–1860).

The most important commentary on the whole Talmud was that made by Rashi. Rashi's insights were so valuable that his comments are, in the traditional Talmud, printed on one side of the text. Rashi was influential in another way. His sons-in-law and grandsons developed a study of the Talmud called *tosafot*, or additions. These men founded various schools that used this study. The collections of the comments are included on the other side of the text opposite Rashi's.

RESPONSA

However valuable the commentaries on the Talmud were, many who wished to be observant were unable to understand some of the legal conclusions to be drawn from the extensive arguments in the talmudic text. Additionally, contemporary problems arose that were not directly discussed by the Rabbis. Unsure of what to do, many individuals and leaders of communities began to write to halachic authorities with questions about Jewish law. The halachic authorities would then provide a response to those questions. These questions and answers were frequently gathered and published, either by the halachic authorities themselves or their disciples. There are thousands of volumes of these questions and answers, which go by the general term *responsa*. They are valuable not only for their legal comments but for their insights into the social histories of the places and time in which they occur.

CODES

Codes of Jewish law present systematic arrangements of halachic decisions from the Talmud brought up-to-date by including material from, for example, the Responsa and specific legal decisions from a *Bet Din*, or law court. The first major code, *Hilchot ha-Rif*, was made by the Rif (Isaac Alfasi, 1013–1103). The most complete, and one of the most influential codes, was the *Mishneh Torah* produced by Maimonides, which covered every aspect of Jewish law. The most authoritative code was produced by Joseph Caro (1488–1575). Caro's *Shulchan Aruch*, or Prepared Table, published in 1564–5, while attempting to unify what Caro saw as the existence of many views, tended to favor the views of those Jews who lived under Muslim rule (the Sephardim). In 1569–71, Moses Isserles added notes, the *Mappah* ("tablecloth"), to the *Shulchan Aruch*, and it become the code that was used by halachic authorities. Its popularity may also have arisen perhaps because it was the first code devised after the invention of the printing press and so could be quickly and widely distributed. To this day, the *Shulchan Aruch* is the code followed by Orthodox Jews.

There were, in turn, many commentaries on the various codes.

OTHER WRITING

There is a tremendous amount of literature available about the Jewish religion. In addition to the material cited above there are also the following:

• Liturgical works, collections of Jewish prayers. In many ways the traditional Jewish prayer book, the *Siddur*, is the most valuable text for understanding the religion, for it includes the ideas and feelings that most deeply touched ordinary people. The *Siddur* puts those ideas and feelings into words and songs that were said and sung daily or on a regular basis and so became profoundly embedded in all Jews who recited those prayers, which until relatively recently included almost all Jews. There are special books of prayers for particular holy days, such as the Haggadah for Passover, which will be discussed later.
• Moralistic literature, which provided codes for ethical living. One well-known example of such works is *The Duties of the Heart* by Bachya ibn Pakuda, who wrote in the eleventh century.
• Philosophical and theological works. Philosophy among Jews was relatively late in its arrival and was used most often to justify Judaism in a language used by thinkers of other cultures. One early Jewish philosopher, Philo, attempted to make Judaism understandable to Greek philosophers. Moses Maimonides wrote *The Guide for the Perplexed* (1190), to explain how the principles of Aristotelian philosophy could be understood by traditional rabbinic Judaism. Maimonides stressed that God could be loved through reason, and that philosophy and religion were not inherently contradictory.

There have been many other significant philosophical works.

• Kabbalistic literature, or the material produced by Jewish mystics. *Kabbalah* means a "received tradition" and focuses on secret interpretations of the biblical text. The most important of kabbalistic texts is the *Zohar*.

• Chasidic literature, produced by a movement that will be discussed in the history section and includes a variety of literature, perhaps the most interesting of which are the various tales told about chasidic leaders.

• Secular literature. Jews have produced large amounts of poetry and fiction. Among the most famous of Jewish novelists who use Jewish themes in their works are Saul Bellow, Bernard Malamud, Philip Roth, and Chaim Potok.

• Other types of literature, including autobiographies, tales of travel, especially to the land of Israel, history, and many other works.

11
Jewish History:
A Brief Outline

Jewish history relies on the Bible for a re-creation of its formative years. While Orthodox Jews continue to believe in the literal historical accuracy of the Bible, other traditionalists and most modernists believe that the Bible is a religious rather than an historical document, that it is sacred but not necessarily scientifically accurate. Such traditionalists and modernists supplement biblical evidence with, for example, archeological and other evidence. It is impossible, even with this supplementary evidence, to verify the accuracy of every biblical account. Nevertheless, most Jewish historians see no reason to doubt the major outlines of history as detailed in the Bible.

ABRAHAM AND SARAH

The history of the Jewish people begins with Abraham, who lived about the year 1900 B.C.E. (Before the Common Era). Abraham lived in a highly civilized area in what today is Iraq, but what was then called Ur, in southern Mesopotamia. Later his father moved northwest to Haran. Abraham's crucial contribution to religious thought

119

was his challenge to paganism, and his worship of one God over all the cosmos. After his father's death, Abraham received a revelation from God to go with his wife Sarah and his family to the land of Canaan, a land promised by God to Abraham's descendants, who would be a great nation, and a blessing for all humanity.

Late in life, Sarah gave birth to Isaac. Abraham later received an instruction to sacrifice Isaac to God, but such a sacrifice (known as the *Akedah*) is stopped by an angel. Many Jewish interpreters see this incident as Judaism's separating itself from the common pagan practice of sacrificing the firstborn son. Isaac married Rebecca, who bore twin sons, Jacob and Esau. Jacob, using his father's failing vision and following his mother's wishes, tricked Isaac into granting him the blessing reserved for the firstborn son.

Jacob, later called Israel after wrestling with an angel, had two wives, Leah and Rachel, and twelve sons and a daughter. Joseph was Jacob's favorite son, and his love, exemplified by Jacob's gift of a coat of many colors to Joseph, led Joseph's brothers to plot against him. The brothers sold him to a caravan of traders who took him to Egypt. Jacob, seeing the coat covered with blood, believed the brothers' story that Joseph had died.

LIFE IN EGYPT

Canaan experienced a famine, forcing the children of Israel to go to Egypt for sustenance. Unknown to them, Joseph had arisen to a position of power through his uncanny abilities to interpret dreams and spare Egypt from economic disaster. The family was reunited.

Unfortunately, however, a new Egyptian dynasty arose and enslaved the Jewish people. Eventually there arose a great Jewish leader named Moses. Despite his own hesitancy, Moses led the Jewish people out of slavery in the Exodus. He led them across the Sea of Reeds, to Mount Sinai.

A DATELINE OF JEWISH HISTORY

1900 B.C.E.	Abraham
1280	Exodus from Egypt under Moses' leadership.
1250	Conquest of Canaan under Joshua's leadership.
1200–1020	Era of the Judges (e.g., Deborah, Gideon, Samson, and Samuel).
1020	Saul, the first king
1004–965	Rule of King David; Jerusalem is made the capital of the nation.
965–928	Solomon rules as king; The First Temple is built.
922	The Israelite Kingdom is divided into two nations, Judah (two tribes) and Israel (ten tribes).
ca. 850	Elijah, the prophet
ca. 750	Amos
ca. 735	Hosea
ca. 725	Isaiah and Micah
722	The Assyrians conquer Israel and send its inhabitants into exile, marking the disappearance of the nation.
639–609	Josiah
ca. 600	Jeremiah
586	Judea is captured. The Temple is destroyed and most of the inhabitants are sent into exile in Babylonia.
ca. 590	Ezekiel
ca. 550	Second Isaiah (author of chapters 40–66 in the biblical book Isaiah).
538	First return from Babylonia.
515	The Temple is rebuilt.
ca. 444	Ezra reads the Torah publicly.
332	Alexander the Great conquers the land of Israel, leading to Greek influence.
167	Antiochus IV outlaws Judaism.
164	Judah Maccabee captures Jerusalem and rededicates the Temple, a story remembered during the holiday of Hanukkah.

ca. 100	Scrolls are written by members of a community living near the Dead Sea.
63	The Romans take control of Jerusalem.
37–4	King Herod rules under Roman control.
ca. 10 C.E.	Hillel dies.
26–36	Pontius Pilate is prefect.
30	Jesus is crucified.
70	The Second Temple is destroyed by the Romans. Yohanan ben Zakkai founds a learning center at Yavneh.
73	Fall of Masada.
ca. 80–110	Gamaliel heads Yavneh. The Hebrew Bible is put into its final form. The rabbis develop an order for prayers.
132–35	Bar Kokhba war.
ca. 200	Judah Ha-Nasi edits the Mishnah.
ca. 220	The Sura academy in Babylonia is founded by Rab.
ca. 400	Jerusalem Talmud completed. Its final editing is completed by ca. 700.
ca. 600	Babylonian Talmud completed.
630–640	Moslems conquer the Middle East.
1040	Birth of Rashi.
1096	The First Crusade. Many Jews are killed in Rhineland.
1138	Birth of Moses Maimonides.
1190	Jews massacred in York, England.
1233	The Inquisition forces Jews to convert or die.
1290	Jews are expelled from England.
1349, 1394	Jews are expelled from France.
1348–1350	The Black Death; Jews are blamed. Many begin moving east to Poland.
1492	Jews expelled from Spain.
1516	The institution of the ghetto is begun in Venice. Jews must live separately from others.
1520	The Babylonian Talmud first appears in print.
1567	Joseph Caro publishes *Shulchan Aruch*.
1648	Jews massacred in Poland and Ukraine.
1654	Jewish community founded in New Amsterdam.

1665	Shabbetai Zevi proclaimed as Messiah.
1760	Death of Baal Shem Tov, founder of Chasidism.
1786	Death of Moses Mendelssohn, key thinker of *Haskalah* (Jewish Enlightenment).
1789	French Revolution gives freedom to Jews; United States Constitution provides for religious freedom.
1807	Napoleon calls a Sanhedrin for rulings.
1881	Czar Alexander II killed in Russia; Jews blamed, leading to attacks (pogroms). Many Jews emigrate, with most going to the United States.
1882	Founding of BILU, movement of students to settle in the land of Israel (see p. 134).
1885	Pittsburgh Platform of Reform Judaism.
1886	Jewish Theological Seminary founded to train rabbis in the new Conservative movement.
1888	Death of Samson R. Hirsch, German Orthodox leader.
1896	Theodor Herzl publishes *The Jewish State* advocating the creation of a Jewish nation to combat hatred of the Jews.
1897	Herzl convenes the First Zionist Congress.
1904	Death of Herzl.
1909	Tel Aviv is founded.
1917	Balfour Declaration issued marking Britain's support for a legal homeland for the Jews.
1933	Hitler is chancellor in Germany.
1935	Nazis promulgate Nuremberg Laws stripping German Jews of their legal rights.
1938	November 9—*Krystallnacht*. German synagogues are burned.
1939–1945	Jews are murdered in death camps, in massacres, through starvation, and other methods. The Holocaust results in the death of 6 million Jews, including 1½ million children.
1943	Warsaw Ghetto uprising.
1947	United Nations votes to partition Palestine.

1948	May 14. Israel is an independent nation. Arabs go to war.
1967	Six Day War. Jerusalem is reunited. The Western Wall, the last remnant of the Temple, comes under Jewish control.
1973	Yom Kippur War.
1978	September 5–18. Prime Minister Begin meets with President Anwar Sadat of Egypt at Camp David.
1979	March 26. Prime Minister Begin and President Sadat sign peace treaty.
1982	Israeli incursion into Lebanon.
1991–1992	Peace talks between Israel and Arabs.
1993	Israel and the Palestine Liberation Organization recognize each other and begin talks on Palestinian-Arab self-rule.

It was at Mount Sinai that Moses transformed a people into a religious movement. The Israelites collectively experienced God's presence. Through Moses they received the ethical teachings that were to guide their lives. The Israelites understood these teachings as expressing the will of God. For forty years the Jews wandered through the desert, shedding their heritage of slavery, coming to terms with their religious vocation as a holy nation and a kingdom of priests, and preparing to reenter their promised land.

THE PROMISED LAND

As the Israelites reached the Jordan River, Joshua became their leader after Moses' death. Joshua conquered much of Canaan, and twelve tribes were established, each named after Jacob's sons. External threats sometimes forced these tribes to unite and find a common leader. Those common leaders were called Judges. The Judges, including Deborah and Samson, were military rather than political leaders or legal scholars as in the modern meaning of the word. Eventually, it was decided that the tribes would be safer if they became more officially united. Samuel, last of the Judges, chose Saul to be the first king of this new nation.

The kingship in Israel was unusual. Saul was subject to the same religious laws as other people; his voice was not always the final word. Two important groups of people sometimes challenged the king. These were the priests, who were in charge of religious laws, and the prophets, who believed themselves and were accepted as messengers of God, having as their mission the transmission of God's will to the people. The prophets emphasized God's desire for all people to be moral, including kings, priests, prophets, and ordinary citizens.

Saul was instrumental in helping the Israelites fight their hated enemy, the Philistines, but he died in battle with his enemy. Saul was succeeded by King David, who had a series of military triumphs. After capturing Jerusalem, which stood outside the land owned by any of the tribes, David established his political capital in this politically neutral city. Jerusalem simultaneously became the center of religious activity.

David was succeeded by the wise king, Solomon, who built the Temple in Jerusalem. As prosperous and culturally enriching as Solomon's reign was, however, the kingdom had many problems. Different tribal units had retained their own sense of identity and felt that tax money had been gathered unfairly, and that their inhabitants had provided too much of the labor force.

Solomon's son Rehoboam could not hold the united kingdom together. In 922, ten of the twelve tribes in the north left the kingdom under Jeroboam and established a nation called Israel. The remaining two southern tribes formed a nation called Judah.

Israel, the northern kingdom, was constantly in ferment. No ruler lasted very long, due to assassinations and other forms of violence. Finally, in 722, the internally weakened Israel was captured by the Assyrians. While some of the citizens of Israel no doubt fled to Judah or elsewhere, the vast majority were forcibly taken to the Assyrian Empire. There, the "ten lost tribes" vanished from history, probably through a slow assimilation.

BABYLONIAN EXILE

The tiny kingdom of Judah was all that was left of the Jewish people. Too weak to resist powerful empires, it finally fell to Babylonia. In 586 B.C.E., the citizens of Judah were sent into their Babylonian exile after their Temple had been destroyed.

The Babylonian exile might have marked the death of Judaism. Robbed of their land, their Temple, their religious services involving sacrifices, the Judeans could easily have assimilated just as their Israelite cousins had. Instead, however, just the opposite happened. The Judeans remained a united group. They discovered that God was a "portable God." As lord of all the universe, God was present in Babylon as well as Judea. The exiles developed a set time for prayer. They found religious institutions, later called synagogues, to take the place of the Temple. They discovered that some Babylonians found the Jewish religion attractive and became converts. Their prophets, especially Isaiah, told them of their future glory, of the time when God would be worshipped by all people.

RETURN TO JERUSALEM

After almost fifty years in exile, in 539, the Jews found themselves under new control. The Persian King Cyrus, after conquering the Babylonians, gave permission in 538 for Jews to return to their land. Such a return was enormously difficult because Jerusalem lay in ruins. Nevertheless, many Jews did return. The Temple was rebuilt during a five-year period and was completed by 515.

Ezra, a scribe, was responsible for the enforcement of Jewish law. He struggled against the high rate of intermarriage, ordered that the Torah be read in public and be studied. Some modernists believe Ezra actually edited various existing manuscripts into what is called the Torah. As a scribe, he and his students made copies of the Torah and went out to the people explaining its contents.

The Persian Empire was defeated by Alexander the Great in 333; Alexander eventually conquered Judah and tried to impose the Greek beliefs on the captive peoples. Most Jews were offended by the central precepts of Hellenism, or Greek thought, which emphasized the physical over the moral, the pleasurable over the ethically correct. After Alexander's death, Judea was fought over until 198 when the Syrians got control. The Syrians decided that Hellenistic ways should be forced upon the Jews. In 169, the king, Antiochus, forbade worship on the Sabbath, circumcision, and other religious rituals and sent troops to insure that Greek, not Jewish, ways were followed. A Jewish priest, named Mattathias, and his five sons led the rebellion. One son, Judah, the Maccabee became the leader of the fight. Judah recaptured Jerusalem and cleansed the Temple of pagan influences. This cleansing took eight days, and forms the origin, along with the triumph over foreign influences, of the festival of Hanukkah.

The Hasmoneans succeeded the Maccabees as leaders of the people. Judah remained an independent nation, growing in both size and influence, reinvigorating the monotheistic idea in the world. Judaism also spread rapidly during this time, in part through forced conversion of the Idumeans by John Hyrcanus in 125. Hyrcanus also forcibly converted the Edomites, and his son Artobulus I forced the Itureans to convert in 105. More commonly, however, Judaism spread because its message was widely viewed as morally superior to the pagan view. Synagogues were visited by pagans. Jewish merchants often answered questions about their religion. Many people became Jewish during the era.

The Jewish people, expanding as it was, was internally divided. The people separated into groups. One group, the Sadducees, were the upper-class descendants of the priest. They wished to retain the Temple services and so generally wished to conserve the political order. The Sadducees did not believe that the dead would be resurrected, in an afterlife, or in the coming of a messiah. Nor did they believe that the oral traditions that would be put down in the Mishna had the same divine origins as the Written Law of the Torah. Their major opponents were the Pharisees, who were made up of the common people. The Pharisees emphasized the holiness of the oral law, which they saw as necessary to explain the new circumstances of Jewish life. They were particularly active in seeking converts to Judaism. The Essenes were a group of ascetics who seem to have separated themselves from the main community. The Hasmonean empire eventually weakened from within.

ROMAN RULE

The Romans took control over the area and made Herod the king. Herod was a great builder, but a cruel tyrant. He died in the year 4 B.C.E. The Romans seized complete control, not even appointing a king, but having a Roman-appointed governor put in charge. The Jews were oppressed. They lost their freedoms. While the Sadducees, fearful of losing their religious power, supported submitting to Roman rule, and the Pharisees expanded their study of religious law and expounding it through education, another group known as the Zealots emerged. The Zealots wished to use violence to overthrow the Roman rule. Many people expected the Messiah to arrive to liberate the country. Indeed, many people claimed to be that Messiah.

Jesus lived during this period of Jewish history. The Romans thought he was associated with the Zealots and the Sadducees thought he was a threat to priestly power. Jesus was put to death by the Romans by the normal Roman method—crucifixion.

Jewish life became more and more unbearable, until open rebellion began in 66 C.E. Of course, the Romans were the mightiest military power in the world. It was only a matter of time before the Romans crushed the Jewish rebellion, cruelly killing thousands of Jews and selling many thousands of others into slavery.

In the year 70, the Romans destroyed the Second Temple. (This destruction took place on the same date on the Hebrew calendar— the 9th of Av—as the destruction of the First Temple. Other tragedies also occurred on that date, and it is now a holy day of mourning).

As Jerusalem was being attacked by the Romans, one rabbi, Yohanan ben Zakkai, used a trick to escape, went to a Roman general, and asked permission to establish a small academy for the purpose of teaching the Bible to children. Vespasian agreed, and Rabbi Yohanan went to Yavneh where, while the Temple fell, an academy grew.

At Yavneh, the Rabbis faced an incredibly difficult task. They had to preserve their religion at the very moment that its central institution, the Temple, and its nation were being destroyed.

Other Jews continued to rebel against the Romans. The Zealots went to Masada, a fortress in the Judean hills. There, in the year 73, the Jews took their own lives rather than become slaves to the Romans. Another rebellion took place in the years 132–135 under the leadership of Bar Kochba. This rebellion also failed.

The Romans then sought to eradicate Jewish life. The name of the country was changed from Judea to Palestine, a Latinated form of the Jews' worst enemy, the Philistines. A series of anti-Jewish laws were passed. Many Jews were forced to leave the land. A Jewish nation in the land of Israel was destroyed for almost 2000 years.

The learning at the academies went on, and by 200, the Oral Law had been gathered into the Mishnah. While the Romans ruled, the Jews continued to study and apply the religious laws to their daily life. Rome, however, was crumbling from within. Emperor Constantine converted to Christianity in 313 and new anti-Jewish legislation began.

THE GAONIC AGE

There were in Babylonia especially active Jewish scholars, such as Rav and Samuel, who established academies. By the year 500 the Babylonian Jewish rabbis had produced the Gemara, which, together with the Mishna was known as the Talmud. (Another less frequently used Gemara was produced in the land of Israel.)

After the Talmud's completion, the heads of the various academies (each head was called Gaon) ruled Jewish religious life. The years 600–1000 are frequently called the Gaonic Age.

The era was marked by the rise of Islam in the seventh century and its rapid spread across the area. The Jews, under Muslim rule, had a great creative period. One Gaon, Saadia (882–942) produced a book titled *Beliefs and Doctrines*, which was the first major medieval work of Jewish philosophy. Saadia defended Jewish religious doctrine as compatible with both science and philosophy, saying Judaism represented one source of truth.

THE GOLDEN AGE

By the eleventh century, the center of Jewish religious life shifted west, from Babylonia to Europe, and especially Spain. For several centuries Jews had what is called "The Golden Age," despite some conflicts between Jews and the Muslims who ruled the land. Much religious literature, poetry, philosophy, and other work were produced. Jews entered into high social levels, and, in general, led productive lives. Perhaps the two greatest writers of the era were Judah Ha-Levi (ca. 1085–1140) and Moses Maimonides (1135–1204). Ha-Levi wrote poetry, such as *Ode to Zion*, recounting his passionate attachment to the land of Israel, and philosophy, including his great work, *Kuzari*, about the conversion of the Khazar tribe after the Khazar King listened to the arguments from proponents of varying religions and found Judaism to be the most congenial. Maimonides wrote the previously mentioned *Guide for the Perplexed* and *Mishneh Torah*.

EXPULSION FROM SPAIN

The Golden Age lost its luster when Christians forced the Muslims from Spain. The Catholic Church was not tolerant of nonbelievers such as Jews. Jews faced persecution, forced exile, and intense pressure to convert. Some Jews pretended to convert and lived secretly as Jews. Eventually, in 1492, Jews were officially expelled from Spain.

The Jews who had lived in Spain became known as Sephardim (Hebrew for Spain). Other Jews, though, had not lived in Spain. They had gone from the land of Israel not to Babylonia and Spain, but especially to Rome and from there to such places as France and Germany. They became known as Ashkenazic (Hebrew for German) Jews.

The Jews in Europe lived in insecure positions, religiously rejected, without political power outside their own communities, at the mercy of various powers and authorities, unprotected from the ignorance and hatred of people brought up to believe the Jews were inherently evil.

THE CRUSADES

The year 1096 was a turning point in Jewish life. That was the year of the first crusade, a religious war by which the Christians sought to remove the Muslims from rule in the Holy Land. The armies that marched on the crusade attacked Jewish communities on their journey, committing massacres in such places as Worms and Cologne in the Rhineland. The crusade ushered in an era of ever-increasing attacks on Jews. By 1144 there was the emergence of the blood libel, a charge that Jews made *matzah* used at Passover by using Christian blood. Jews were also blamed for starting and spreading the Black Plague, which swept across Europe in 1348–50, killing almost a third of the population. Anti-Jewish legislation continued. The Fourth Lateran Council in 1215 was especially crucial in spreading such rules—including one that Jews had to wear special hats or badges. This practice would be revived by the Nazis in the twentieth century. The Talmud was burned by Christians as anti-Christian. In England, Jews—who had arrived with William the Conqueror in 1066—were expelled in 1290. France produced Rashi (1030–1105), the great commentator on the Bible and Talmud, and the Jews would remain there until expelled in 1349 and again in 1394.

LIFE IN EASTERN EUROPE

Jewish reactions to this wave of hatred were varied. Some Jews stayed and engaged in physical and spiritual resistance. Another group focused on mysticism, using meditation and prayer, searching for the hidden meaning in the Bible. Jewish mysticism, or Kabbalah, had as its central text the *Zohar*. Another group of Jews traveled to the East, to Poland and Lithuania, where the leaders welcomed Jews for their experience and sought their help in developing those lands. While hatred soon followed them, and they often had to encounter prejudice, in general the Jews fared fairly well for a few centuries. In particular, the Jews developed their creative scholarship until 1648 when Bogdan Chmielnitzki led a massive attack against the Jews.

In the 1660s, suffering from persecution, buoyed only by their religious fervor, thousands of Jews responded to the call of Shabbetai Zevi, a Turkish Jew who claimed to be the Messiah. Jewish life suddenly seemed filled with hope. However, the Turkish Sultan forced Zevi to choose between becoming a Muslim and being put to death, and Zevi chose conversion. His followers felt betrayed and crushed.

Broken-hearted, dispirited, poverty-stricken, betrayed by false messiahs, the Jews of Eastern Europe were at a low point. It was at the beginning of the eighteenth century that there arose a leader named Rabbi Israel ben Eliezer (1700–1760), known as the Baal Shem Tov, the Master of the Good Name. The Baal Shem Tov founded the chasidic movement. The *chasidim* stressed joy in their spiritual lives, that religious fervor could come from dance and not just from study, that the feeling of Jewishness, of serving God with love, was crucial. The chasidic movement attracted many followers, but also opponents (called *mitnagdim*), who believed the *chasidim* focused too much on the subjective emotions of the Jew and not enough on the intellectual rigors of Talmudic study.

MODERNITY

Meanwhile, the external world was changing rapidly. Martin Luther began to reform Christianity. Science was intruding into areas where once religion held complete control. Toleration as a political idea was gaining force and would enter into Jewish life especially after the 1789 French Revolution. These changes are grouped under the general term *modernity*.

After the Revolution, Jewish life in Europe changed tremendously. Jews were given political rights for the first time in many
places. Because they were nationless, and therefore having no special loyalty to a particular nation, they were trusted in international
economic activities. Jewish communities still operated according to
talmudic law, especially as promulgated in the *Shulchan Aruch*. Despite this traditional religious life, modernity also radically changed
Jewish life. Intellectual efforts by philosophers led to the *Haskalah*,
the Jewish enlightenment. Those Jews who called themselves enlightened sought to reform Jewish life according to the political, religious,
and social life around them. They wanted to change the religious
forms of traditional Jewish life, the way Jews dressed, the foods they
ate, the books they studied. These efforts greatly weakened traditional
control over Jewish life. Some Jews assimilated, intermarried, or left
Judaism. Others sought to maintain a Jewish identity but attached
themselves to what they saw as the virtues of modernity. Such a view
led to the birth of the Reform movement.

Of course there was a traditional reaction to those who wished
to reform Judaism. Samson Raphael Hirsch (1808–1888) founded a
movement to preserve the traditional way of life, but said such a way
of life was compatible with living a modern life. This neo-Orthodoxy
attracted many followers. The Conservative movement also sought
to retain belief in Jewish law while saying such law could and should
be adapted to fit the needs of modernity rather than discarded.

Jews were still small in number in the United States, but its revolutionary birth, its religious ideals, its lack of an anti-Jewish past made
it more and more attractive. Many of Poland's Jews meanwhile had
come under Russian control after Poland was partitioned at the end
of the eighteenth century.

RUSSIAN POGROMS

Russia was the setting for the next crucial turning point in the tor-
tured history of hatred of the Jews. In 1881, Czar Alexander of Russia was assassinated. Jews were blamed, and horrible attacks on Jews,

called pogroms, which had existed sporadically, became widespread. The eradication of the Jews through emigration, starvation, and conversion became national policy in Russia. Millions of Russian Jews eventually traveled to the United States.

The resurgence of anti-Semitism (a term coined in 1879 by a Jew hater named Wilhelm Marr) in the modern world was deeply troubling, especially to those enlightened Jews who believed modernity would bring an end to medieval religious hatred. Some of these Jews concluded that only through a political revolution grounded in socialism could Russia be free from hatred.

THE LAND OF ISRAEL

A small number of Jews, mostly university students, took another approach. They concluded that they had no future in Russia and that any other country of the Diaspora (that is, any country outside the land of Israel in which Jews were dispersed) would at some point duplicate what had happened in Russia. These Jews decided to move back to their ancient homeland, then called Palestine. At the time Palestine was not a nation but part of the Turkish empire. The land was unfit for farming; the swamps were filled with malaria; the people were mostly nomadic, or relied on monies sent from outside. These students started a group called BILU and began to see a new future for Jews as independent workers in their own land. BILU is an acronym for the Hebrew words *Bet Yaakov lechu ve nelcha*, which translate as "House of Jacob, come and let us go." This is a quotation from Isaiah 2:5.

THE RISE OF ANTI-SEMITISM IN A NEW FORM

Anti-Semitism, meanwhile, was appearing not only in backward Russia but in the very centers of European civilization such as Austria and France. The nature of anti-Semitism itself was changing. During ancient times, some pagans resented Judaism because it attacked basic pagan beliefs. During the Middle Ages and on into the nineteenth century, Jews were seen by many Christians as religious enemies, charged with deicide and with renouncing Christ. This theological anti-Semitism lessened as religion's hold on society lessened. Anti-Semitism, however, took on a new form. Jews were considered to be a race among the various races of the world, but an inferior race, one that endangered the other races. This racial anti-Semitism in a way was even more dangerous than theological anti-Semitism because according to theological anti-Semites Jews might convert, be saved, and live. Racist anti-Semites, however, allowed for no such conversion. People could not convert from their "race." For Jews, there was no escape. This racial hatred, building on centuries of theological hatred, aimed at a people deprived of a nation that would provide communal self-defense and a haven from persecution, eventually found its most deadly proponent in Germany in the 1930s.

One early example of anti-Semitism was the Dreyfus Affair in France. Colonel Dreyfus was wrongfully accused of treason just because he was Jewish. Although his innocence was known, there was a deliberate attempt by the military to protect their mistaken accusation of Dreyfus. The affair was widely reported.

ZIONISM

One of those who did the reporting was a Hungarian-born Austrian journalist, lawyer, and playwright named Theodor Herzl (1860–1904).

At a ceremony of military degradation, in which Dreyfus' military insignias would be removed, Herzl was shocked as the crowd yelled not "Death to the traitor," but "Death to the Jews." The horrible conclusion for Herzl, and many others, was that even in the heart of civilized Europe anti-Semitism would not simply disappear. Herzl cast about for a solution, trying several improbable ones, until he came to the conclusion that the Jews would have to have their own state.

While others had come to this conclusion, Herzl did more than write about the idea, though he did that in his striking pamphlet *Der Judenstaat* (The Jewish State) in 1896. After the pamphlet's appearance, Herzl began slowly to put together a political movement that could transform his idea into reality. He began a newspaper, and, in the boldest of strokes, organized the First Zionist Congress, a gathering of Jews purporting to speak on behalf of all world Jewry and calling for political restoration of power. Such a daring gesture was opposed by liberal Jews who believed their newly given rights as citizens in their own countries would be rescinded as they were accused of double loyalties. Very traditional Jews thought it blasphemous that Herzl would take the task historically assigned to the Messiah of ingathering the exiles. Nevertheless, the Congress was called in 1897, setting up an organization that aimed at a Jewish nation.

In some sense the history of European Jewry for the next fifty years was an historical race between the poor, weak, divided Zionists and the forces of anti-Semitism. Several crucial world events intervened. The Zionists failed to get the approval of Turkey, the country controlling Palestine, to cede land, but young Jews continued very slowly to enter the land. The Jews thought the Arab inhabitants would welcome them. Most of the Arabs were nomads, unsettled on the land because of its unsuitability for farming. The Jews were in a majority in Jerusalem and other areas.

World War I ended with the British seizing control of Palestine and getting a mandate from the League of Nations to administer the territory.

This revolutionary change brought with it a change in Zionist fortunes. The British, seeking help from international Jewry during World War I, had issued its Balfour Declaration supporting the idea of a Jewish homeland. The British Zionist Chaim Weizmann emerged to lead the Zionist movement. In Palestine, the Jewish community was also organizing under the leadership of David Ben-Gurion. However, soon after British control was solidified, Britain gave away 80 percent of historic Palestine to form what is now Jordan. The Zionists, citing the Balfour Declaration, were angry at this action, but could not prevent it. The Arabs, meanwhile, were beginning to oppose Zionism. Arabs had begun to move into Palestine, attracted by the economic opportunities the Zionist presence had brought, and stayed. Many of them had already lived in the general area. In addition, religious Arabs believed the land, especially Jerusalem, to be holy and unfit to be held by non-Muslims, whether Jewish or Christian.

THE HOLOCAUST

World War I had an important impact in Germany as well. There was an explosive rise in anti-Semitism, in part because Jews were blamed for Germany's defeat. Germans were bitter about the peace forced on them at Versailles and disillusioned with democracy as an effective form of government. Seeking an outlet for their rage, the Germans found it in a weak people, who could not fight back, who had been the subject of attack for a thousand years. After the 1929 worldwide depression, anti-Semitism grew even faster. By January 1933 Adolf Hitler had become chancellor of Germany.

The Nazis began a systematic attack on the Jewish community. There were boycotts of Jewish-owned businesses, burning of books, dismissal of Jews from government employment, and increasing legal restrictions. School curricula were changed. The media began publishing anti-Semitic materials. In 1935 the infamous Nuremberg Laws were passed. These laws stripped Jews of their rights as German citizens, forbidding them to marry Christians, for example.

Jewish reaction came swiftly, but, without help from outside powers, without a national home to which German Jews could emigrate, the efforts were insufficient. While German Jews organized and a World Jewish Congress convened to urge a boycott of German products, the international community stood by silently. Nations would not take in Jewish refugees. Hitler took such indifference to the Jews' fate as a sign that he could continue with his program of eradicating the Jewish presence from Germany.

On November 9, 1938 the Nazis organized what became known as *Krystallnacht*, the Night of Broken Glass. Synagogues and Jewish businesses were destroyed. Twenty-five thousand Jews were sent to concentration camps.

The Nazis continued to pursue their dream of expansion. Hitler had annexed Austria in 1938. Then he annexed the Sudetenland. It was only when he invaded Poland on September 1, 1939 that Britain declared war. The Nazi takeover of Poland was fateful because two million Polish Jews fell under Nazi control. Most of them died during the Holocaust.

The word *Holocaust* refers specifically to the Nazi aim of exterminating world Jewry physically, not just culturally or religiously. It was attempted genocide—the killing of an entire people.

The attempt was called by the Nazis "the final solution." At the Wannsee Conference in January 1942, the Nazis decided on the official policy of extermination. The random mass killings by death squads that had occurred, especially in Russia following the Nazi invasion in June 1941, were replaced by systematic mass transporting of Jews to concentration camps where they were gassed or starved to death. There were frequent attempts by the Jews to resist, most notably in the Warsaw Ghetto uprising, but also by revolts in such camps as Sobibor. Without weapons, weakened, concerned by the brutal Nazi retribution, the Jews who made these attempts were not finally able to stop the killing. The outside world seemingly stood by without attempting to save the Jews. The Catholic Church, led by Pope Pius XII, did not protest. Great Britain refused to let Jewish refugees into Palestine because of the objections of the Arabs. The United States withheld information about the Holocaust as it built up internal support for the war.

By the European war's end in April 1945, almost six million Jews had been killed. Jewish life since the Holocaust has attempted to make sense of the crime. Simple psychological, historical, and economic arguments are dwarfed, however, by the enormity of the evil. Jews who believe in a just God must confront God's silence. Those who believe in the goodness of humanity must confront the world's silence and indifference as well as the inexplicable drive to genocide by so many under the Nazis' leadership.

THE STATE OF ISRAEL

There can be redemption from the Holocaust's haunting questions, but many people have noted the simple historical fact that only a few years after the end of the Holocaust, the State of Israel was born. The Jews, one-third of whom had been killed, had a revived nation in their ancient land after almost two thousand years.

The British had continued to refuse Jewish immigration even after the war. Finally, the British turned over the problem to the United Nations, which recommended partitioning the land into a Jewish and an Arab state. The Jews accepted this proposal; the Arabs did not and vowed to fight. The United Nations voted for partition in November 1947. In May 1948 David Ben-Gurion issued a proclamation of independence. Israel was born. The next day, however, the British left and the Jews began a war to keep their independent nation.

The nation of Israel won the war, but the war's aftermath included bitterness that has not yet fully ceased. Significantly, the nations around Israel refused to sign peace treaties. Many Arabs claimed they had been made refugees. Instead of being absorbed by neighboring Arab countries, these Arabs were put into terrible camps living in horrible conditions. The Arabs began over time to establish their own identity, to call themselves Palestinian (a term they had at first disliked because it was mainly used to refer to Palestinian Jews). These Palestinian Arabs began to grow in number and demanded that Israel be destroyed and be replaced by an Arab-controlled nation.

In 1956 there was another war. In 1967, the Arab nations, vowing the destruction of Israel, massed to attack. Israel, noting that the Arab actions legally constituted war, decided to strike first. Israel won a lightning victory, taking over all the territory west of the Jordan River, the Sinai desert, and the Golan Heights, adjacent to Syria and Lebanon, which had been used to launch rockets onto the settlements in the north of Israel. Most importantly, the Jews took the eastern part of Jerusalem, the site of the Western Wall (at one time called the Wailing Wall; its name change implies that Jewish control over the Wall demands a ceasing of the wailing), the only remaining part of the Second Temple. For years, Jews had been forbidden to pray at the Wall. The 1967 war was also crucial because it gave Israel control over what, over time, would be more than a million more Palestinian Arabs who were generally hostile to Israeli administration.

Even the decisive victory by Israel in 1967, however, did not deter the Arabs from refusing peace. In 1973, on Yom Kippur, the holiest day of the Jewish year, the Arabs attacked. During fierce fights, the Israelis eventually managed to hold onto their land. The Arabs had fought more forcefully than anyone expected, restoring some pride to Arab peoples.

Egypt became the first nation to sign a peace treaty with Israel. President Anwar Sadat of Egypt met Prime Minister Menachem Begin of Israel at Camp David in the United States in September 1978. By 1979, the peace treaty was signed.

The peace with Egypt did not immediately lead to peace with other Arab countries. In 1982, acting on provocation, Israel entered Lebanon to remove the Palestinian Liberation Organization, the movement organized to fight Israel. In the mid-1980s the Arabs in the administered territories west of the Jordan, sometimes called the West Bank, and in Gaza, near the Sinai, began attacking Jewish civilians and soldiers in an uprising called the intifada.

By 1991–1992, with the Soviet Union disintegrated and the Cold War over, with the sense by the Arabs that military parity with Israel was not possible without the Soviet Union, with pressure brought by the United States both on Israel and the Arabs, a peace process was begun.

The end of the Soviet Union also brought a million Jews to Israel, with the possibility of millions more one day choosing to emigrate to the Jewish state.

AMERICAN JEWRY

American Jewry, the most populous and the most prosperous Jewish community in the world, had secured its own place, especially after

World War II. It had been enormously important in building up Israel, in fighting worldwide anti-Semitism, in forcing the Soviet Union to allow Jews to emigrate, and in many other ways. American Jews continue in their leadership role, trying to work out a partnership with Israel to guide Jewish life into the next century.

12
Jewish Practices

American Jews vary greatly in the types and intensity of the ways they observe Jewish practices. This section includes an overview of a large number of Jewish practices. Many traditional Jews, including Orthodox and some Conservative Jews, observe all or most of these age-old customs. Many Conservative and Reform Jews observe some or many of these practices. A sizable minority of Jews observes very few of the traditional practices.

Practices for many Jews have become a matter of personal style and choice, rather than the traditional notion of commandments or ethical teachings that God has ordained. There are many reasons for this decline in observing traditional practices. Many Jews have come to understand religion as an act of personal autonomy, so that Jews are not compelled by religious law to practice but choose among the traditions to find those most resonant to the lives they lead. For such Jews, the practices in this section are a traditional smorgasbord, a table of delicacies, which can be sampled to find individual tastes.

On such a view, there are many doors that lead to the house of Judaism. Some Jews find their way in by Jewish music, or the grandeur of Judaism's ethical teachings, or the poetic study of the Bible as a substitute or adjunct to traditional practices.

Jewish identity is elastic in the modern world. It is no longer simple to describe Jews as people adhering to specific beliefs or people who follow specific practices. It was Rabbi Mordecai M. Kaplan, the founder of the Reconstructionist movement, who termed Judaism a religious civilization—with all the components of any civilization, including language, land, and culture.

In that sense, it makes more sense when describing contemporary Jews to discuss a people, so that Jews who do not have traditional beliefs and do not follow religious practices may still be legitimately called Jewish by virtue of their membership as part of a people.

Modern Jewish identity, minimally, is a sense of belonging to that people, identifying with its past and its fate. For some Jews, such an identity does not include practices.

This section is presented for those who wish to follow more traditional practices, or to sample Judaism's age-old ways. It is often suggested for those reluctant to follow practices, that they are depriving themselves of one of religion's central opportunities.

Jewish practices are not meant to be simply religious behaviors. They were designed and meant to function as supplements to profound belief and ethical concern. The Jewish practices described here are the regular reminders of our relationship to God and our moral duties.

IN THE JEWISH HOME

Jewish religious practices are centered in the home and the synagogue. Practices in Jewish homes vary widely, but there are central symbols and prayers in many Jewish homes.

The first of the symbols in a Jewish home is the *mezuzah*. The *mezuzah* (a Hebrew word meaning "doorpost") is a small container attached to doors. The container might be made of stone, metal, wood, or other materials. Inside the container is a parchment with various biblical passages (Deuteronomy 6:4–9 and 11:13–21) on one side and the Hebrew word *Shaddai* (meaning "Almighty") on the other side. Usually, the container includes a hole making the word *Shaddai* visible, although sometimes the container has *Shaddai* or its first Hebrew letter, *shin*, on the front.

By tradition, the *mezuzah* is placed on every door in a house except for rooms specifically set aside for certain personal needs such as a bathroom. Many Jews just have a *mezuzah* on the front door leading into the house. There are specific religious laws concerning how the *mezuzah* is to be attached, the prayers, the timing to put it up, and the checking of the *mezuzah*.

Some Jews consider the *mezuzah* simply a good-luck charm (a fact that led many Reform Jews to abandon its use) although another, more religious meaning, is that the *mezuzah* is a constant reminder of our duties as Jews, both in our homes (as we are reminded when we enter the house) and in the world (as we are reminded when we leave the house).

A *mizrach* is an object such as a cloth or wall hanging that is put on the eastern wall in a house as a reminder of the correct direction in which to face while praying. The word *mizrach* (Hebrew for east) is always included in the object.

There are many ritual objects found in Jewish homes. These include, for example, candlesticks used for Shabbat and holy days, a cover for *challah* (the traditional braided bread used for the Sabbath and holy days), a *menorah* (a candelabra, especially one used during Hanukkah), a plate used for the traditional meal, the *seder*, at Passover, a goblet for the blessing over the wine, spice boxes used for the ceremony of *Havdalah*, which concludes the Sabbath, objects with a Star of David (a six-pointed star, also called the *Magen David*, or Shield of David, which, also not of biblical origin, increasingly became a symbol of Judaism after the seventeenth century) and others, depending on the home and the tradition.

In addition, many Jewish homes include examples of Jewish art, a collection of Jewish music, Jewish videotapes, and, most importantly, Jewish books. The reading list at the end of this book includes some specific reading suggestions, but most Jewish homes include at least the Bible and the *siddur*, the prayer book.

The food eaten in a Jewish home is also important. The Jewish attitude toward food is discussed in the section Through the Day, below, but traditional Jews emphasize the importance of keeping a ritually pure, kosher home. There are also many prayers said in the home. These, too, will be discussed below.

The home is both a holy place and a sanctuary. It is a place of peace, a respite from the turmoil of the world. Jewish ethical teachings were designed to enhance peace in the house. Such obligations as honoring parents, avoiding family violence, having children, and other mitzvot involving family life all serve to make for a whole, happy family.

The home's designation as holy and as sanctuary also includes the obligation to welcome guests. This ethical obligation is sometimes forgotten, or like so many ethical obligations, handed over to social institutions designed for that purpose. However, this Jewish obligation (which, by extension, can be met through such efforts as volunteering at homes for the dispossessed and the hungry) was seen as vital for the moral development of people.

The home, then, is one of the crucial centers of Jewish life. It is there that children learn their values, follow the role models of their parents, siblings, aunts, uncles, cousins, and grandparents, absorb Jewish learning, and come to understand the beauty of their Jewish heritage.

In many ways, the home is the most important Jewish religious institution. At the very least, however, it is the companion to that other central Jewish religious institution, the synagogue.

IN THE SYNAGOGUE

Even in the home, the individual is part of a community. The obligations to marry and have children and to invite guests are meant to prevent a person from becoming isolated. It is unsurprising, therefore, that in Judaism there is great emphasis on community worship, people getting together to pray. Additionally, this communal nature of Jewish prayer is emphasized by the use of common prayers, found in the siddur.

The word *synagogue* comes from the Greek for "bringing to-gether." In contemporary American society, *synagogue* is often used interchangeably with the word *temple*, although at one time there was a dispute over *temple*, which was used by those as a statement that they no longer expected that the Temple in Jerusalem would be re-built. The term *Jewish center* also came to be used, especially among Conservative Jews, to designate the expanding role of the synagogue in American life, not just as a religious institution but as a commu-nal gathering place for significant meetings and functions as well. The Yiddish word *shul* is also used by some traditionalists to refer to the synagogue.

The amount of Hebrew used in synagogues varies greatly. Learn-ing Hebrew is vital for following the prayers. The boredom some people report in attending synagogue services often arises from the fact that these worshipers do not know the prayers or the order of services. A basic course in Hebrew supplemented by learning several prayers will make the synagogue experience more meaningful. Because the services include several basic prayers, learning only a few would be a significant start in understanding the service.

Prayer may be said in any language. There is a famous story of a little boy who could not read Hebrew, and did not know the prayers, so while the others were praying he stood and kept repeating the alphabet. His father asked him why he did that, and the boy replied that since he did not know the prayers, he would just say all the let-ters and God would put them in the right order.

However adept God may be at interpreting our prayers, the use of Hebrew both in the synagogue and at home can be especially mean-ingful because of its ability to connect individual worshipers and congregations to other Jews in history and currently throughout the world. When we pray in Hebrew, we identify with the long history of the Jewish people. We know that as we pray, people all over the world are saying those exact same words.

In traditional synagogues, there are a variety of significant rules about appropriate behavior. These rules include not carrying any objects such as handbags, not carrying money (so it is inappropriate to bring, for example, *bar* and *bat mitzvah* gifts to the synagogue), not smoking, not writing, and not riding to services. Positive requirements include wearing the appropriate religious attire. The rules of synagogues vary tremendously, especially among the different religious groupings.

The religious attire worn by Jews is sometimes worn at home and elsewhere as well as in the synagogue. There are several important pieces of attire. All Orthodox Jews and Conservative Jews are obliged to wear these. Reform Jews are not compelled to do so, but some find attachment to tradition and beauty in these symbols, and so do wear them.

One such piece of attire is the *kippah*, or head covering, also called a yarmulke. The *kippah* is worn at all times by some traditional Jews. Others use it at set times. Orthodox and Conservative Jews wear a *kippah* at all times in their houses of worship. It is voluntary or not used in many Reform houses of worship. While a *kippah* is worn by men, women cover their heads with a *kippah*, hat, scarf, or in other ways in many synagogues. In others, such a head covering is optional.

The *tallit* is a prayer shawl once worn only by married males, but now worn in traditional synagogues by all men (and, in some places, women). The *tallit* is often optional in Reform congregations. It consists of two parts, the shawl itself and its fringes, called *tzitzit*. (It is from the colors of the *tzitzit* that the blue and white flag of Israel was derived.) The *tallit* is worn during the morning service at home or in synagogue except on the holy day of Tisha B'Av when it is worn during the afternoon service. It is not worn at night. The *tallit* is held at its top with outstretched hands. The following blessing is then said:

בָּרוּךְ אַתָּה יי, אלהינו מלך הָעוֹלָם, אֲשֶׁר קדשָׁנוּ
במצוותיו, וצונו להתעטף בַּצִיצִית.

Baruch attah Adonai, Eloheinu melech ha-olam, asher kideshanu be-mitzvotav, vitzivanu le-hitatef be-tzitzit.

(Blessed be You, Lord our God, Ruler of the universe, who sanctified us through Your teachings and taught us to wrap ourselves with
these fringes.)

(Note: I have translated *mitzvot* and its linguistic variations as "teachings"; many other translators render it as "commandments." Jews have
an ethical obligation to perform these tasks according to tradition,
however the concept is translated.)

Very traditional Jews also wear a small *tallit* (a *tallit katan*) under
their clothes during the day.

The *tefillin*, or phylacteries (from the Greek "safeguard") is also
worn by traditional Jews. The *tefillin* is made up of two black leather
boxes that look like cubes. The boxes contain parchments with biblical passages. One of the boxes has the Hebrew letter *shin*, standing
for *Shaddai*, another name for God. This box is placed on the forehead
using the leather strap attached. The other box is put on the arm.
The *tefillin* are worn during morning prayers at home or in synagogue
by traditional Jews. They are optional for Reform Jews. The *tefillin*
are not worn on the Sabbath or during festivals. Depending on
the religious tradition, there are other days when some Jews do not
wear them. By tradition, the *tallit* is worn by males when they reach
bar mitzvah age. Increasingly, women are observing this mitzvah as
well.

The *tallit* is put on before the *tefillin*. Putting on *tefillin* is easier
than the following description makes it sound. It is most useful for
someone, a rabbi for example, to take a few minutes and illustrate its
use. The hand, or arm, *tefillin* is put on first—on the left arm if you
are right-handed, and the right arm if you are left-handed. After roll-
ing up any shirt or blouse and removing a watch, unwrap the leather
straps of the hand *tefillin*. The box is put on the top of the arm's bicep
and the strap pulled tightly. The following prayer is then recited:

בָּרוּךְ אַתָּה יְיָ, אֱלֹהֵינוּ מֶלֶךְ הָעוֹלָם, אֲשֶׁר קִדְּשָׁנוּ
בְּמִצְוֹתָיו, וְצִוָּנוּ לְהָנִיחַ תְּפִילִין.

Baruch attah Adonai, Eloheinu melech ha-olam, asher kideshanu be-mitzvotav vitzivanu le-haniach tefillin.

(Blessed are You, Lord our God, Ruler of the Universe, who sanctified us through Your teachings and taught us to wear *tefillin*.)

The strap is then wound around the arm seven times clockwise in the Ashkenazi tradition, counterclockwise in the Sephardic tradition, with the remaining part of the strap wound around the palm. The straps of the head *tefillin* are than unwound, with the box placed on the head underneath the hairline. The following blessing is then said:

בָּרוּךְ אַתָּה יְיָ, אֱלֹהֵינוּ מֶלֶךְ הָעוֹלָם, אֲשֶׁר קִדְּשָׁנוּ בְּמִצְוֹתָיו, וְצִוָּנוּ עַל מִצְוַת תפלין.

Baruch attah Adonai, Eloheinu melech ha-olam, asher kideshanu be-mitzvotav vitzivanu al mitzvat tefillin.

(Blessed are You, Lord our God, Ruler of the Universe, who sanctified us through Your teachings and gave us the teaching of *tefillin*.)

At this point, the strap around the palm is unwound. It is rewound around the palm, then the middle finger, and then the ring finger forming the letter *shin*.

The synagogue also has traditional books. The *siddur* is the prayer book for each weekday and for the Sabbath. The *machzor* is the special prayer book for holy days. Additionally, synagogues have the *Chumash*, a book containing the Torah. The Torah is traditionally read in individual portions with each portion called a *parashah*. There are fifty-four traditional sections in the Torah. One section (sometimes two) is read and studied each week (along with a section called the *Haftarah* from the Prophets section of the Bible) in most synagogues, although this tradition varies as well.

The synagogue has its own geography. The holiest object in the synagogue is the Torah, which, when it is not being used, is housed in the holy Ark (*aron ha-kodesh*), which is located on the eastern wall of the synagogue, facing Jerusalem. In many synagogues the Ark has a curtain called a *parochet* hanging in front of it. Behind the *parochet* there are often doors to the Ark and inside the doors a cabinet holding the Torah scrolls, and there are usually more than one because several are needed on certain holy days. The Torah scrolls are covered with mantles that are open at the bottom but closed at the top except for two holes for the rollers around which the Torah parchment is rolled. The Torah also might have a crown of silver, a breastplate, a pointer to help readers keep their place while reading the Torah, and decorative objects on the tops of the rollers. The Torah parchment itself has been written by an expert called a *sofer*, or scribe. The words on the Torah scroll are written in columns with breaks in the text.

An eternal light (*ner tamid*) hangs above the Ark. Depictions of the Ten Commandments are also often found above the Ark as are depictions of lions, which in the Bible were often used to symbolize strength. Synagogues also have a raised platform, or stage, called the *bimah*. (Sephardic Jews refer to this platform as a *teivah*). In many synagogues, the *bimah* is indeed like a stage with the congregation facing it. In other traditional synagogues the *bimah* is in the middle of the congregation. In both cases the *bimah* holds a table on which the Torah reader can read and from which prayers can be said. In Orthodox houses of worship there is a separation in seating between men and women. Either women sit above the men in a gallery or the two genders are divided by an object of varying design known as a *mechitzah*. In Conservative and Reform congregations men and women sit together.

The synagogue also has people who perform specific functions.

The rabbi is perhaps the best known of those people. A rabbi (from the Hebrew "my teacher") gives the blessings, provides an explanation of the service, often including announcing the page for those having trouble following the service, and gives a sermon. Outside the synagogue, the rabbi provides general leadership, advice, counseling, and help to the congregants and others in the Jewish community. In general, a rabbi is consulted for issues regarding Jewish religious rules. The Reform, Conservative, and Reconstructionist movements have women rabbis, while the Orthodox have exclusively male rabbis.

The cantor (in Hebrew, *chazzan*) sings and chants the service and leads the congregation in prayer. Most cantors are professional, although any congregant is allowed to serve. A congregant serving as a cantor is called a *baal tefillah*. Cantors frequently train youngsters for *bar* and *bat mitzvah* ceremonies. As in the rabbinate, the non-Orthodox movements have women cantors.

The *gabbai* helps run the service such as by assisting the person reading the Torah, arranging for the order of those going up to the Torah, and in other ways. Sometimes when the *gabbai* receives a salary, the *gabbai* is called a *shammash*.

The Torah reader, or *baal korei*, reads from the Torah during the Sabbath, on holy days, and on Monday and Thursdays at morning services when the Torah is read.

Ushers may help people find a seat or provide a *siddur* and *Chumash*.

Services in different synagogues vary greatly. In traditional synagogues, a quorum of ten people (or, in Orthodox and some Conservative synagogues ten men) called a *minyan* is necessary for reading the Torah in the synagogue and reciting certain prayers.

Traditional Jews pray three times each day, whether in synagogue or at home.

The morning service on weekdays, called *Shacharit*, which requires *tallit* and *tefillin* by Orthodox and Conservative Jews, includes various Morning Blessings, Verses of Song, the *Shema* (the crucial prayer emphasizing the oneness of God), the *Amidah* (also known as the *Shemoneh Esrei*, which consists of nineteen blessings and prayers and is in many ways the core and central prayer of each service), various Supplications on weekdays, *Hallel* (hymns of thanksgiving taken from the Book of Psalms) on holy days, the Torah (on Sabbaths, Mondays, and Thursdays only), the *Musaf* (from the Hebrew "additional") on the Sabbath, holy days, and *Rosh Chodesh* (the first day of every lunar month), various Psalms and hymns, and the concluding prayer *Aleinu*.

The afternoon service, called *Minchah*, consists of Psalm 145 (called *Ashrei*), the *Amidah*, and *Aleinu*.

The evening service, called *Maariv*, consists of the *Shema* and the blessings used for it, the *Amidah*, and *Aleinu*. In many synagogues, the *Minchah* and *Maariv* services are held together.

The Torah service is particularly important. It includes removing the Torah from the Ark, reading from the Torah and Prophets, and returning the Torah to the Ark. The Ark is open. The Torah is then taken out carried around the synagogue, and the congregants approach the Torah and some touch it with their prayer book and kiss the book. The Torah is then taken back to the *bimah* where it will be read. Before different parts of the Torah portion are read, a congregant is given the honor of coming up to the *bimah* and reciting blessings before the part is read and after. This activity is called an *aliyah* (from the Hebrew "ascent"; the word is also used to describe someone who moves to Israel). There are a varying number of *aliyot* (plural of *aliyah*) depending on the service and the synagogue. By tradition the initial *aliyah* is set aside for a *kohen*, a person descended from the first high priest, Aaron. The second *aliyah* for a levite, descendants of the ancient priests. The third *aliyah* is for Israelites, that is all other Jews.

People honored with an *aliyah* are usually notified beforehand. They are called by their Hebrew name or by number and, in traditional synagogues, wearing a *tallit*, they go to the *bimah*. A person having an *aliyah* stands to the right of the Torah reader. The reader then points to the place in the Torah where the reading is to begin. The *aliyah* recipient then takes the end of the *tallit*, touches the place in the Torah, brings the *tallit* to the lips, and kisses it. The recipient then says:

בָּרְכוּ אֶת יְיָ הַמְבֹרָךְ.

Borchu et Adonai Ha-mevorach.

(Praised be God, the One Who is Blessed.)

The congregation responds by saying:

בָּרוּךְ יְיָ הַמְבֹרָךְ לְעוֹלָם וָעֶד.

Baruch Adonai Ha-mevorach la-olam va'ed.

(Praised be God, the One Who is Blessed, for ever and ever.)

The recipient repeats this line.
Then the recipient continues with the following:

בָּרוּךְ אַתָּה יְיָ, אֱלֹהֵינוּ מֶלֶךְ הָעוֹלָם, אֲשֶׁר בָּחַר
בָּנוּ מִכָּל הָעַמִּים, וְנָתַן לָנוּ אֶת תּוֹרָתוֹ. בָּרוּךְ
אַתָּה יְיָ, נוֹתֵן הַתּוֹרָה.

Baruch attah Adonai Eloheinu melech ha-Olam, asher bachar banu mi-kol ha-amim, ve-natan lanu et Torato. Baruch attah Adonai, notein ha-Torah.

(Blessed are You, Lord our God, Ruler of the universe, Who has chosen us from among all people and given to us the Torah. Blessed be You Who has given us the Torah.)

(Note than in Reconstructionist and some Sephardic services there is some difference in wording. In many synagogues, there is a large chart with the words in the original Hebrew and transliterated Hebrew for the *aliyah* recipient to read from.)

At this point the Torah reader reads.

After the reading has been concluded, the *aliyah* recipient touches the Torah again. A final blessing is then said:

בָּרוּךְ אַתָּה יְיָ, אֱלֹהֵינוּ מֶלֶךְ הָעוֹלָם, אֲשֶׁר נָתַן לָנוּ
תּוֹרַת אֱמֶת, וְחַיֵּי עוֹלָם נָטַע בְּתוֹכֵנוּ. בָּרוּךְ אַתָּה
יְיָ, נוֹתֵן הַתּוֹרָה.

Baruch attah Adonai, Eloheinu melech ha-olam, asher natan lanu Torat emet, ve-chayyei olam nota betocheinu. Baruch attah Adonai notein ha-Torah.

(Blessed are You, Lord our God, Ruler of the universe, Who has given us a Torah of truth and put within us eternal life. Blessed be You, Lord, Who gave us the Torah.)

After the final blessing, the *aliyah* recipient moves to the right side of the *bimah*, where there may be a prayer said. The recipient stays there while the next person has an *aliyah*. After the next person has concluded, the recipient usually shakes hands with the reader and others such as the rabbi. Different synagogues have different traditions. Many Jews, for example, walk in a path that is longer back to their seats than they originally took when they came up to the *bimah*. This is to illustrate their reluctance to leave the Torah.

After the Torah reading has been completed (in the Ashkenazic tradition; in Sephardic congregations it is more common to display the Torah scroll prior to the reading), the Torah is lifted up (*hagbah*) and rolled (*gelilah*). *Hagbah* ("elevation") is done by unrolling the Torah scroll. There should be several columns showing with a seam in the middle (so that, if the Torah tears, it will do so at a seam). Holding each roller, the person performing *hagbah* then slides the Torah until the bottom rollers are off the table. The Torah is then lifted. Sometimes it is helpful to bend the knees before lifting. The Torah scroll is held upright. The person then turns around so that the congregation can see the writing on the scroll. The congregation (depending on the tradition) then chants:

Ve-zot ha-Torah asher sam Mosheh lifnei B'nei Yisrael al pi Adonai be-yad Mosheh.

(This is the Torah that Moses set before the Children of Israel.)

The person, still holding the Torah up, sits down.

The person doing *gelilah* rolls the Torah scroll using the rollers, puts the sash (or buckle) around the scroll, covers the scroll with the Torah cover, and puts on any of the silver ornaments. The Torah will be returned to the Ark after the *Haftarah* has been completed.

Note that in Reform temples, much of this service might be shortened or altered. More modern ways of praying might be substituted. In general, it is advisable to watch other congregants and follow their lead.

THROUGH THE DAY

Besides the daily prayers, traditional Jews offer a wide variety of blessings during the day. Blessings can be recited, for example, over bread, rain, when a new house is built, and on numerous other occasions.

Ethical behavior is meant to supplement the system of prayers. The Jewish values of faith, learning, family, involvement in the wider society, love, work, purpose, justice, compassion, benevolence, holiness, and others are meant to be practiced on a daily basis. Performing the *mitzvot*, giving to charity, and helping the ill and those unable to provide for themselves are the moral materials out of which are shaped the Jewish day.

Traditional Jews start the day by a ritual washing of the hands, and then recite the first prayer of the day, which praises God for restoring life after sleep. This is followed by the morning prayers.

Mealtimes are a crucial part of the day. Like all else in life, especially all else that is central to living, Jewish thinkers have pondered how to make the act of eating into a holy act. As early as in biblical times, Jews are directed about appropriate animals to eat and how such animals are made fit to be eaten. In the Bible, Jews are directed to keep the ritual dietary laws so that they might become a holy nation, apart from the idol-worshipers in other lands. Later scholars, such as Maimonides, emphasized the health values in keeping kosher. Other thinkers emphasized that keeping kosher made eating itself holy. Because kosher slaughtering is, as far as possible, aimed at kill-ing the animal without pain by severing the trachea and esophagus in one motion, there was an ethical argument made.

The general rules for appropriate eating are called *kashrut*. More familiarly, the word *kosher* is used. (Actually, while the word *kosher* is most often applied to food, it does mean "ritually correct" so that it can also apply not only to food but to, for example, the utensils with which we eat, and all religious articles including a *tallit*, *tefillin*, and so on).

Kosher foods include the following:

• Any fruit or vegetable that is naturally grown from the earth.
• Animals that chew their cud and have split hooves. Some examples of kosher animals are cattle, goats, and sheep.
• All fish with fins and scales. Some examples are bluefish, carp, flounder, mackerel, rainbow trout, salmon, tuna, and whitefish.
• The fowl that have been named by the Torah as kosher. Some examples are chicken, turkey, duck, and geese.
• All dairy products.

There are also a variety of unfit foods. (These are, as usually pro-nounced, called *trefah*.)

Non-kosher foods include the following:

• Certain fish such as shellfish, including crab, lobster, and shrimp, eels, shark, frog, turtle, and others.
• Birds of prey and carrion eaters. Examples of excluded birds include ostrich, pelican, swan, and vulture.
• Animals that chew their cud but do not have split hooves. Examples include camels, horses, and rabbits.
• Animals that have split hooves but do not chew the cud. The most notable example in this category is the pig.

It is important to note that even if the animal is allowed, there are still many rules that must be followed before it can be considered kosher. For example, the animal must be ritually slaughtered by a *shochet*, a professional who understands the various rules. Meat cannot have any blood on it, so the animal is inspected after it is slain; its meat is soaked in water, salted, and then soaked in water again.

Kosher foods are certified as such by various rabbis and agencies. Consumers are often careful to select only foods marked kosher by a rabbi and agency they respect. They also become aware of the contents of food.

Another important element of keeping kosher is not mixing meat products (called *fleishig*) and milk products (called *milchig*). There is a period between permissibly eating meat and milk; the period varies from one-half hour to six hours depending on the food and the tradition. Food that is neither meat nor milk is called *pareve*. *Pareve* foods include, for example, all fruits, vegetables, and cereals. In order for traditional Jews to keep this rule, they must do more than just avoid cheeseburgers. A kosher home maintains separate sets of dishes, a set for meat products and another set for milk products. This separation extends as well to flatware, pots, and pans. Still other utensils are sometimes bought for preparing *pareve* foods.

Observance of kosher eating laws varies very widely. Reform Jews are not bound by the *halachah* and so are free to decide whether to keep kosher or not. Some do so to maintain a Jewish tradition, to feel part of a wider Jewish community, or for other personal or religious reasons. Conservative Jews are supposed to keep kosher, but many Conservative Jews, like many Reform Jews, keep it selectively or not at all. For example, some Jews will abstain from pork products but eat all other foods. Others might keep kosher at home but eat in non-kosher restaurants. Still others buy kosher meat but do not separate meat and milk products.

There are many blessings associated with food.

The *Ha-motzi*, the blessing over bread, is recited at meals that have bread:

בָּרוּךְ אַתָּה יְיָ, אֱלֹהֵינוּ מֶלֶךְ הָעוֹלָם, הַמּוֹצִיא לֶחֶם
מִן הָאָרֶץ.

Baruch attah Adonai Eloheinu melech ha-olam, ha-motzi lechem min ha-aretz.

(Blessed are You, Lord our God, Ruler of the Universe, who brings forth bread from the earth.)

After the meal, the Grace after Meals (*Birkat Ha-mazon*) is traditionally recited.

In general, then, at meals and at each moment of the day, a Jewish life is meant to be endowed with spiritual purpose and a sense of holiness.

A SPECIAL DAY: THE SABBATH

The Jewish Sabbath (*Shabbat*, or *Shabbos* according to the Ashkenazic pronunciation), beginning on Friday evening by lighting a candle, and ending on Saturday evening by the lighting of another candle, is so central to Judaism that it is mentioned among the Ten Commandments. We are commanded to "remember the Sabbath Day and keep it holy." The Sabbath is crucial, then, in a religious sense, providing a weekly commemoration of God's resting after creation. In that sense, the Sabbath is a day of reflection on creation itself, and, by inference, on our own creations and life during the last week and our plans for the future week. The day is holy in being separated from the other six days.

Probably the most famous ethical demand that Judaism makes upon its people concerning the Sabbath is that the day is devoted to rest. The Talmud lists thirty-nine separate forms of work that are to be avoided. Many contemporary Jews have differing interpretations about what constitutes work, or whether Jews should or should not drive on the Sabbath, or even whether this commandment can be followed in the demanding modern world with its economic pressures and its recreational allures, both of which can and do intrude on the peace of the Sabbath. Discussions of the ethical dilemmas of such choices both with our ourselves and our children are part of the

ongoing dialogue of Judaism. Many Jewish parents view Sabbath decisions as moments of ethical growth for their children who must
decide, for example, whether to play on a sports team, or keep religious tradition. Such difficult moments can provide an opportunity
for the entire family to discuss their own identities and choices.

While choices about if and how to observe *Shabbat* vary very
greatly among American Jews, it is a common occurrence that those
who do not practice any *Shabbat* observances are often surprised by
the beauty of the traditions when they choose to begin to follow some.
This is so, in part, because the Sabbath is not a bleak day of prohibited behaviors, but a day conceived to be set aside for religious traditions. The Sabbath is an island in time, a spiritual refuge. It is an active
release from the cares of the world, an obligatory time of relaxation,
a time to forget the ordinary worries of the week. Indeed, many modernist Jews, seeking additional justifications for the Sabbath, note the
physiological and psychological benefits that are derived from taking
time out during the week. It was just such a modernist, using the
pseudonym Ahad Ha'am, who said that it was not so much that the
Jewish people had kept the Sabbath, but that the Sabbath had kept
the Jewish people. The Sabbath, like other religious practices, binds
Jews to God, to their own history, their spiritual ancestors, and to
their own identities.

Very traditional Jewish families follow a series of prescribed practices. Below are some of the most important of the traditions that can
be used to begin or continue keeping the Sabbath.

The Sabbath traditions begin before sundown on Friday evening
with the lighting of two Sabbath candles. There are set candle lighting times, about eighteen minutes before sunset. The eyes are covered by holding a hand over them, the candles are lit, and then the
blessing is recited:

בָּרוּךְ אַתָּה יְיָ, אֱלֹהֵינוּ מֶלֶךְ הָעוֹלָם, אֲשֶׁר קִדְּשָׁנוּ
בְּמִצְוֹתָיו, וְצִוָּנוּ לְהַדְלִיק נֵר שֶׁל שַׁבָּת.

*Baruch attah Adonai, Eloheinu melech ha-olam, asher kideshanu
be-mitzvotav, vitzivanu le-hadlik ner shel Shabbat.*

(Blessed are You, Lord Our God, Ruler of the universe, Who has sanctified us through your teachings and taught us to kindle the Sabbath light.)

There are customary blessings over children offered by parents on *Shabbat*. For sons, the blessing is:

יְשִׂימְךָ אֱלֹהִים כְּאֶפְרַיִם וְכִמְנַשֶּׁה.

Yesimcha Elohim ke-Ephraim ve-chi-Menasheh.

(May God make you like Ephraim and Menasheh.)

For daughters, the blessing is:

יְשִׂימֵךְ אֱלֹהִים כְּשָׂרָה, רִבְקָה, רָחֵל, וְלֵאָה.

Yesimech Elohim ke-Sarah, Rivkah, Rachel, ve-Leah.

(May God make you like Sarah, Rebecca, Rachel, and Leah.)

The following blessings are then said for all the children:

יְבָרֶכְךָ יהוה וְיִשְׁמְרֶךָ.
יָאֵר יהוה פָּנָיו אֵלֶיךָ וִיחֻנֶּךָּ.
יִשָּׂא יהוה פָּנָיו אֵלֶיךָ וְיָשֵׂם לְךָ שָׁלוֹם.

Yeverechecha Adonai ve-yishmerecha
Ya'er Adonai panav elecha ve-chunecha
Yisa Adonai panav elecha ve-yasem lecha shalom.

(May God bless you and keep you.
May God's countenance shine on you and be gracious to you.
May God care for you and bring you peace.)

Some families sing a traditional song, such as "*Shalom Aleichem*" at this point.

The next crucial blessing is *Eshet Chayil*, "The Woman of Valor," said by husbands to their wives. These verses from the Book of Proverbs praise the wife's virtues. Some homes include just the repeating of the words *eshet chayil*. Other homes include the traditional blessing.

The blessing over the wine, the *Kiddush*, is then recited. Traditional homes cite the usual verses. In many homes, the only line recited is:

בָּרוּךְ אַתָּה יְיָ, אֱלֹהֵינוּ מֶלֶךְ הָעוֹלָם, בּוֹרֵא פְּרִי
הַגָּפֶן.

Baruch attah Adonoi, Eloheinu melech ha-olam, borei pri ha-gafen.

(Blessed are You, Lord our God, Ruler of the universe, Who created the fruit of the vine.)

In traditional homes, the hands are then washed and a blessing recited. This is followed by the blessing over bread. This blessing, called the *motzi*, is made over bread called *challah*. While historically, *challah* referred to any bread used for the *motzi*, today that term is usually applied to an egg bread that is braided. The *challah*, with its cakelike taste and attractive appearance, is a favorite part of the meal in many homes. The *motzi* blessing is:

בָּרוּךְ אַתָּה יְיָ, אֱלֵהֵינוּ מֶלֶךְ הָעוֹלָם, הַמּוֹצִיא לחם
מִן הָאָרֶץ.

Baruch attah Adonai, Eloheinu melech ha-olam, ha-motzi lechem min ha-aretz.

(Blessed are you Lord, our God, Ruler of the universe, Who brings forth bread from the earth.)

The meal is then eaten. Usually, the table has been made up to look especially attractive. The Friday evening meal is the highlight of the week. Some popular foods include chicken, fish (including gefilte fish), cholent (made up of meat, beans, potatoes, and other vegetables heated before the Sabbath, since, by tradition, cooking itself was not allowed on the Sabbath), and *tzimmes* (a vegetable or fruit casserole using various recipes and sometimes including meat).

Between courses of the meal, stories are told or the Bible is discussed, and favorite Sabbath songs are sung.

The traditional blessings after the meal (*Birkat Ha-mazon*) are then said in many traditional homes.

Friday evenings also include a synagogue service. In some synagogues this service is the most important of the week. Other synagogues emphasize the more traditional Saturday morning service. A favorite tradition is the *Oneg Shabbat* celebration that follows the Friday evening services. For those Jews who do not attend a synagogue service, Friday can be a time for simple relaxation or for study from the Torah or a Jewish book. One mystical tradition focused on Friday evening as the most spiritually nourishing time to make love.

There is a Sabbath morning and afternoon service. Again, traditions vary greatly about how the Sabbath day is celebrated. Traditionalists frequently have a meal about noon and another after the *Minchah* service. Traditionalists also favor using Saturday afternoons for study. Many, for instance, begin on the Sabbath after Passover to study the tractate of the Talmud we have discussed called *Avot* (more well known as "Ethics of the Fathers").

The Saturday evening service, which ends the Sabbath, includes the service known as *Havdalah* (Hebrew for "separation"). This ceremony includes drinking wine and using spices. In many synagogues the song "*Eliyahu Ha-navi*" is sung.

THROUGH THE YEAR

The Jewish calendar is significantly different from the Gregorian one we use daily. For example, according to the Jewish calendar the new day begins at sunset, the new week begins after *Havdalah* on Saturday night, and the new month begins with a new moon on the 15th of each new month. (The first day of every lunar month is known as *Rosh Chodesh*, or "head of the month.") The Hebrew months are, in order, *Tishrei, Cheshvan, Kislev, Tevet, Shvat, Adar* (in seven out of every nineteen years there is also *Adar* II), *Nisan, Iyar, Sivan, Tammuz, Av,* and *Elul.* Such crucial events as Hebrew holy days and the date of death are calculated according to the Hebrew calendar. They therefore change each year according to the Gregorian calendar. Thus, for example, while Hanukkah begins on the 25th day of *Kislev* every year, that day varies, sometimes widely, on the Gregorian calendar.

Rosh Hashanah

The Jewish New Year begins on the first and second days of *Tishrei* with Rosh Hashanah. The New Year is celebrated on two days because of a talmudic decision resulting from a need to make sure that the holy day was celebrated on the correct day, because witnesses saying they had seen the new moon were frequently delayed. Most Reform temples follow the biblical rather than the talmudic tradition and celebrate Rosh Hashanah for one day.

    The holy days are filled with communal worship. Several Jewish terms are used in relation to holy days. For instance, the word *yontif* is Yiddish for a holy day, so that the greeting "*Gut yontif,*" meaning literally to have a good day, is often used by Ashkenazic Jews. The Hebrew word for prayer is *tefillah*, and Rosh Hashanah services include some special prayers found in the *machzor*. For example, there are special prayers for penitence that are called *selichot* that are said during Elul and on the Saturday night before Rosh Hashanah. Many synagogues have a late service on that Saturday night and invite speakers to supplement the service.

    In the United States, it is common for Jews to send Rosh Hashanah cards. These cards are often inscribed with the Hebrew words *Le-Shanah Tovah Tikateivu* ("May you be inscribed for a good year"). This traditional greeting stems from the talmudic tractate describing this holy season as one in which we are judged and our names entered in the Book of Life. That is, by tradition, our fates are entered in the Book on Rosh Hashanah and the Book is sealed on Yom Kippur. The ten days between these two holy days, when our fate is suspended, are therefore known as the Days of Awe.

Customs surrounding Rosh Hashanah vary greatly. Orthodox Ashkenazic Jews observe a ceremony called *Tashlich*, which is a symbolic casting of sins into a body of water. The ceremony is done on the afternoon of Rosh Hashanah's first day (or the second day if the first falls on the Sabbath). Because of the seriousness of the Days of Awe, many people use that time to contemplate and to study. It is common for Jews to give *tzedakah*, or charity, during this season.

Rosh Hashanah, as the beginning of the year, carries with it the connotation of all beginnings: the opportunity to change ourselves, to evaluate our past, reckon our mistakes, decide that we must change, declare our intention to change, and act on that declaration. Rosh Hashanah, however, is different from a secular New Year. The secular New Year is a time for revelry, for letting go. The Jewish New Year is a time for quiet prayer. The secular New Year celebrates only the beginning of one year. The Jewish New Year commemorates nothing less than an anniversary of the world's creation. Indeed, some Jews in trying to explain the holy day to their children, use a cake and have the children sing "Happy Birthday" to the world.

There are other activities for children as well. In many Jewish homes children have apples dipped in honey as a hope for a sweet new year. Children and adults alike enjoy the sounding of the *shofar*, or ram's horn, as well.

Yom Kippur

It is during the ten Days of Awe that God passes judgment on all people. That judgment period is completed on Yom Kippur, the Day of Atonement. Atoning for our sins, trying to improve ourselves, is not easy. Jewish tradition emphasizes the Days of Awe as opportunities to atone for our sins against God. By tradition, though, our sins against other people must be atoned by going back to those we have hurt. God, that is, does not simply absolve our sins against other people through our prayers. We continue to have the ethical obligation to go directly to those we have sinned to atone.

There are several observances associated with Yom Kippur. Orthodox Jews, for example, follow a tradition called *kapores* as a way to atone for their sins. *Kapores* is performed on the day before Yom Kippur by waving a live fowl three times over one's head and reciting a prayer. The fowl is then taken to a ritual slaughterer known as a *shochet* to be killed. Other Jews performing this ceremony substitute money for the fowl.

Probably the best known of those observances is fasting, refraining from food and drink. This *mitzvah* is traditionally obligatory for adult Jews and not for children (that is, those who have not celebrated a *bar* or *bat mitzvah*). In addition, those who for medical reasons cannot fast are not obliged to do so.

The meal prior to the beginning of the fast traditionally includes such foods as *kreplach*, or dumplings filled with chopped meat and onions as well as favorite foods.

There are five services held on Yom Kippur. The first service, held in the evening, is called *Kol Nidre* (from the Hebrew "all vows"). The morning service, *Shacharit*, is followed in some synagogues by *Musaf*, an additional service, and then by the *Yizkor*, or memorial, service. It is during *Yizkor* that prayers for the dead are offered. *Minchah*, the afternoon service, is next, and it includes a reading from the Book of Jonah. The final prayer is known as *Ne'ilah*, which refers to the closing of the Temple gates. After *Ne'ilah*, comes the last of the blasts from the *shofar* and the conclusion of the Days of Awe. Many synagogues follow the tradition of having congregants call out "Next Year in Jerusalem" after the sounding of the *shofar*.

After Yom Kippur's completion, there is a meal to break the fast that frequently includes salty foods, such as herring, deliberately intended to get people to drink the water necessary for replenishing their bodies.

Sukkot

Five days after Yom Kippur is the holy day of Sukkot (or Succos in the Ashkenazic pronunciation), the Feast of Tabernacles. In ancient times on Sukkot Jews would come from all over the land of Israel to the Temple where sacrifices would be offered. (Sukkot was one of three such "pilgrim" festivals; the others are Passover and Shavuot). Sukkot was a time for thanksgiving as the final harvest was gathered. Indeed, the American tradition of Thanksgiving had its origin in Sukkot. Sukkot is observed for seven days, with varying traditions in Israel and among the different denominations. Sukkot is also a time for remembering the wanderings of the Jews in the desert after they escaped from slavery in Egypt. The prime symbol at Sukkot is a *sukkah*, a hut or booth where food is eaten and, for some Jews, a place even to sleep, during the week.

One popular Jewish tradition is that the first nail of a *sukkah* is sunk immediately after the end of Yom Kippur. The *sukkah* is often made of wood panels, canvas, or other materials and has fruits or vegetables within. The roof by tradition consists of branches from trees, straw, or similar material. Many religious stores offer a prefabricated *sukkah*.

Sukkot also is symbolized by four plants: the citron, or *etrog*, a palm branch called the *lulav*, a myrtle, or *hadas*, and the willow, or *aravah*. Blessings are recited over these. It is also traditional then to wave the *lulav*.

The last day of Sukkot is called Hoshana Rabba. In ancient times, seven processions went around the altar while verses were sung and the *lulav* waved. Today, some congregations have the worshipers walk around the synagogue seven times.

Shemini Atzeret

Shemini Atzeret (the Eighth Day of Assembly) is celebrated after the last day of Sukkot as a closing festival of the season. Outside Israel, Shemini Atzeret is celebrated on two days except by the Reform movement, which, like in Israel, celebrates it on one day. Shemini

Atzeret is one of four holy days on which *Yizkor* is recited aloud in Orthodox and Conservative Ashkenazic synagogues.

Simchat Torah

The second day of Shemini Atzeret is called Simchat Torah (or "Rejoicing in the Torah"). It is on Simchat Torah that the cycle of reading the Torah is completed and is begun again. In synagogues, the Torah scrolls are carried around the synagogue.

Hanukkah

Hanukkah has become a very important holiday in the United States. Because of when it is celebrated, it functions almost as the Jewish counterpart to Christmas. Religiously, however, Hanukkah—because it was not mentioned in the Torah—is less important than the preceding holidays mentioned. Despite this, it has acquired a social potency; it is widely celebrated by Jews who do not observe some of the more religious holy days.

Hanukkah has become a very useful time to discuss Jewish identity with children, to sit down as a family and talk about how a Jewish identity differs from a Christian one, to discuss how Jews understand God, as such an understanding differs from how Christians do, and to explore the psychological and social implications of minority group membership in a way appropriate for the age level of the child. This is especially important for children because American children's culture is saturated with Christian content during December. It is the time that children are most acutely aware of their differences, a time when some Jewish children want a Christmas tree, a visit from Santa, or to take part in the other attractive elements of the Christmas season.

One tactic some Jewish parents have resorted to is to engage in a competition. Thus, lavish presents are presented. Instead of this approach, the educational one described above is more useful. Hanukkah, like all Jewish holy days, has its majesty and beauty. This is what should be emphasized.

The story of Hanukkah is especially exciting for children, with its heroes and miracles. The story begins after Alexander the Great died in 320 B.C.E. His divided kingdom was ruled over by generals who sought to impose Greek (Hellenistic) ways upon the peoples they had conquered, including the Jews. In particular, the Hellenists who ruled Syria and the land of Israel defiled the Temple. Their ruler, Antiochus Epiphanes, commanded that sacrifices to pagan gods be made in the Temple. In 165 B.C.E., Jews, under the leadership of Mattathias and his five sons, including Judah the Maccabee ("Judah, the Hammer"), revolted. The Hellenists were forced from the country. The Temple was rededicated. By tradition, the Jews found one jar of sacred oil meant for the menorah (the seven-branched candelabrum). The oil was only enough to last for one day, but instead the flame burned brightly for eight days.

Hanukkah is celebrated by lighting candles in a menorah. There are eight candles (one for each day of the miracle) and a ninth called the *shamash* (or "servant"), which is used to light the other candles.

Two blessings are said over the candles each night. A third blessing, the *shehecheyanu*, is added only on the first night.

The blessings for lighting the candles are the following:
First blessing:

בָּרוּךְ אַתָּה יְיָ, אֱלֹהֵינוּ מֶלֶךְ הָעוֹלָם, אֲשֶׁר קִדְּשָׁנוּ
בְּמִצְוֹתָיו, וְצִוָּנוּ לְהַדְלִיק נֵר שֶׁל חֲנֻכָּה.

Baruch attah Adonai, Eloheinu melech ha-olam, asher kideshanu be-mitzvotav vitzivanu le-hadlik ner shel Hanukkah.

(Blessed are You, Lord our God, Ruler of the universe, who has sanctified us through Your teachings and taught us to kindle the Hanukkah lights.)

Second blessing:

בָּרוּךְ אַתָּה יְיָ, אֱלֹהֵינוּ מֶלֶךְ הָעוֹלָם, שֶׁעָשָׂה נִסִּים
לַאֲבוֹתֵינוּ בַּיָּמִים הָהֵם בַּזְּמַן הַזֶּה.

Baruch attah Adonai, Eloheinu melech ha-olam, she-assah nisim lavoteinu, ba-yamim ha-hem ba-z'man ha-zeh.

(Blessed are You, Lord our God, Ruler of the universe, who brought miracles for our ancestors in ancient years at this time.)

The *shehecheyanu* is the third blessing (recited only on the first night):

בָּרוּךְ אַתָּה יְיָ, אֱלֹהֵינוּ מֶלֶךְ הָעוֹלָם, שֶׁהֶחֱיָנוּ,
וְקִיְּמָנוּ, וְהִגִּיעָנוּ לַזְּמַן הַזֶּה.

Baruch attah Adonai, Eloheinu melech ha-olam, shehecheyanu, vikiyemanu vehigiyanu la-z'man ha-zeh.

(Blessed are You, Lord our God, Ruler of the universe, who has kept us alive, and sustained us, and allowed us to reach this day.)

After reciting these prayers, it is customary to sing *Ma'oz Tzur* ("Rock of Ages") and other songs.

Note that on Sabbath, the Hanukkah candles must be lit prior to lighting the *Shabbat* candles.

There are many customs associated with Hanukkah. For instance, it is common for children to receive Hanukkah *gelt* (Yiddish for "money") either literally or in candy (usually chocolate) form. As discussed, this tradition has expanded in contemporary America to include sometimes lavish presents on each of the eight nights. One useful practice for parents is to ask children to sacrifice one of their presents and use the money for *tzedakah*, such as to buy presents for children in Israel who would otherwise do without. (Each year the Israeli newspaper *The Jerusalem Post* has a Toy Fund dedicated to providing gifts for such children).

Traditional foods at Hanukkah include potato pancakes (called *latkes*). Israelis often use jelly doughnuts called *sufganiyot*.

The most notable game is played with a *dreidl*, a four-sided top. Each side has a Hebrew letter. The four letters are *nun, gimel, hey,* and *shin* (an acronym for *nes gadol hayah sham*, "a great miracle happened there," an allusion to the Hanukkah oil miracle). Israeli *dreidls* have substituted the letters *nun*, *gimel*, *hey*, and *pey* as an acronym for *nes gadol hayah po*, "a great miracle happened here," an allusion to the miraculous revival of the modern Jewish nation of Israel. While there are various rules for playing the *dreidl* (sometimes made up as the game goes on), usually each child places a piece of candy in the "pot" in the middle and then takes a turn spinning a *dreidl*. If the *nun* comes up, each player must put in another piece of candy. If a *shin* (or *pey* in Israel) comes up, only the person spinning adds a candy to the pot. If a *hey* comes up, the person spinning removes half of all the candy. If a *gimel* comes up, the person spinning takes all the candy.

Asarah B'Tevet

Asarah B'Tevet (the tenth day of the month of *Tevet*) is a remembrance of the day the Babylonians began their siege of Jerusalem in 586 B.C.E.

Tu B'Shevat

Tu B'Shevat (the fifteenth day of the month of *Shevat*) is celebrated in the middle of winter. It was meant in ancient times to mark the end of winter rains in the land of Israel and the emergence of trees. In general, it was celebrated as a way to maintain spiritual and now physical contact with Israel. Israeli schoolchildren use the day to plant trees. Many American Jews have trees planted for them in Israel through the Jewish National Fund or in other ways focus on building in Israel. Other Jews celebrate by having a seder (not to be confused with the more common seder at Passover). Still others use the opportunity to contemplate the relationship of people to the environment. Fruits and carob are common Tu B'Shevat foods.

Purim

Purim, described in detail in the Book of Esther, tells the story of the wicked minister Haman who served King Ahasueros in ancient Persia. Haman intended to destroy the Jews. He cast lots (*purim*) to decide on which date to start his plot. His plans to eradicate the Jewish people (so resonant after the Holocaust) were stopped by Esther, who because of her beauty had become Queen, and her cousin Mordecai. Haman was hanged, and the Jews saved.

Purim is celebrated on the 14th of *Adar*, most often in March. Because Esther called on the Jews to fast prior to her efforts to save her people, traditional Jews fast on the 13th of *Adar* from dawn to dusk. The Book of Esther, called the *Megillah* (a Hebrew word for any scroll), is read in synagogue on Purim. Perhaps the favorite part of the reading occurs when Haman's name is mentioned, because each time it is said, the congregants make noise either booing or hissing, stamping their feet, or shaking a noisemaker called a *grogger*. The noise is intended to blot out Haman's name.

Purim is a popular holiday because one widespread custom is for children (and adults, including rabbis) to dress up in a costume. Some synagogues have fairs or carnivals. Drinking and gambling are an accepted part of the celebration. *Hamantaschen* (from the German "Haman's pocket" alluding evidently to Haman's acceptance of bribes), which is a triangle-shaped pastry (a shape supposedly reminiscent of Haman's hat), is eaten. It is often filled with prune, fruit, or poppy seeds.

Passover

Passover (or *Pesach*, in Hebrew) is one of the most popular of Jewish holidays, in part because it is centered in the home and focuses on the family.

Passover is the annual commemoration of the liberation of the Jewish people from slavery in Egypt. The Exodus story, retold each Passover, tells of Moses, the Jewish child saved by the Egyptian princess and raised among royalty, who grew up to lead the people. Moses confronted the Pharaoh, the Egyptian leader, to free the Hebrew slaves. When Pharaoh refused, ten plagues descended upon Egypt, including the final one, the slaying of Egyptian firstborn sons. Before this final plague, the Jewish people were told to consume a lamb and place part of the lamb's blood on the posts of their doors. In this way, as the firstborn were dying, the Jewish homes were identified, "passed over," and spared this plague. Eventually, Moses led the people across the Sea of Reeds, to Sinai where they received the Torah, and across the desert toward the land of Israel.

Passover is also the celebration of human freedom, a reminder of our ethical obligation to free those still enslaved, and a reminder that freedom did not and does not just occur, but requires us to re-member slavery and to continue our struggle for freedom.

Originally, Passover was celebrated for seven days (as it still is in Israel and in many Reform homes), but an eighth day was added after the beginning of the dispersion of the Jewish people in the year 70 C.E. because of a possible calendar confusion.

While some contemporary Jews use Passover simply as a time for a large meal with the extended family, there are many religious traditions associated with the holiday. For example, there are prohi-bitions against eating leavened bread and food with yeast and against using the same dishes and utensils ordinarily used to eat such food. These forbidden foods, dishes, and utensils are called *chametz*, or "sour."

Traditional Jews go through a ceremony of selling their *chametz* to a non-Jew. Houses are cleaned thoroughly. In many homes there is a search for *chametz* on the night before Passover begins. Those concerned with eating correctly may have separate milk and meat dishes just for Passover. Others use paper plates and plastic utensils for the holidays. Many people shop for "Kosher for Passover" foods.

The most famous of traditions associated with Passover is the *seder*, a combined family meal and religious service. The service is contained in a special prayer book called the *Haggadah*.

The *seder* plate is special for the holiday and marked with places for each item. The foods on the *seder* plate, which are not eaten, include:

1. *Karpas*, a vegetable, usually green, which is dipped in salt water.
2. *Charoset*, a mixture of nuts, chopped apples, spices, and wine. The *charoset* represents the mortar slaves used to make bricks.
3. *Maror*, or bitter herbs. Frequently, horseradish is used for the *maror*. The *maror* represents the bitter lives led by the Jews in slavery.
4. *Beitzah*, a roasted egg, representing a festival offering that was brought to the Temple.
5. *Zero'a*, a roasted bone, most often a shank bone. It represents a Passover sacrifice. (Jewish vegetarians sometimes substitute a broiled beet.)

Some *seder* plates include a sixth section for the *chazeret*, a vegetable even more bitter than the *karpas*.

Three pieces of matzoh, or unleavened bread, are also used to represent the three groups of Jews, the *kohanim*, Levites, and Israelites. There are four cups of kosher-for-Passover wine that are drunk during the seder. Additional items used at a seder include salt water in which to dip the *karpas* and Elijah's Cup, a special cup of wine set aside for the prophet Elijah, who, by tradition, visits every home on Passover and drinks from the cup. It is traditional practice to recline while eating because doing so was a symbol of freedom in the ancient world.

The service is outlined in the *Haggadah*. Here is a typical outline of a service:

- Candles are lit.
- *Kiddush* is recited over the first cup of wine, which is then drunk.
- There is a ceremonial hand washing.

• A blessing is recited over the *karpas*, which is dipped in salt water and tasted by everyone.

• The middle *matzah* (called the *afikomen*) of the three is broken. The larger piece of the broken *matzah* is hidden, and children look for it after the *seder* meal.

• The story of Passover is told.

• The Four Questions are asked. By tradition, these questions are asked by the youngest child at the *seder*. However, anyone may recite these questions, not just children. Here are the Four Questions:

Introduction:

מַה־נִּשְׁתַּנָּה הַלַּיְלָה הַזֶּה מִכָּל־הַלֵּילוֹת?

Mah nishtanah ha-lailah ha-zeh mi-kol ha-leilot?

(Why is this night different from all other nights?)

First question:

שֶׁבְּכָל־הַלֵּילוֹת אָנוּ אוֹכְלִין חָמֵץ וּמַצָּה, הַלַּיְלָה
הַזֶּה כֻּלּוֹ מַצָּה?

She-be-chol ha-leilot anu ochleen chametz u-matzah, ha-lailah ha-zeh kulo matzah?

(Why is it that on all other nights we eat either bread or *matzah*, but on this night we only eat *matzah*?)

Second question:

שֶׁבְּכָל־הַלֵּילוֹת אָנוּ אוֹכְלִין שְׁאָר יְרָקוֹת, הַלַּיְלָה
הַזֶּה מָרוֹר?

She-be-chol ha-leilot anu ochleen she'ar yerakot, ha-lailah ha-zeh maror?

(Why is it that on all other nights we eat all vegetables, but on this night we eat only bitter herbs.)

Third question:

שֶׁבְּכָל־הַלֵּילוֹת אֵין אָנוּ מַטְבִּילִין אֲפִלוּ פַּעַם אֶחָת,
הַלַּיְלָה הַזֶּה שְׁתֵּי פְעָמִים?

She-be-chol ha-leilot ein anu matbileen afilu paam echat, ha-lailah ha-zeh shetei fe'amim?

(Why is it that on all other nights we do not dip even once, but on this night we dip twice?)

Fourth question:

שֶׁבְּכָל הַלֵּילוֹת אָנוּ אוֹכְלִין בֵּין יוֹשְׁבִין וּבֵין
מְסֻבִּין, הַלַּיְלָה הַזֶּה כֻּלָּנוּ מְסֻבִּין?

She-be-chol ha-leilot anu ochleen bein yoshveen u-vein mesubin, ha-lailah ha-zeh kulanu mesubin?

(Why is it that on all other nights we eat when we are sitting or re-clining, but on this night we eat while reclining?)

- A parable is told about the Four Sons.
- The Ten Plagues are named. As each of the plagues is named, a drop of wine is spilled from each glass.
- Songs are sung.
- The second cup of wine is drunk.
- The hands are ceremonially washed while reciting a blessing.
- There is a blessing over the *matzah*.
- There is a blessing over the bitter herbs.
- The herbs are dipped into the *charoset* and eaten.
- The meal is served.

- The *afikomen*, found by a child, is ransomed with a gift and then eaten by all.
  - The Blessings after the Meal are sung.
  - The third cup of wine is drunk.
  - The door is opened so that Elijah may enter.
  - Psalms of praise called *Hallel* are sung.
  - The fourth cup of wine is drunk.
  - The seder concludes with the traditional words "*Le-shanah ha-ba'a b'Yerushalayim,*" or "Next Year in Jerusalem," the hope that Jews will be free in their homeland.

Yom Ha-Sho'ah (Holocaust Remembrance Day)

Yom Ha-Sho'ah commemorates the 6 million Jews who died during the Holocaust. Many synagogues hold special services on the 27th day of Nisan. There are lectures about the Holocaust in many places. On the morning of Holocaust Remembrance Day in Israel, sirens are sounded. People stop their cars and stand outside, radio and television shows are suspended, work ceases. There is a national silence for two minutes.

Yom Ha-Atzma'ut (Israel Independence Day)

Israeli independence is celebrated each year on the fifth of *Iyar* because on that date in the Hebrew year 5708 (May 14, 1948), the Jewish people proclaimed their independence in the modern nation of Israel. If Yom Ha-Atzma'ut falls on either a Friday or a Saturday, it is celebrated on the preceding Thursday so as not to interfere with *Shabbat*. In Israel, Yom Ha-Atzma'ut is preceded on the fourth of *Iyar* by a day of remembrance for those Israelis who gave their lives in defense of their country. Yom Ha-Atzma'ut is celebrated by parades and prayers. The date is often used by Jews to rededicate themselves to Israel and to give to an Israeli charity, to buy an Israel bond, to donate to the Jewish National Fund, or in some other way help Israel.

Lag B'Omer

The second day of Passover begins a counting of the forty-nine days between Passover and another holy day, Shavuot. The "counting of the *omer*" is done to connect these two crucial days. An *omer* was a measure of the grain put aside especially for the Temple. Each day, a part of that grain is given to God.

These forty-nine days are associated with pain in Jewish history, evidently because in about the year 135 C.E. a plague killed many of Rabbi Akiba's students. Others noted the period had been a time when the Jews had been particularly persecuted. Traditional Jews mourn during this time. Many rabbis, for example, will not conduct a wedding service on most days during these weeks. One exception is Lag B'Omer ("thirty-three days into the *omer*").

That day, the 33rd day of *omer*, the 18th of *Iyar*, a day on which the plague was supposed to have lessened, is a break in the forty-nine days of mourning. Rabbis perform weddings. Israeli schoolchildren go on picnics. In the United States, some synagogues hold field games, such as races or softball games.

Yom Yerushalayim (Jerusalem Day)

Yom Yerushalayim is celebrated on the 28th day of *Iyar* because on that date in the year 5727 (June 7, 1967), the holy city of Jerusalem was reunified and under Jewish control for the first time since the year 70 C.E.

Shavuot

Shavuot (the Feast of Weeks) was a celebration of the early wheat harvest in Israel. It also commemorates the giving of the Torah at Mount Sinai, when God and the Jewish people entered into a covenant. Shavuot is celebrated for two days in the Diaspora by Orthodox and Conservative Jews. It is celebrated for one day (the 6th of

Sivan) in Israel and by Reform Jews. Shavuot is the holy day on which Jews rededicate themselves to the Torah.

Shavuot is a companion holiday to Passover in its insistence that current Jews think of themselves first (at Passover) as having been slaves and then (at Shavuot) as having been at Mount Sinai to enter into the covenant.

At Shavuot, many homes and synagogues are especially decorated with flowers. The most traditional preparation involves study, especially a tractate of the Talmud called *Pirke Avot* ("Sayings of the Fathers"), which is filled with wise aphorisms.

Shavuot is a special holiday for converts, for on this day the Book of Ruth is read. This book, about a woman who chose to become Jewish, is sometimes said to be read on what was originally an agricultural holiday to show that converts are a worthy harvest for Israel. Ruth's non-Jewish birth and her attachment to Judaism show her loyalty not just to a people but to the Torah, an attachment that Shavuot emphasizes.

Shivah Asar B'Tammuz (The 17th of Tammuz)

This is a day of fasting from morning until night for traditional Jews to commemorate the day when the Babylonian army first breached the walls of Jerusalem in the year 586 B.C.E.

Tisha B'Av (The 9th of Av)

For three weeks after the Babylonians breached the wall, they attacked Jerusalem. On the ninth day of *Av*, the Babylonians reached the Temple and burned it. Tragically and ironically, the Temple (after being rebuilt) was destroyed again on the 9th of *Av* in the year 70 C.E. by the Romans. Other terrible events in Jewish history also became associated with this day.

Tishah B'Av is a fast day. The Book of Lamentations is read in synagogues.

THROUGH A JEWISH LIFE

Birth

The first *mitzvah* in the Torah is to "be fruitful and multiply." It is therefore unsurprising that the birth of a new Jewish baby is greeted with such joy and hope. Perhaps especially for a people burdened with a history punctuated with persecution, with the recent slaughter of one-third of its population, with a current population that is less than 1 percent of the world's population, the Jewish people prizes each infant.

There are particular ceremonies for both newborn girls and boys. Girls are named, often in synagogue. Conservative Jews have the naming on the first Sabbath after birth or within several months after birth. Reform Jews have a Covenant of Life service on the eighth day after the girl's birth, or sometime thereafter. There are also many emerging home ceremonies for naming a newborn baby daughter.

Naming the child is an important decision. It is very common among Jews to give each child, girl and boy, a secular name to be used for public life and a Hebrew name for the specifically religious moments in life, such as an *aliyah* to the Torah, signing a marriage contract, and at other times. There are many popular Hebrew names for girls and boys. Some popular ones for girls include Leah, Naomi, Rachel, Sarah, Miriam, and many others. Some popular ones for boys include David, Daniel, Michael, and many others. Many Hebrew names have become popular since the birth of Israel.

Many Ashkenazic Jews choose to name a newborn after a relative who has died. Sometimes this tradition is carried on by just using the first letter of a name. Thus a child named after a grandfather named Morris might be named Michael. Sephardic Jewish practice allows a person to be named after someone alive and therefore to be a Junior.

The Hebrew name given to a child (or names, if a middle name is also provided) is part of the way the child is called for religious occasions. Children are also identified by the Hebrew name of their parents. Thus a boy with the Hebrew name Mosheh Avraham whose father had the Hebrew name Simchah Yaakov would be called Mosheh Avraham ben Simchah Yaakov. *Ben* means "son." A girl with the name Ruth Tamar would be Ruth Tamar bat Simchah Yaakov, *bat* meaning "daughter." It is also important to know the mother's Hebrew name, which is included by many synagogues when the father is named. Thus, the full name might be used as Ruth Tamar bat Simchah Yaakov ve-Shulamit Zipporah (*v'* means "and").

In Conservative and Orthodox Judaism, there is also consideration given to the baby's lineage, whether *kohen*, Levite, or Israelite. By tradition, the baby's lineage comes through the father so that children of a kohen are each a *kohen*. Reform Judaism does not use the lineage system. As was discussed previously, all branches of Judaism recognize that a child's Jewishness comes from the maternal side. Thus, all children born of a Jewish mother are Jewish. Reform Judaism recognizes that a child born of a Jewish father and non-Jewish mother (that is, a woman who was not born Jewish and did not convert to Judaism) may be considered Jewish if the child is raised in the Jewish tradition and through public acts identifies as a Jew. This view coheres with the Reconstructionist views. Conservative and Orthodox Judaism, however, believe that the child of a Jewish father and non-Jewish mother is not Jewish and must convert in order to become Jewish.

Newborn boys have a special ceremony called a *brit milah* during which they are circumcised to represent their entrance into the Jewish covenant with God. Although this religious obligation was at one time almost universal, some contemporary parents are concerned about the need for circumcision and the pain involved. There has been a medical debate about its value, with recent findings in favor of it. This is so, in part, because of the rarity of medical complications resulting from circumcision. For Judaism, however, medical arguments are secondary to the religious significance of the *brit milah*. This ceremony takes place, health permitting, on the eighth day after the boy's birth. The person who performs the circumcision is called a *mohel*. The circumcision ceremony itself involves several traditional stages, although these stages vary according to local customs. The godmother stays with the mother and child until the godfather brings the baby to the *mohel* who takes it and calls out *Baruch Ha-ba* ("Blessed is this arrival"). The *mohel* then blesses the child (in some services the child is put on Elijah's Chair, a special chair put aside for the prophet who visits, like on Passover). The *mohel* gives the child to the father who hands the boy to a person called the *sandek*. The *sandek* (Greek for "godfather," because the *sandek* is the boy's second godfather) holds the child on a pillow or a table for the circumcision. The father of the son then recites a blessing:

בָּרוּךְ אַתָּה יְיָ, אֱלֹהֵינוּ מֶלֶךְ הָעוֹלָם, אֲשֶׁר קִדְּשָׁנוּ
בְּמִצְוֹתָיו, וְצִוָּנוּ לְהַכְנִיסוֹ בִּבְרִיתוֹ שֶׁל אַבְרָהָם
אָבִינוּ.

Baruch attah Adonai, Eloheinu melech ha-olam, asher kideshanu be-mitzvotav vitzivanu le-hachniso bi-verito shel Avraham avinu.

(Blessed are You, Lord our God, Ruler of the universe, who has sanctified us with Your teachings and taught us to bring this boy into the Covenant of Abraham our father).

The circumcision is then performed. Then the *mohel* recites a blessing over wine and the boy is named. The *mohel* then puts a piece of cotton or similar material into the wine and puts the cotton to the baby's lips. Many parents are pleasantly surprised at how quickly the boy stops crying.

The happy moment of the boy's entry into the covenant is followed by a meal to celebrate.

There is another ceremony followed by Orthodox and Conservative Jews, but, because the ceremony depends on lineage, is not followed by Reform Jews. This ceremony is called *Pidyon Ha-ben*, or Redemption of the Firstborn Son.

In this ceremony the first son is redeemed from his biblical obligation to devote his life totally to God when the boy's father pays a *kohen* five *shekelim*, or five silver dollars. *Pidyon Ha-ben* does not apply to a *kohen* or Levite; they have the obligation to serve. Therefore, if the boy's father is a *kohen* or Levite there is no need for the ceremony.

Education

All children have a difficult time establishing an identity, learning about the world they inhabit, developing social relationships, and a variety of other developmental tasks. Integrating a Jewish identity into the totality of identity is not always an easy task for a child. Sometimes they are confused as they try to differentiate themselves from their non-Jewish friends and neighbors.

It is the aim of Jewish education to make Jews literate about their own history and culture, to prepare them to lead Jewish lives in their homes, synagogues, and in the world, and to understand their identity as a Jew.

It is important not to confuse "education" with "schooling." Without question, the central Jewish education children receive comes from their homes. It is in the homes that they acquire values, attitudes, and behaviors. They find the role models to follow. Knowing this, many Jewish parents who had been otherwise unobservant or minimally observant use the birth of a child to start or increase their practice of Jewish customs. For example, many parents begin to light candles on *Shabbat* and perform other customs, especially blessing the children, keeping kosher, giving their children a *lulav* on Sukkot, marching on Simchat Torah with flags, lighting Hanukkah candles with the child, taking part in a seder, reading stories to their children about holidays or Israel or, in general, on Jewish subjects, singing songs, watching appropriate videos, building a *sukkah*, or any of a wide variety of other ways to help a child. Parents can impart the central ethical values of caring for others, of providing charity to the needy, of caring for the sick, and many other such acts.

The home nurturing of children and the sprouting of their Jewish identities can be helped by activities outside the home as well.

Many synagogues, YM-YWHAs, and Jewish community centers have established day care and preschools. Such programs vary widely, especially in their Jewish content, but are useful for finding a community for children in which many or most members of the community celebrate Hanukkah. The Christmas season is often particularly confusing for young Jewish children (and sometimes for their parents as well) as they try to understand why they do not celebrate Christmas, which judging by the cartoons and programs on television, the excitement of their classmates, and the decorations they see around them, everyone ought to be celebrating. A day-care center or preschool that helps children through such confusion can be particularly helpful for parents.

As Jewish children grow, their parents have various educational options. One option, of course, is to ignore the Jewish education of the child completely. Such an act, of course, insures that the child will grow up ignorant of Jewish customs and feel alienated from those who are familiar with the customs and with the wider Jewish community generally. Other parents arrange for a tutor, or provide Jewish education themselves if they are learned.

Other parents send their children to a Jewish religious school that meets after the secular school on weekdays, weekends, or some combination of both. There are also some Jewish nonreligious schools that characteristically stress ethics, or Jewish culture, or Yiddish, rather than traditional Jewish religious traditions. Finally, other parents send their children to day schools in which the child receives an integrated Jewish and general education. The Conservative, Orthodox, and Reform movements all have day schools, and there are day schools that are nondenominational, serving members from all movements. In some places, there are also Jewish high schools. The Jewish education in such schools varies widely.

There are a variety of other ways for Jewish children to learn about their heritage. For example, there are a large number of Jewish camps run by religious, Zionist, secular, and other groups as well as Y's. Jewish adolescents can also join various youth groups. Major youth groups include the North American Federation of Temple Youth (NFTY), which is the Reform Jewish youth movement, United Synagogue Youth (USY), which is run by the Conservative movement, and the B'nai B'rith Youth Organization (BBYO), which is sponsored by chapters of the service organization B'nai B'rith. There are also a variety of Zionist and other youth organizations.

Bar and Bat Mitzvah

Jewish boys are considered adults at the age of thirteen years and one day. Jewish girls are considered adults at the age of twelve years and one day. The entry into Jewish adulthood means taking on more religious tasks. These tasks might include being counted as part of a *minyan* (Orthodox and some Conservative Jews only count males as part of the *minyan*), following the commandments, fasting on the appropriate days, and other religious obligations.

While it is not legally necessary to have a ceremony to mark this occasion, it has been customary to do so. That is, a Jewish boy becomes a *bar mitzvah* ("son of the commandments") at the appropriate age with or without a ceremony or party.

The *bat mitzvah* ("daughter of the commandments") ceremony is not celebrated by Orthodox Jews. Conservative, Reconstructionist, and Reform Jews do celebrate this ceremony. The first *bat mitzvah* was Judith Kaplan, the daughter of the founder of Reconstructionism, Rabbi Mordecai Kaplan. Her *bat mitzvah* was held in 1922. Many Jewish girls delay having the ceremony until they reach thirteen.

The *bar* or *bat mitzvah* ceremonial requirements are relatively simple. The young person has an *aliyah* and, if he or she can do so, reads from the Torah, chants from the *Haftarah*, the section from the Prophets, and, depending on the person and custom, may lead various parts of the liturgy. Other widespread practices include parents reciting a blessing and the child giving a speech, perhaps about the Torah portion, or on some other issue of Jewish concern. Many of those becoming *bar* or *bat mitzvah* pledge to donate a portion of their gifts for charity.

The *b'nei* and *b'not mitzvah* in the United States are most often associated with large, expensive parties. Rabbis have frequently noted that such lavish parties are contrary to tradition. One popular alternative is to use the money that would have been spent on the party and take the *bar* or *bat mitzvah* person to Israel for a ceremony at Masada, the Western Wall, or some other equally memorable place.

One unfortunate misconception about the *bar* or *bat mitzvah* is that it is often deemed to represent the end of a child's Jewish education. Unfortunately, thirteen is an age in which intellectual curiosity is rapidly emerging and so much of the opportunity to extend formal learning into those educationally productive years is lost. Both Jewish parents and youngsters retain the religious responsibility to continue learning. In Judaism, learning is sacred and a lifelong task and joy.

Most Reform and some Conservative congregations also have a confirmation ceremony. The confirmation ceremony was initially introduced in the nineteenth century to replace the *bar mitzvah* ceremony and was held at a later age to allow for a fuller Jewish education. Today, the ceremony is often used to reaffirm the young man or woman's commitment to Judaism.

Marriage and Family Life

Marriage is a central event in Jewish life in large part because it perpetuates a central institution of continuity: the family. Judaism constantly stresses the value of individuals not separating themselves from the wider community. Whatever contribution individuals have to make on their own, they also, in Jewish tradition, have a responsibility to make a contribution as a member of their community. This sense of communal responsibility begins by getting married so as to begin a family. Communal responsibility is somewhat at odds with the modern sensibility that prizes love only as a reason for marriage. Judaism, without dismissing the crucial notions of love and caring, sees marriage, however, as more than an arrangement between two individuals. The marriage for love only can fail when love fades or changes its object of affection. In the Jewish concept of marriage, the couple has an obligation to God and to the Jewish community. A marriage is holy, not just legal. In Jewish life, the family becomes the source of solace and protection, of education and support.

Because of marriage's central role in Jewish life and continuity, the Talmud has four extensive tractates devoted to its regulations. There are many rules about prohibited partners, mostly having to do with what would be considered incestuous marriages.

One central regulation that is particularly pertinent to modern life is that intermarriage is not allowed. All the movements within Judaism are officially opposed to intermarriage. Reform and Reconstructionist rabbis may choose to perform an intermarriage at their discretion. It is important to stress that a marriage between someone born Jewish and a convert to Judaism is not an intermarriage. (Because Orthodox Jews do not generally recognize Conservative and Reform conversions, they may argue that a person converted by one of these movements was not converted at all.)

There are many symbols associated with a Jewish wedding, including the following:

• The *chuppah*, or wedding canopy, which represents the Jewish home. Sometimes a *tallit* is used in place of the *chuppah*. The *chuppah* is optional in Reform services.

• The ring. Traditional Jewish wedding rings are very simple bands without ornamentation. The purpose of this was to show that the bride was not marrying because of an expensive ring. Also, the simple ring allowed the poor, who could not afford expensive rings, to feel unembarrassed about their own wedding ring.

• The *ketubah*, or marriage contract. The *ketubah* is a guarantee by the bridegroom to the bride that she will be protected financially, even in case of the bridegroom's death or if a divorce occurs.

There are many ceremonies associated with the Jewish wedding. Actually, the first ceremony in traditional synagogues takes place on the *Shabbat* before the wedding in a ceremony called the *Ufruf*. In Orthodox and Conservative synagogues the groom (and, in many

Conservative synagogues the bride also) is given an *aliyah* to the Torah. After the *aliyah*, the congregation throws candy, raisins, or nuts to symbolize a wish for a sweet marriage.

On the wedding day, traditional women visit the *mikveh*. Later, the *ketubah* is signed. Traditional synagogues also have a veiling ceremony called *Badeken*.

The families walk to the *chuppah*. Usually the groom and his escorts (often his parents, but not necessarily) walk down the aisle and face the rabbi. Sometimes the rabbi delivers a blessing. The various other members of the wedding party such as bridesmaids then walk down the aisle and take their appointed places. The bride, escorted by her parents or others, walks down the aisle to stand on the groom's right side. Sometimes, only the bride's father walks her most of the way, pauses, and waits for the groom to continue walking her to the *chuppah*. Orthodox and some Conservative brides walk around the groom seven times. Some psalms may be recited at this point. The official performing the service then recites a blessing over wine. The bride and groom drink from the same cup. The groom puts the ring on the bride's right index finger and recites the blessing:

הֲרֵי אַתְּ מְקֻדֶּשֶׁת לִי בְּטַבַּעַת זוֹ כְּדַת מֹשֶׁה
וְיִשְׂרָאֵל.

Harei at mekudeshet li be-tabat zu ke-dat Mosheh ve-Yisrael.

(Behold, you are consecrated unto me with this ring, according to the law of Moses and Israel.)

Many contemporary marriages include a double ring ceremony in which the bride gives a ring to the groom. In Reform ceremonies, the bride might repeat the same blessing to the groom as the groom offered to her.

Some couples make personal statements after which the *ketubah* is read aloud, or at Reform services a Certificate of Marriage is noted. The Seven Wedding Blessings (the *Sheva Berachot*) are recited. The groom and bride drink from the second cup of wine, and the ceremony concludes. Perhaps the rabbi or other religious official says a few words at this point or offers a prayer. The rabbi then, by tradition, puts a glass wrapped in paper or similar material on the floor and the groom uses the heel of his shoe to break the glass. The breaking of the glass has been explained in various ways. Some say it is done to recall the destruction of the Temple, to remember even in moments of supreme joy that happiness is fragile and can be broken. It is a reminder to be vigilant in love. Everyone then shouts *Mazel Tov* (Good luck) and the bride and groom kiss. The wedding party then leaves the *chuppah*. Some weddings include the throwing of rice. Orthodox and some Conservative Jews then follow a custom called *Yichud* ("union") in which they go to a private room. Because Orthodox and some Conservative Jews fast on their wedding day, the *Yichud* is a time to break the fast.

Finally, there is a large wedding meal.

The marital life that follows the wedding ceremony has its own ethical ideals within Judaism. All movements are united in understanding marriage as sacred. Marriage was traditionally regarded within Judaism as the appropriate and healthy institution for sexual satisfaction. The sex drive was never seen as somehow immoral but as perfectly human, a drive best satisfied through partnership with a single, married partner. For this reason, Jews are united in their opposition to adultery or sexual experimentation outside marriage.

Orthodox and some Conservative Jews follow laws of family purity, which include abstaining from sexual relations at the time of menstruation and seven days afterward. Following the seven days, these traditionalist women go to a *mikveh* to be immersed. The *mikveh* symbolizes the new cycle, with its possibilities of a new life. After immersion in the *mikveh*, the woman has been ritually purified and can again engage in marital relations.

Marriage was also prized because it provided the institution for bearing and rearing healthy children, the sanctuary from the ordinary world, the source of support and strength, an opportunity to enhance love, a source of creativity. Most of all, of course, it is a chance to follow a central ethical teaching of the Torah.

Unfortunately, not all marriages are happy ones. In a society saturated with sexual symbolism and prizing individual desire above communal responsibility, it is unsurprising that many Americans, and many American Jews, have pursued their own interests at the expense of their marriages. It is also the case, of course, as Judaism has always recognized, that some marriages are intolerable, whether because of physical or mental abuse, adultery, mental illness, refusal to support the family, or some other equally compelling reason.

All the movements within Judaism recognize that divorce is sometimes necessary even while maintaining that marriage is the ideal. Divorce is not considered sinful by Jewish law. Indeed, divorce can be seen in the Book of Deuteronomy.

In general, all movements agree that the first step in getting a divorce is to get a decree from the state. This civil divorce is sufficient as a complete divorce within Reform Judaism. Both Orthodox and Conservative Judaism, however, require a religious divorce following a civil one. The religious divorce requires the husband to give his wife a *get*, a legal document. The *get* is written by a *sofer*, a scribe either before or when a *Bet Din*, or religious court, is convened (Orthodox and Conservative practices differ), at which time the divorce is religiously granted. There are other Conservative practices as well, including a husband's appointing the court to give the *get*.

Orthodox and Conservative Judaism do not allow remarriages after a divorce unless a *get* has been obtained. Reform Judaism does allow such remarriages.

The Ideal Jewish Life

It is probably not possible to describe an ideal Jewish life and harder still to live one. Still, it is possible to list some of the ideals. At the heart of such an ideal is the view of each Jew as expressing a Jewish identity through each thought and action. The ideal Jewish life is the one in which all aspects of the life are unified into a whole that is at its core Jewish. Thus, home life, work life, communal life, ethical practices, religious behavior—all would be intertwined in that ideal Jewish life. That life is marked by certain recurring themes. The ideal Jewish life is defined by attachment to tradition, as understood and practiced, by the Jewish community to which Jews choose to belong. It is a life filled with study, of the Bible and other sacred texts, but also of the world created by God, of the history of God's creation, humanity, and the societies and cultural products those humans produced. It is a life marked by charity, concern for others, a struggle to become a better person. It is a life that finds love in marriage, fulfillment in raising and educating Jewish children, participating in synagogue and Jewish communal life, developing the ethical habits that will lead to compassion, benevolence, justice, and holiness, and, above all, maintaining a faithful relationship with God.

Death

As all religions must, Judaism, too, faces the most profound questions. These include, among others, the nature of and reasons for death. In many ways death tears at belief. We fear extinction, we know the heartache that accompanies the death of someone we care about or love, we want to cling to our lives, to continue seeing sunsets, to watch our children grow, to follow the plots of our own lives. We want to continue our efforts, to play music, to work, to be creative. We feel deprived of paths we did not take. We worry about the future without us. We wonder if we have seen justice in our lives, if we have been treated fairly.

There are many traditional Jewish practices meant to take us through the difficult times after a death. From the moment of death until the burial, the grief is accompanied by the responsibility of burial.

Although there are widely varying customs within Judaism, there are some traditional practices that should be noted:

- *Taharah* is the preparation of the body.
- *Shomrim* (watchers) stay with the body, often reciting Psalms.
- *Tachrichim* are the simple white shrouds in which traditional Jews are dressed.

• Traditional Jews do not allow embalming, with the exception of legally or medically required autopsies, such as accidental deaths. Traditional Jews also believe it is disrespectful to have the body in view.
• The coffin should be modest, of unadorned wood. Jewish tradition frowns on expensive or showy coffins.
• Cremation is contrary to Jewish law.
• The funeral service and burial should be as soon as possible after death, allowing for the appropriate relatives and friends to be notified.

While a burial at a funeral chapel is not legally required, it is a common practice. There are several traditions associated with the funeral chapel:

• While it is most appropriate for a funeral service to take place at a Jewish funeral chapel, a non-Jewish funeral parlor may be used if there is no Jewish one available and there are no non-Jewish religious symbols.
• It is traditional to have a closed casket. It is not considered a sign of respect to view the deceased.
• Traditionalists do not allow flowers or music.
• The *Keriah* ceremony is widely practiced at the chapel or before burial at the cemetery. Sephardic Jews often perform the ceremony after the funeral when they have returned to their homes. Reform Judaism allows the family the choice about whether to perform this ceremony. The ceremony consists of the cutting of a garment or black ribbon. *Keriah* is a symbol of the acceptance of the death. After *Keriah*, it is customary to recite the following blessing:

בָּרוּךְ אַתָּה יְיָ, אֱלֹהֵינוּ מֶלֶךְ הָעוֹלָם, דַּיַּן הָאֱמֶת.

Baruch attah Adonai Eloheinu melech ha-olam dayan ha-emet.

(Blessed are you, Lord our God, Ruler of the Universe, the true Judge.)

At the funeral itself, after the coffin is placed in the ground, some earth is placed onto the coffin. Among Orthodox Jews, it is a tradition that the entire casket be covered. Conservative and Reform Jews usually put only some earth on the coffin, allowing cemetery workers to complete the task. One widely followed tradition is for members of the immediate family, and others who wish to, to take turns putting earth on the coffin. Some mourners turn the shovel around using its reverse side when they do this to separate this task from other tasks. Additionally, some place the shovel in a pile of dirt rather than handing it to the next person.

The shoveling of earth by the deceased's loved ones is meant to symbolize a sign of respect and a mature understanding of the reality of death. Death, in Jewish life, is not a fact to be hidden away or avoided, but a reality to be faced directly as an inevitable part of life.

The rabbi recites some psalms. The prayer *El Malei Rachamim* is then recited. The traditional prayer *Kaddish* is then recited.

The *Kaddish*, which does not mention death, is a central Jewish prayer. It is in Aramaic, not Hebrew. This is the *Kaddish* prayer with a Sephardic pronunciation; in general Ashkenazic pronunciation would have an *s* instead of a *t* so the first word would be *Yisgadal*:

יִתְגַּדַּל וְיִתְקַדַּשׁ שְׁמֵהּ רַבָּא בְּעָלְמָא דִּי בְרָא
כִרְעוּתֵהּ, וְיַמְלִיךְ מַלְכוּתֵהּ בְּחַיֵּיכוֹן וּבְיוֹמֵיכוֹן
וּבְחַיֵּי דְכָל בֵּית יִשְׂרָאֵל בַּעֲגָלָא וּבִזְמַן קָרִיב,
וְאִמְרוּ, אָמֵן.
יְהֵא שְׁמֵהּ רַבָּא מְבָרַךְ לְעָלַם וּלְעָלְמֵי עָלְמַיָּא.
יִתְבָּרַךְ וְיִשְׁתַּבַּח, וְיִתְפָּאַר וְיִתְרֹמַם, וְיִתְנַשֵּׂא
וְיִתְהַדָּר, וְיִתְעַלֶּה וְיִתְהַלָּל שְׁמֵהּ דְּקֻדְשָׁא, בְּרִיךְ
הוּא, לְעֵלָּא (וּלְעֵלָּא) מִן כָּל בִּרְכָתָא וְשִׁירָתָא
תֻּשְׁבְּחָתָא וְנֶחֱמָתָא, דַּאֲמִירָן בְּעָלְמָא, וְאִמְרוּ אָמֵן.
יְהֵא שְׁלָמָא רַבָּא מִן שְׁמַיָּא, וְחַיִּים עָלֵינוּ וְעַל כָּל
יִשְׂרָאֵל, וְאִמְרוּ, אָמֵן.
עֹשֶׂה שָׁלוֹם בִּמְרוֹמָיו, הוּא יַעֲשֶׂה שָׁלוֹם עָלֵינוּ
וְעַל כָּל יִשְׂרָאֵל, וְאִמְרוּ, אָמֵן.

Yitgadal ve-yitkadash shmei raba be-olma divra chirutei. Ve-yamlich malkutei be-chayeichon uve-yomeichon uve-chayei de-chol beit Yisrael baagala uvi-z'man kariv ve-imru, Amen.
Yehei shmei raba mevorach lei'olam ule-olmei olmaya.
Yitbarach ve-yishtabach, ve-yitpaar, ve-yitromam, veyitnasei, veyithadar, veyitaleh, veyit'hallal shmei dekudesha brich Hu. Le-eiyal min kol birchata ve-shirata tushbechata ve-nechemata, damiran be-olma ve-imru, Amen. Oseh shalom bimromav, Hu yaaseh shalom aleinu ve-al kol Yisrael, ve-imru Amen.

(May God's name be sanctified throughout all the world, which the Lord has created according to Divine Will. May God establish the Divine within your lifetime and within the lifetime of all the house of Israel and let us say Amen.
May God's great name be a blessing to all of eternity.
Praised and exalted, glorious and adored, may all revere God's name, and may God be blessed, and let us say, Amen.
May life and peace come down from heaven upon us and all the people Israel, and let us say Amen.
May God, who created peace, give peace to us and to all of Israel, and let us say Amen.)

After returning home from the cemetery, traditional Jews first wash their hands before entering the house. Immediate family members observe a mourning period called *Shivah* for seven days. *Shivah* begins with the burial and the day of the burial is counted as the first day of mourning. By tradition, friends and neighbors prepare the first meal served at the *Shivah* house. It is common to wear the cut ribbon except on *Shabbat*. Traditional Jews have prayer services in the house of mourning, services that, for traditionalists require a *minyan*. There are different customs about observing *Shivah*, but all agree that it is time of reflection and guests should show support. Some widely observed traditional practices include lighting memorial candles, not wearing leather shoes, covering mirrors in the home, sitting on low stools, doing without haircuts and shaving, not having an *aliyah* in synagogue, and, if at all possible, not working.

While historically women were not required to recite the *Kaddish*, it is today a very widespread practice among Reform, Conservative, and even some Orthodox Jews for women to recite *Kaddish* as well.

Sometimes, converts face a dilemma about sitting *shivah* or reciting *Kaddish* for their natural, non-Jewish parents. Religious authorities disagree over the propriety of such an act since it is a commandment to honor one's natural parents, and it is unclear which is appropriate. Beyond the general agreement that it is inappropriate for a convert to mourn within the religious traditions of the non-Jewish parents, guidance is not always clear. Many traditionalists conclude that converts are not required to follow traditional Jewish mourning practices, but may do so if they wish.

After the *Shivah* period, *Kaddish* is recited for eleven Hebrew months, but, for traditionalists, only when there is a *minyan* present. After *Shivah*, is a period called *Shloshim*, which lasts for twenty-three additional days (making for a total of thirty days). During this period, the mourner avoids festive events such as weddings or parties.

Jewish law does not require that there be a special unveiling ceremony for a tombstone, but such ceremonies are often held, usually about one year after the death.

There is in synagogues a special service intended to remember those who have died. This service, called *Yizkor* (or May God Remember) is traditionally included on Yom Kippur, Shemini Atzeret, the last day of Passover, and Shavuot. Some Reform Jews say *Yizkor* only on Yom Kippur and the last day of Passover.

The anniversary of death is marked by a *Yahrzeit* observance, which includes lighting a memorial candle that burns for 24 hours and attending the synagogue to say the *Kaddish*.

It should be noted that, because practices and the nature of adherence to tradition vary so greatly among American Jews, the ceremonies surrounding death and burial arrangements can result in very painful decisions. One typical dilemma, for example, is that the deceased may have had a final wish for a practice that violates Jewish law, as for example a desire to be cremated. Some people wish to have a particular funeral home that other members of a family think inappropriate. Some want to be buried in a favorite suit or dress rather than in traditional garb. In such circumstances, consultation with a rabbi is vital.

Judaism emphasizes this world. There is a reluctance within the tradition to contemplate the world to come after we die, so as to keep our focus where it belongs, on living in and improving this world.

Nevertheless, there is within the Jewish tradition a clear vision of life beyond death. According to classical Jewish tradition, a tradition frequently challenged by modern Jews, the sequence of events will be the following: the souls of the dead go to Heaven; at some future time the Messiah will arrive; after a time the dead will be resurrected so that their souls will be reunited with their physical bodies. Many modernist Jews who believe in life after death do not accept this physical resurrection but focus on the soul's eternity.

The Jewish conception of the afterlife emphasizes, in a way that we obviously cannot fully comprehend, the closeness of souls to God.

There have been Jewish conceptions of Hell, most often as a state of being remote from God, of the soul at a great distance from the Almighty. Other thinkers, especially Maimonides, suggest that the soul of an evil person can be destroyed so it cannot spend eternity in Heaven. Indeed, one of the central Jewish views of the afterlife is its possibility for the final reckoning of justice, that, after death, the unpunished wicked and the unrewarded good will get what they morally deserve.

13

The Ethnic Dimension in Jewish Life

Many observers of Jewish life who were reared in a non-Jewish religion are confused about the nature of Jewish identity. Judaism is often inaccurately conceived of only as a religion so that simply following Jewish religious observances ought to make a person Jewish. Conversely, outsiders are sometimes confused when they see people who are nonreligious Jews feel deeply attached to their Jewishness.

A Jewish identity is an intertwined collection of identities. One central strand in that collection is the notion of Jewish ethnicity.

An ethnic group consists of those who believe themselves to be united and belong to the same people. Such unity may, in fact, be tenuous or even mythic, but it is the sense of attachment that is crucial. Ethnic identity comes from a person's attachment to the ethnic group. For such a person who identities with the Jewish people, such an ethnic identity may arise from other than a common religious belief. Some people identify ethnically with the Jewish people out of a loyalty to family, out of an identity with Jewish history, out of pride in Jewish accomplishments, out of a sense that there is a common Jewish consciousness that they share, out of a stubbornness not to let anti-Semites define who is Jewish or try to eradicate Jews such as what happened during the Holocaust, out of an attachment to the products of Jewish culture including language or linguistic expressions, out of an identification with Israel and the fate of the Jewish people, or for some other reason. A complete Jewish identity includes both a religious and ethnic component, although it is important to stress that for many American Jews the religious component is less important than the ethnic.

This fact makes conversion even a more difficult process than it already seems to be. It is one matter to search through a religious identity and discover Judaism's religious attractiveness, but it is another to change religions only to feel (or worse, be told) that Jewish identity cannot just be acquired through a religious conversion.

Conversion, that is, requires not only an educational process to learn about Judaism but an extended time of adaptation to become part of the Jewish community, to join the group.

Such acculturation requires patience. It requires an effort to absorb a new vocabulary (see the glossary at the end of this book for a start) and new foods. But there is a harder, much more crucial dimension in acquiring a Jewish identity.

A JEWISH CONSCIOUSNESS

The most difficult task in acquiring a Jewish identity after accepting Judaism's religious tenets, interpreted as they are in various ways, is to develop a Jewish consciousness.

The convert has not just found God as understood by Judaism, or found a romantic partner who is Jewish, or found a new set of religious practices. The convert has found a new set of concerns. As a new Jew, the convert needs to identify with the Jewish community so deeply that the community's concerns are absorbed by the convert. The Jewish community cares about the survival and security of Israel. So must the convert. The Jewish community cares about preserving the memory of the Holocaust so as to firm its resolve to fight anti-Semitism. So must the convert. The Jewish community cares passionately about Jewish survival in the United States. Such passion finds expression in an emphasis on Jewish education and marriage to someone Jewish. However difficult it may be for a convert, this too must be integrated into the new Jewish personality; converts must emphasize to their children the importance of marrying someone Jewish.

Feeling Jewish will, of course, take time. Ultimately, however, the conversion that will be most successful is the one in which the converts see their own future and the futures of their children as identical with the future of a thriving, secure Jewish community.

This effort by converts is difficult. Born Jews need to understand this difficulty and help converts—both before and after the conversion ceremony—adjust to the contours of a Jewish identity. Because converts so frequently bring a religious zeal missing in some born Jews, the combination of converts bringing spirituality and born Jews bringing ethnicity can only result in Jews with a fuller, more satisfying Jewish identity.

III
AFTER THE CONVERSION

14
Making Jewish Choices

The postconversion joy, tempered with the continuing need to learn, has another dimension as well. The transforming nature of a conversion allows a convert to see the world through a different set of eyes. Seeing the world through Jewish eyes means making Jewish choices. These choices are large and small, vital and peripheral, but all add up to the definition of a new life. It is a Jewish choice to join a synagogue or Jewish organizations, contribute to charities, continue to learn about Judaism, raise the children in a Jewish environment, visit Israel, or get involved politically on behalf of Jewish causes. It is possible to do all this, and it is possible to do none of it. That is the nature of choice. Entering into the covenant, however, implies the keeping of an agreement. As each new convert focuses on that agreement, choices have to be made.

15
Choosing a Synagogue

One important question after becoming Jewish is deciding first whether to affiliate with a synagogue or not and, if so, which synagogue to join.

There are large numbers of Jews who are not members of a synagogue. Some of them do not know very much about the service and do not wish to learn; some do not like to pray; some associate the synagogue with unpleasant early memories; others have still different reasons. Some nonmembers seek to enhance their Jewish attachments by joining other, more secular, Jewish groups, perhaps a Jewish cultural group, or a group devoted to protecting Jews against anti-Semitism, or a YM-YWHA. Others believe themselves to be simply Jewish, feel no need to affiliate, and are Jewish on their own personal terms. Indeed many conversionary families, following the pattern of all American Jewry, do not affiliate after the conversion process is over.

Despite the large unaffiliated Jewish population, it is especially important that new Jews get at least a taste of synagogue life. Synagogues are the religious focal point of the Jewish community. Joining a synagogue provides an opportunity for a regular prayer community, a place to teach children, a source for adult learning through courses and lectures, a resource to ask questions about Judaism, an emotional tie to the Jewish community, and a spiritual home.

Indeed, it is possible to find the synagogue as a source of spiritual experience. As Leslie Kahan (not her real name) puts it:

> The first time I walked into a synagogue I had an experience like sudden enlightenment. I didn't know anything about Judaism, but I knew immediately that it was for me. I was enthralled with what I saw and heard. The meditative, musical sounds of the prayer pleased me. The philosophical bent of the rabbi's talk impressed me. I couldn't begin to figure out what page we were on in the prayer book, but I wanted to learn.

Choosing a synagogue is not always very easy. In part this is so because synagogues and rabbis can vary greatly. In addition, learning the prayer service can be a challenge. The first decision is the determination about which religious grouping to join. As indicated in Part One, there is substantial disagreement among the movements within Judaism about the status of converts. In addition, there is considerable difference among the movements (and synagogues within each movement as well) about the nature of the service. It would be useful to read about each movement that sounds interesting and attend one or two different houses of worship within those movements. American Jewry is, if anything, pluralistic, so that there is a spiritual place on the synagogue continuum for all worshipers. The only problem is finding that place.

THE CONVERT'S RELIGIOUS NEEDS

In part, it is necessary for worshipers to determine their religious needs. Each service has its own style. In some synagogues there is a lot of noise, in others there is more decorum. Some synagogues have a lot of Hebrew, others much less. Some have frequent participation by the congregants, such as through responsive reading, singing, and even dialogue with the rabbi, while others focus on the rabbi's performance. Some follow a traditional liturgy very closely, while others are more playful with the tradition and incorporate new ideas, for example, in celebrating the holidays. Some synagogues have congregants who are very friendly, while others have congregants who are more aloof. Some synagogues are large and beautiful, while others are small and plain. Some synagogues focus on the routine of the service, while others focus more on the individual spiritual experiences of the worshipers.

It is important to determine your own needs and then look for a synagogue to meet them. It is, of course, possible to attend services in various synagogues looking for one that matches spiritual expectations. It should also be noted that sometimes a synagogue that does not provide a program you need will do so if asked.

There are frequently cited problems about joining a synagogue. One problem often mentioned is the expense of joining. Some synagogues provide reduced or even free membership for new members for a set period of time, so it is worthwhile to inquire. Some people wonder whether they should join a synagogue if they do not yet have children. Although this is obviously an individual choice, the arguments given above can be supplemented with the obvious fact that new Jews will feel more comfortable teaching their children about Judaism and the synagogue if they are already familiar with rituals, the synagogue service, and other matters before a child asks such questions.

In general, it is true that those people who attend a synagogue they like regularly will come to feel most at home. As the tunes and prayers become familiar, their repetition will have the same soothing effect as hearing a favorite song over and over. The prayers that are used come to be so loved, in part, because they provide that experience, that sense of warmth at hearing the familiar again.

That is why attendance becomes valuable. It is possible to hear the service so frequently that it becomes comfortable.

SYNAGOGUE PROGRAMS

For new Jews, different synagogues will provide different programs. Many synagogues now have learner's services, during which the ser-

vice is explained and gone over slowly. Some synagogues have conversion support groups.

One excellent idea done in some synagogues is to have host families invite new Jews for a Sabbath dinner or a seder, help the new
Jew journey through the prayer book, answer questions about Judaism, the synagogue, the rabbi, the congregants, or the community.
Host families can take new Jews on a local Jewish tour to find such
places as a kosher butcher and bakery store, local Jewish bookstores,
which frequently carry Jewish religious articles that supplement those
articles that might be sold in the synagogue itself, the Jewish community center, Jewish schools, and local Jewish organizations.

Some synagogues have intensive adult education courses so that
the new Jew, like all Jews, can take part in lifelong learning. Such
courses should be in basic Judaism, of course, such as Hebrew, Bible,
and Jewish history, but also valuable are courses in such matters as
Jewish songs, dances, cooking, embroidery, conducting a seder, and
so on. Some synagogues extend the notion of education to include
such activities as weekend retreats, lecture series, visits to local Jewish historical sites, and so on.

The rabbi can make a big difference in making a new Jew feel
comfortable. It is important to hear different rabbis. Attend *Shabbat*
services and hear the sermons, the explanations of the Torah portion, possibly a discussion of contemporary issues such as about Israel
or American culture. The rabbi is at heart a teacher, frequently
offering courses. Determine if you can learn from the rabbi, feel comfortable asking questions, even ones for which you think you are supposed to know the answers. Even a learned rabbi may not be the right
kind of teacher for you. It is also important to see if the rabbi is a
good person, a *mensch*. If you or your family need help, would you
feel comfortable going to the rabbi? These are not easy questions to
ask, and perhaps it will take a visit to several synagogues before a
choice is made, but the "synagogue shopping" is well worth the time
and effort if it can result in a spiritual home for you and your family.

For new Jews who prefer the intimacy of a small group, there
may be a *chavurah* within your community or even within a synagogue.

Usually, a *chavurah* functions independently as a group meeting in homes and emphasizing participation by all members. The word *chavurah* means "communal spirit." The idea actually began with the Essenes and Pharisees in ancient times. In modern times, the idea of a community praying together emerged in the United States primarily because of a feeling that large synagogues prevented the emergence of a true community spirit and that such synagogues focused on the outer forms of prayer rather than the spiritual needs of those praying. There are various types of *chavurot* (plural of *chavurah*), either of devout and knowledgeable people who get together to study, or a community that essentially lives together as a group and so studies together, or as a group or groups functioning within a larger synagogue. Members of a *chavurah* study together, celebrate holy days together, and, in general, provide a spiritual support group. You should ask if a *chavurah* exists in your community.

WHAT CONVERTS BRING TO A SYNAGOGUE

Converts have a tremendous amount to offer a synagogue. At first, before the conversion, they bring an outsider's perspective, which can be particularly valuable. One convert speaking before a Jewish audience asked them pointedly why they did not love their religion enough to share it. Such a statement carries enormous moral weight when spoken by someone brought up in another religion. Because of this, public conversion ceremonies are valuable not only for the convert but as an educational experience for all Jews. Converts can take the lead in their synagogue in such activities as including articles on conversion in the synagogue bulletin, setting aside in the library a collection of books on the subject, forming the support groups described above, lecturing to students about the place of the convert in Jewish history, and much else. Naturally, no new Jew should feel obligated to do any of these; some people who have converted understandably desire simply to become part of the spiritual community, not to be looked upon as somehow a different kind of Jew.

The synagogue and its congregants have complementary obligations. They must sincerely welcome converts, integrate them into the synagogal community, help them when help is needed, and learn more about the role of converts in Jewish life precisely so they see converts as genuine Jews and not somehow as second-class Jews.

Additionally, converts can affect indifferent born-Jewish spouses. Almost all rabbis tell stories of how a lax congregant found renewed Jewish interest because of the gentle support by the converted spouse.

16
Continuing to Study

In Judaism study is tantamount to prayer. While some traditionalists understand "study" to be limited only to the great sacred religious texts, many modernist Jews believe that studying Judaism involves studying any part of it.

The crucial aspect of learning about Jewish life is incorporating the learning into everyday experiences. The following sections describe some possibilities.

JEWISH NEWSPAPERS

Start with the Jewish papers for your community and expand to include national papers and, from Israel, the *Jerusalem Post*. Regular reading of Jewish papers is a crucial way to stay informed about the key issues of the day in Jewish life. If you do not know the name or address of your local paper, you can call a local synagogue asking for the librarian or someone else at the synagogue to provide that information.

JEWISH MAGAZINES

There are many excellent Jewish magazines. Among the most valuable are the intellectual *Commentary*, which includes a good deal of non-Jewish political and social analysis from a neoconservative point of view, the more particularly Jewish *Moment*, the slick and interesting magazine from Israel *The Jerusalem Report*, the Zionist-oriented *Midstream*, the lively newsletter publication *Sh'ma*, the diverse and interesting *Jewish Spectator*, the controversial *Tikkun*, which provides analysis usually from a liberal to leftist point of view, the scholarly *Judaism*, and the magazine centering on issues concerning Jewish women *Lilith*. In addition such major organizations as Hadassah, B'nai B'rith, and Women's American ORT publish important magazines. Each religious movement also publishes important religious journals. These magazines might be read in synagogue libraries. Some are available in public libraries. Read some to see which interest you.

JEWISH BOOKS

It is vital to read Jewish-oriented books to learn in depth about Jewish matters. Jews have taken the name given to them as "the people of the book" very seriously. Almost any subject in Jewish life is covered in a wide variety of reading materials. Specific suggestions for reading are included at the end of this book in a reading list.

Locate a good Jewish bookstore in the area and go in to see what is available. Many synagogues stock at least some titles.

It is also extremely valuable to become a member of the Jewish Book Club and to get a catalog of Jewish books from Jason Aronson Inc. Other book catalogs are also available.

JEWISH MUSIC AND ART

There are many collections of Israeli music, Yiddish songs, and music by well-known Jews. Although some well-known musicians who were Jewish did not always write specifically Jewish material, a Jewish flavor can be felt underneath much of their work. It is valuable to listen to works by such popular masters as Harold Arlen, Irving Berlin, Leonard Bernstein, Bob Dylan, and others. For a more specifically Jewish flavor, Shlomo Carlebach and Debbie Friedman are particularly exciting performers.

There are books of art with specifically Jewish themes by such well-known artists as Marc Chagall, Sir Jacob Epstein, Chaim Gross, Jacques Lipchitz, Amedeo Modigliani, Camille Pissarro, Larry Rivers, Ben Shahn, and many others.

POPULAR CULTURE

Learn about Jewish life from other products of popular culture. There is a list of Jewish-oriented films at the end of the book. Individual episodes of television shows can also be very insightful. Some of the famous Jewish-oriented series were "The Goldbergs," "Menasha The Magnificent," "The Gertrude Berg Show," "Bridget Loves Bernie," which caused a stir because the couple was intermarried, "Rhoda," "Busting Loose," "Lanigan's Rabbi," "Chicken Soup," which starred Jackie Mason, and others. There were important recurring characters on large numbers of television programs, including "thirtysomething." Some of this material is becoming available on videotape or even in reruns. Other series with Jewish characters include such shows as "Sisters," which has a character who converts to Judaism, "L.A. Law," and many others.

Many Jews are particularly interested in what they learn about being Jewish from humorists and comedians. The list of Jewish comedians is enormous, from Don Adams and Woody Allen to Henny Youngman. Many Jewish women are including Jewish material in their comedic performances as well.

CONTINUING EDUCATION COURSES AND INDEPENDENT STUDY

Formal study is also available. Check local synagogues, colleges, continuing education programs through high schools, Y's and Jewish community centers, and other institutions for instruction. These institutions also sometimes have Jewish lecturers. There are traditional and other institutions in Israel for learning, and retreats offered by various Jewish organizations. Much of the material is advertised in Jewish newspapers, adding to the already important value of those papers.

Traditional Jewish study has been in groups more than as individuals, so that communal study is very much in keeping with how the Jewish people has studied through its history. It is useful to remember the image used to describe the study of Talmud: its learning is so vast that students often feel that they are only in one spot in a very large sea. All Jewish learning is like that; it is difficult and it is enjoyable. The difficulty lies in ever feeling finished, while the joy is that there is so much to pick from and the supply of materials so seemingly inexhaustible that one can enjoy studying aspects of Judaism throughout life.

Some people enjoy cooking and learning new kosher recipes. Others like folk dancing, or a beginning course in Hebrew, or a history of Jewish ritual objects, or any of the variety of subjects that go into making a Jewish life. Virtually any important subject of interest has a Jewish angle.

Additionally, it is possible to cull Jewish material from the non-Jewish media. Many major newspapers and magazines include material about Jews, Judaism, and Israel. *The New York Times* and other publications have frequent material pertaining to Jewish life. Reading articles about Israel, for instance, is a quick way to get into the flow of Jewish conversation. It will not take long to look for Jewish materials on television news and entertainment programs. Listening to and watching the popular media presentations of Jewish life is an important way to know what is happening in Jewish life, or at least the media's understanding of what is happening.

It is possible to embark on an effort at independent study. There is considerable sacred material translated into English. There are Hebrew–English bilingual editions of many texts as well. The various commentaries available are also important. You can start by reading some of the materials in the reading list at the end of this book.

Many born Jews and those new to Judaism feel overwhelmed by the sheer amount of material. The idea, though, is to start where you are interested and get what you can. In education, students are sometimes told to pretend that what they are learning is water coming from a pump. They put their hands under the pump to catch all the water they can. Inevitably, most of the water will fall over their hands; they will only be able to grasp a bit of the nourishing water. That is what it is like to study Judaism. It is all nourishing. Study, and grab what you can. The pump will always be there for you to get some more water.

17
Raising Jewish Children

EDUCATION

There have been many explanations for the Jewish love of learning. Perhaps such a love arose because the revelation to the Jewish people came through words and was transmitted in part through study of the written Torah and in part through passing on the oral Torah. Another explanation is that the persecution of Jews fostered admiration for learning, which was consistently portable. Jews may have had to leave their homes, their goods, their jobs, but they could carry their religion and their learning, no one could steal those from them.

Whatever the origin of the Jewish attachment to learning, it runs deep in the Jewish soul. Learning about Judaism is an important life-long goal for Jews; learning is so sacred it is considered a form of prayer. It was the scholar, not the wealthy merchant, who was accorded the greatest admiration. It was the scholar who was the preferred marriage partner.

While traditionally, the notion of study applied most specifically to the Torah and Talmud, that notion of study has expanded today to include the broad range of what was once considered secular studies. The sciences illuminate God's natural creation, the social sciences the depth of the crowning creation—human beings, and the humanities show the imaginative struggle of those humans to understand themselves, the natural world, and the sublime mysteries that earlier ages identified with religion.

Because learning has so central a place in Judaism, it is obvious that the teaching of young Jews about their heritage is a vital parental and communal responsibility. The very act of education for Jews is an act of survival, for separated from their unique worldview and way of life, Jews would assimilate into the larger cultures among which those Jews in the Diaspora live. With education, the distinctiveness and value of Judaism remain alive for another generation.

It is a sad fact to note the failures of educational efforts. Some Jews do not educate their children at all in basic Judaism. Others send their children to a Jewish school but do not provide support for the learning at home. Others believe all Jewish education is over after a *bar* or *bat mitzvah* ceremony. These are not ways to perpetuate Judaism effectively. Imagine asking a child to know history, but never teaching it, or letting a child study it several hours a week for a few years but not after age thirteen, or ignoring or even belittling the subject at home. Clearly, a child would have limited knowledge of or respect for history. It is vital in the transmission of the Jewish heritage, then, that parents prize the activity, learn along with their children, helping them as they might in secular subjects, and reinforcing the values learned in religious schools.

Not all religious schools do a good job of teaching. Parents in this situation need to consider their alternatives: working with the teacher or school to improve the school, joining another synagogue, hiring a private tutor, or even starting a school. Above all, it is crucial to remember that the responsibility for education involves teamwork between school and parents.

For general information about Jewish education, contact local synagogues or a local Board of Jewish Education.

Many Jewish institutions have begun to realize the desperate need for Jewish-oriented day-care facilities. Sometimes, Y's, Jewish community centers, or synagogues have day-care available; often a half-day of nursery school is also available. There are Jewish providers of day-care available who are licensed but not part of an institution. For day-care facilities, ask those with infants, or check the local Jew-

JESNA works with all denominations and has information about local boards of Jewish education and other educational institutions.

For schools associated with specific movements, contact the congregational organizations of each movement included in the addresses at the end of this book.

For those who do not wish to or cannot attend a day school, a supplementary Jewish education is often the only other choice. Most supplementary education is run through synagogues, although there are local parent-run schools and schools run by the Workmen's Circle in which Yiddish language and culture is stressed and Jewish religious obligations not stressed.

Most American Jewish children receive their Jewish education in this supplementary way. Many American Jewish educators, parents, and students find the way unsatisfactory, in large part because the students do not have adequate time to be taught (parents enroll students often only until the *bar* or *bat mitzvah* and the entire school time is, while varying widely, usually no more than eight hours a week and often even less) and because their education takes place after a full school day when they are tired and when other activities (homework, playing with friends, taking music lessons, engaging in other recreational activities, and so on) compete for attention and time. Given these limitations, supplementary schools work hard, often under difficult financial constraints, to educate American Jewish youth.

There are an increasing number of educational opportunities available for Jewish children with learning disabilities. Those with visual problems can obtain books in braille and in large print as well as cassette recordings and other valuable materials from:

Jewish Braille Institute of America
110 East 30th Street
New York, NY 10016
(212) 889-2525

As with day school education, a successful supplementary school education requires parental inclusion. Parents must make it clear that

Jewish schooling is as important as soccer or gymnastics, that parents prize Jewish learning. Parents should praise their children when they have learned, for example, a new song. Giving children a chance to perform what they have learned at home is very important.

Indeed, it is crucial not to confuse Jewish education with Jewish schooling. Much of what occurs at home is crucial. Parents, though, do not have to take all responsibility upon themselves. They can, for example, send their children to Jewish camps. A list of Jewish camps can be obtained from:

Jewish Community Centers Association of North America
15 E. 26th Street
New York, NY 10010-1579
(212) 532-4949

Parents can join Y's and Jewish community centers. They can make sure their youngsters join youth groups (many of which were mentioned in Part One), which are frequently centered in synagogues. Among major youth groups are the North American Federation of Temple Youth (NFTY), affiliated with the Reform movement, United Synagogue Youth (USY), affiliated with the Conservative movement, the National Conference of Synagogue Youth (NCSY), affiliated with the Orthodox movement, and the B'nai B'rith Youth Organization (BBYO), which is sponsored by local groups affiliated with B'nai B'rith.

Education for Jewish youth need not stop at age thirteen. There are, for instance, Jewish high schools in large cities. Many of these are run by various strands within the Orthodox movement, but non-Orthodox or unaffiliated schools are increasing. Some high-school–level Jewish courses are offered at night at various synagogues.

Choosing a college is also, in part, a Jewish choice. College is a time of adolescent liberation, of the formation of an independent identity, of the questioning of parental and communal values. While such questioning is natural and healthy, there should be appropriate Jewish resources and responses when the questions come. There are various Jewish institutions of higher learning and many colleges and universities offer one or more Jewish courses. Some universities have majors in Jewish studies. It is important to check the catalogs of colleges being considered to determine any Jewish connections, such as courses, or a Hillel or other Jewish student organization. Determining the approximate Jewish student population is also important so that Jewish college youth can have Jewish peers and a large dating pool. Checking with a Hillel at the colleges can be very valuable. Additionally, it should be determined if it is possible to spend a semester or year abroad in Israel. Such a possibility can have enormous educational benefits.

TRAVEL

Families can avail themselves of many travel opportunities. Most observers of the Jewish community believe the very best travel experience is for the family to go together to Israel, to travel, to study, for a *bar* or *bat mitzvah*, or for any other reason. Many parents have reported a marked increase in Jewish identity after such a trip.

My family went to Israel for our daughter Elana's *bat mitzvah*. We had the ceremony at Masada, in a beautiful and deeply moving setting. As we traveled across the country, seeing sites, exploring caves, putting on mud at the Dead Sea, going to the Western Wall at night, and many other experiences, it became clear to me that more than almost any other experience, this trip made our four children feel strongly attached both to a long Jewish past and an exciting Jewish present and future. Check with local synagogues and in Jewish media for groups that travel to Israel. For general information about travel, contact:

Israel Government Tourist Office
350 Fifth Avenue
New York, NY 10118
(212) 560-0650

18
Getting Involved in Jewish Life: How the Jewish Community Is Organized

There are many Jewish organizations of all types. Perhaps the chief characteristic of American Jewish life, in fact, is its diversity. There is no central rabbinical body to cover all Jews, no universally accepted organization.

In local areas there are synagogues, YM-YWHAs, Jewish community centers, bureaus of Jewish education, schools, and other institutions as have been discussed.

The various religious movements each have several central institutions. The following sections list these institutions.

CONSERVATIVE MOVEMENT

United Synagogue of Conservative Judaism
155 Fifth Avenue
New York, NY 10010-6802
(212) 533-7800
This is the organization of Conservative Jewish congregations. It can provide information about such congregations in your area.

225

Jewish Theological Seminary of America
3080 Broadway
New York, NY 10027-4649
(212) 678-8000
This is the rabbinical seminary that trains Conservative rabbis. It has many other services.

University of Judaism
15600 Mulholland Drive
Los Angeles, CA 90077
(310) 476-9777
The University of Judaism, the Los Angeles–based affiliate of the Jewish Theological Seminary, is widely known for its excellent Introduction to Judaism program taken by many who wish to convert.

Rabbinical Assembly
3080 Broadway
New York, NY 10027
(212) 678-8060
This is an organization of Conservative rabbis.

ORTHODOX MOVEMENT

The Orthodox world is more varied than the others, with no one central organization or seminary. For information about Orthodox institutions, contact a local Orthodox rabbi.

RECONSTRUCTIONIST MOVEMENT

Federation of Reconstructionist Congregations and Havurot
Church Road and Greenwood Avenue
Wyncote, PA 19095-1898

This is the congregational organization. The Reconstructionist Rabbinical Association (RRA) and Reconstructionist Rabbinical College (RRC) are at the same address. The telephone number of the RRA is (215) 576-5210 and the number of the RRC is (215) 576-0800.

REFORM MOVEMENT

Union of American Hebrew Congregations
838 Fifth Avenue
New York, NY 10021
(212) 249-0100
The UAHC is the congregational arm of the Reform movement and has information about Reform temples in your area.

Hebrew Union College–Jewish Institute of Religion
3101 Clifton Avenue
Cincinnati, OH 45220
(513) 221-2810
HUC-JIR trains Reform rabbis. It maintains campuses in New York and Jerusalem as well.

Central Conference of American Rabbis
192 Lexington Avenue
New York, NY 10016
(212) 684-4990
The CCAR is the organization of Reform rabbis.

NONDENOMINATIONAL ORGANIZATIONS

There are also, in many places, Jewish federations (also called by other names such as welfare funds or some other comparable name—the United Jewish Appeal is one such organization) that raise money for

nonreligious institutions in the local, national, and international Jewish communities. Nationally, the local federations are part of the
Council of Jewish Federations. New York City is a major exception,
with a combined United Jewish Appeal–Federation partnership that
works differently from other parts of the country. In general, your local
Federation will seek funds to run local Jewish charities as well as funds
for such efforts as Operation Exodus to settle immigrants in Israel from
the former Soviet Union.

Your city may have a family service agency (again called by different names) to offer counseling and referral services, a service for
job information, and other important information. Many communities have a Jewish community council, or community relations council, as an umbrella group embracing local branches of national organizations and other groups in the community. The councils often
coordinate communal activities. The councils join together nationally in the National Jewish Community Relations Advisory Council.

There are also many national Jewish organizations. The presidents of many of those organizations have joined together to form
the Conference of Presidents of Major American Jewish Organizations. This crucial umbrella body focuses on foreign policy issues, most
especially those concerning Israel, and serves as a forum to reach a
public consensus within the Jewish community about Israel in order
to interpret this consensus position to the White House and State
Department.

Of the many national organizations, many are devoted to community relations. Some of these are called "defense" organizations
because they fight anti-Semitism.

Several of the most well known of these are the following:

American Jewish Committee
Institute of Human Relations
165 E. 56th Street
New York, NY 10022
(212) 751-4000

The American Jewish Committee has numerous publications and does a lot of research in the area of Jewish community relations and inter-marriage especially.

American Jewish Congress
Stephen Wise Congress House
15 East 84th Street
New York, NY 10028
The American Jewish Congress is well known for its legal efforts in such areas as church–state separation issues. AJCongress is dovish on Israeli issues and generally liberal on American domestic issues.

Anti-Defamation League of B'nai B'rith
823 United Nations Plaza
New York, NY 10017
(212) 490-2525
The ADL is internationally known for its efforts to monitor and com-bat anti-Semitic groups.

There are many religious, cultural, social welfare, and other national organizations as well. Local synagogues and community coun-cils are the best source for organizations in your area. Some of the best known of these organizations are the following:

B'nai B'rith
1640 Rhode Island Avenue, NW
Washington, DC 20036
(202) 857-6600
This service organization sponsors Hillel organizations and other im-portant activities.

Simon Wiesenthal Center
9760 W. Pico Blvd.
Los Angeles, CA 90035
(213) 553-9036

The Center preserves memory of the Holocaust and combats anti-Semitism.

Finally, there is a large network of organizations devoted to helping Israel. Most of these organizations engage in various fund-raising and educational activities, such as donating to needy Israeli institutions and people, providing speakers, films, program assistance, materials for programs and exhibitions, and publications.

Several of the best known of these organizations are the following:

Hadassah
50 West 58th Street
New York, NY 10019
(212) 355-7900
Hadassah is a women's Zionist organization especially noted for helping Israel meet vital health needs.

Jewish National Fund of America
42 East 69th Street
New York, NY 10021
(212) 879-9300
JNF is the exclusive fund-raising agency of the world Zionist organization for such activities as the reclamation and development of Israel. JNF is most famous for its blue boxes in which money is collected to plant trees, but the organization engages in many other activities to develop Israel.

State of Israel Bonds
730 Broadway
New York, NY 10003
(212) 677-9650
This organization provides large-scale investment funds for Israel by selling State of Israel bonds.

Zionist Organization of America
ZOA House
4 East 34th Street
New York, NY 10016
(212) 481-1500
The ZOA engages in public relations work on behalf of Israel and is active in working with college-age and other youth.

These, and most other major American Jewish organizations, play vital roles in support of Israel. However, the organizations play only a very indirect role in specifically political efforts, such as lobbying for passage of foreign aid bills, on behalf of Israel.

The reason for the reluctance of most American Jewish organizations to lobby or to engage in other political activity is that tax law forbids any tax-exempt religious, educational, or charitable organization from lobbying for Israel or supporting or opposing a candidate for any public office. National Jewish organizations know that they rely on their tax-exempt status and so have removed themselves from political activities.

American Jews had to develop another mechanism to express their pro-Israel sentiment in a politically explicit manner. They have done this through the formation of various organizations.

AIPAC
440 First Street, N.W.
Suite 600
Washington, DC 20001
(202) 639-5200

The American Israel Public Affairs Committee (AIPAC) is the center of pro-Israel political activism in the United States. AIPAC lobbies members of Congress, works with the White House and Cabinet departments, appears before Congressional committees considering legislation affecting Israel, publishes and distributes a wide variety of informational literature, organizes on campus, and mobilizes local pro-Israel individuals on key issues. Information about AIPAC's work, including information about the publication *Near East Report* that is sent to members, can be obtained from the above address.

However involved AIPAC is in lobbying, the organization does not engage in partisan political activity, desiring that pro-Israel activity appeal to Republicans, Democrats, and independents. Thus, AIPAC makes no political endorsements, provides no political contributions, and does not rank politicians on the basis of their votes.

Such direct political activity is undertaken by pro-Israel political action committees, or PACs. (Despite the "PAC" at the end of its name, AIPAC is not a political action committee.)

The National PAC
555 New Jersey Avenue, N.W.
Suite 718
Washington, DC 20001
(202) 879-7710
The National PAC is the pro-Israel PAC that organizes throughout the country.

There are, in addition, many local pro-Israel political action committees. Finding one can help you participate in the exciting world of political action.

All these, and the thousands of other American Jewish organizations, require the contributions and dedication of many American Jews (and non-Jews as well). Entry into a complete Jewish life is immeasurably enhanced for new Jews, and born Jews as well, when they support, join, and work with a Jewish group of their choice.

Jewish life is, perhaps, unique. All Jews are needed. Whatever your interests in life are, there is probably a Jewish group that needs your help. American Jewry is small in number. Every single Jew is therefore not only a precious person, but one whose help is crucial to the community's thriving.

You may be new to Jewish life, you may not have felt that your contribution in your non-Jewish life made a difference, but as a new Jew, you do make a difference. Never before have you been so needed.

Appendix A
A Brief Guide
to Jewish Books

The most valuable single piece of advice a new Jew can be given is to read Jewish books on a regular basis. Jewish writers are prolific; Jewish knowledge is contained in Jewish books. Even for the reader who is limited only to English, there is an enormous treasure of Jewish learning.

Apart from sacred literature, there is no one book that is vital. Books are like building blocks; each one alone is strong but not strong enough, while together the books build a sturdy house of Jewish learning.

The following is a guide to some materials that are available. This is a very limited list, however, and is meant as an appetizer to tempt those tasting Jewish knowledge for the first time to see how nourishing such knowledge is. Many vital and basic books, that is, are not included on this list, in part because there are so many good books that it would take a book just to list them. I have put together a rather subjective guide to what I believe are excellent books to introduce the intellectually yearning to the treasures of the Jewish tradition.

Learning about Jewish books is fun. Visit a local synagogue library or Jewish bookstore and browse. Begin your acquisition by joining The Jewish Book Club.

The Jewish Book Club
230 Livingston Street
Northvale, NJ 07647

You should send for catalogs of books from Jewish publishers. One
such important publisher is:
Jewish Publication Society
1930 Chestnut Street
Philadelphia, PA 19103

   This guidebook is being published by Jason Aronson Inc., which
publishes a large number of books in Judaica. For a catalog, write:
Jason Aronson Inc.
230 Livingston Street
Northvale, NJ 07647

   Starting to read in Judaism is not difficult. For a general overview of Jewish books, see *The Book of Jewish Books* by Ruth S. Frank
and William Wollheim (Harper & Row, 1986) and *The Schocken
Guide to Jewish Books* edited by Barry Holtz (Pantheon, 1993). For
bibliographies and reading suggestions, contact:
Jewish Book Council
15 East 26th Street
New York, NY 10010
(212) 532-4949

   There are many excellent books that cover basic Jewish beliefs.
See, for example, *Basic Judaism* by Milton Steinberg (Jason Aronson,
1987) and *The Book of Jewish Belief* by Louis Jacobs (Behrman House,
1984). For a question-and-answer format, see *The Jewish Book of Why*
by Alfred J. Kolatch (Jonathan David Publishers, 1981). For an especially insightful examination of some of the difficult issues facing
believing Jews today, see *The Nine Questions People Ask About Judaism* by Dennis Prager and Joseph Telushkin (Simon & Schuster,
1981). For an approach to Jewish learning in smaller doses, readers

may want to look at my earlier books published by Jason Aronson Inc., *A Treasury of Jewish Anecdotes* (1989) and *A Treasury of Jewish Inspirational Stories* (1993).

All Jewish libraries must include a copy of the Hebrew Bible. One widely used edition is *Tanakh*, published by the Jewish Publication Society in 1985. There are many commentaries on the Torah. One recent excellent volume is *The Torah: A Modern Commentary*, edited by W. Gunther Plaut and published by the Union of American Hebrew Congregations. This book, from a Reform perspective, includes much modern scholarship.

The Talmud is difficult for many beginning readers. A ground-breaking new translation, published by Random House, is currently being undertaken by Rabbi Adin Steinsaltz. His work will make the Talmud accessible for English speakers. Rabbi Steinsaltz has also written a one-volume introduction to the Talmud called *The Essential Talmud* (Jason Aronson, 1992), which is lucid and very helpful. Another excellent introduction is *Everyman's Talmud* by A. Cohen (Schocken, 1949).

The Jewish prayer book is a compendium of the deepest spiritual yearnings of the Jewish people. Each movement publishes its own prayer books, the ones used in that movement's congregations. After you have selected a congregation to join, obtain a copy of the prayer book for home use.

For an introduction to all sacred Jewish texts, see *Back to the Sources* by Barry Holtz (Summit Books, 1984).

Jewish history is long and rich, not an easy subject to grasp by reading just one book. One interesting approach is to read the novel *The Source* by James Michener (Random House, 1965). For a more scholarly approach, one excellent book is *Jewish People, Jewish Thought: The Jewish Experience in History* by Robert M. Seltzer (Macmillan & Collier, 1980). There are many more widely used history books. There are many fine books on the painful history of the Holocaust. One important book is Elie Wiesel's memoir *Night*. For a more general history, see *The War Against the Jews* by Lucy S. Dawidowicz (Holt, Rinehart and Winston, 1975). For an overview of Israeli history, read

A *History of Zionism* by Walter Laqueur (Holt, Rinehart, and Winston, 1972) and *The Zionist Idea* edited with a magnificent introduction by Arthur Hertzberg (Atheneum, 1972). The novel *Exodus* by Leon Uris is a great way to understand some of the emotions and color of early Israel.

There are many basic reference books to choose from as well. *The Jewish Catalog*, edited by Richard Siegel, Michael Strassfeld, and Sharon Strassfeld (Jewish Publication Society, 1973) and its two subsequent volumes are justly famous for their readable style and practical nature. The best one-volume encyclopedia is *The Encyclopedia of Judaism* edited by Geoffey Wigoder (Macmillan, 1989), which is a remarkably clear and accurate work. Eventually, every serious student of Judaism should try to purchase a copy of *The Encyclopaedia Judaica*, edited by Cecil Roth and Geoffrey Wigoder (Keter, 1972). The sixteen volumes and subsequent year books are scholarly and very strong in certain areas, especially, for example, the Holocaust and the East European communities destroyed by that event.

Many Ashkenazic Jews, especially those of a certain age, sprinkle Yiddish expressions into their speech, expressions that functionally serve as slang, understandable to those who are members of the group, confusing to the outsiders, although some Yiddish expressions have come into general use. For a fun and easy introduction and handy guide to such Yiddish expressions, get *The Joy of Yiddish* by Leo Rosten (McGraw-Hill, 1968).

Those readers attracted to a philosophical approach should try *God in Search of Man* by Abraham Joshua Heschel (Jason Aronson, 1987). This poetically evocative, beautifully written volume has had a profound impact on numerous readers. It can be read simply for the beauty of its language. Although not specifically about Judaism, many readers have been deeply moved by Viktor Frankl's book *Man's Search for Meaning* (Simon & Schuster, 1959), with its first part a memoir of concentration camp life and its second part an explanation of logotherapy, an approach to life that stresses the deep human need for a meaning system. More traditional Jewish philosophy is best introduced in the scholarly volume *The Philosophy of Judaism* by Julius

Guttmann (Jason Aronson, 1988). For a book on Jewish mysticism, see Edward Hoffman's intriguing book *The Way of Splendor* (Jason Aronson, 1992), which applies modern psychology to traditional mysticism.

There is an exciting group of books emerging about Jewish women. Some "classics" in this relatively new field include *Jewish and Female* (Simon & Schuster, 1984) by Susan Weidman Schneider, editor of the Jewish feminist magazine *Lilith*, and *On Being a Jewish Feminist*, by Susannah Heschel (Schocken, 1983). There are many other excellent books in this field such as Judith Plaskow's *Standing Again at Sinai* (Harper San Francisco, 1991).

For books on Jewish religious rituals and practices, there are a variety of valuable guides. See *The Complete Book of Jewish Observance* by Leo Trepp (Summit, 1980), *Living a Jewish Life* by Anita Diamant and Howard Cooper (Harper, 1991), and *The Jewish Home Advisor* by Alfred J. Kolatch (Jonathan David, 1990). Also, look at *How to Run a Traditional Jewish Household* by Blu Greenberg (Jason Aronson, 1989) and *To Be a Jew* by Hayim Donin. Useful cookbooks include Anne London and Bertha K. Bishov's *Complete American-Jewish Cookbook* and Leah Leonard's *Jewish Cookery*. A very useful guide to raising Jewish children is found in *The Jewish Family Book* by Sharon Strassfeld and Kathy Green (Bantam, 1981).

There are an extraordinary number of excellent novels about American Jewish life. Here are some of the books that you will find enriching:

The Promised Land by Mary Antin, *The Rise of David Levinsky* by Abraham Cahan, *Hungry Hearts* by Anzia Yezierska, *Haunch, Paunch, and Jowl* by Samuel Ornitz, *The Old Bunch* by Meyer Levin, *Summer in Williamsburg* by Daniel Fuchs, *Call it Sleep* by Henry Roth, *Passage from Home* by Isaac Rosenfeld, and *Jews Without Money* by Michael Gold are just some of the excellent novels about Jewish immigrant life.

Later Jewish generations (with some overlap) are represented in such works as *Marjorie Morningstar* by Herman Wouk, *Up the Down Staircase* by Bel Kaufman, and the popular novels of such writers as

Belva Plain, Gloria Goldreich, Cynthia Freeman, and many other excellent writers. One interesting approach by some writers is to include information about Judaism in a mystery story. See, for example, Harry Kemelman's Rabbi Small books, especially the first, *Friday, the Rabbi Slept Late*. Other writers to use the mystery approach include Faye Kellerman in such books as *The Ritual Bath*, Joseph Telushkin in such books as *An Eye for an Eye*, and Rochelle M. Krich in *Till Death Do Us Part*.

In the 1940s to 1960s three Jewish writers became well known in mainstream American literature. Philip Roth became infamous in the Jewish community for his scathing sociological profiles of American Jewry in such works as *Goodbye, Columbus* and *Portnoy's Complaint*. Bernard Malamud became famous for his short stories that made suffering Jews symbols of the pain of humanity. His best novel is *The Assistant*, about a poor Jewish grocer, his daughter, and a stranger who comes into their life. Saul Bellow, winner of the Nobel Prize, has written many significant novels, including such works as *The Victim* and *Herzog*. Another Jewish Nobel winner for literature was Isaac Bashevis Singer, beloved for his portrayal of a lost world of Yiddish culture in such works as *Gimpel, the Fool*.

Other significant contemporary writers include Cynthia Ozick, who has written widely and explored Jewish subjects in such works as *The Pagan Rabbi*. The number of other excellent Jewish writers is too long to list.

There are also many excellent books for Jewish children. The best source for information is a Jewish librarian. Go to Jewish book fairs and sample some writers. Some of the favorite novels that have lasted are *The Children of Chelm* by David Adler, *Rifka Bangs the Teakettle* by Chaya Burstein, *The Carp in the Bathtub* by Barbara Cohen, *A Promise Is a Promise* by Molly Cone, *About the B'nai Bagels* by E. L. Konigsburg, *Watch the Stars Come Out* by Riki Levenson, *All-of-a-Kind Family* by Sydney Taylor, *The Best of K'tonton* by Sadie Rose Weilerstein, and many others. A personal favorite in our house is *Molly's Pilgrim* by Barbara Cohen (Bantam, 1990). The Jewish Book Council (address above) has a bibliography of books especially for

Jewish children. There is an increasing number of Jewish children's books being published.

, There are also many important books on the subject of conversion to Judaism. Useful guidebooks include *Your People, My People* by Lena Romanoff, with Lisa Hostein, *Choosing Judaism* by Lydia Kukoff, written from a Reform perspective, *Embracing Judaism* by Simcha Kling, written from a Conservative perspective, and *Becoming a Jew* by Maurice Lamm, written from an Orthodox perspective. The UAHC-CCAR Commission on Reform Jewish Outreach (838 Fifth Avenue, New York, NY 10021; telephone [212] 249-0100) has a list of extremely valuable publications on various aspects of conversion.

For more scholarly studies of conversion, see *Jews by Choice: A Study of Converts to Reform and Conservative Judaism* by Brenda Forster and Joseph Tabachnik (Ktav, 1991), and *New Jews* by Steven Huberman (UAHC, 1979).

For an Orthodox perspective, one critical of Reform and Conservative positions on conversion, see *Who Is A Jew?* by Jacob Immanuel Schochet (Shofar, 1989). One Orthodox writer seeking an end to the interdenominational squabbling is Reuven P. Bulka in *The Coming Cataclysm: The Orthodox-Reform Rift and the Future of the Jewish People*, second edition (Mosaic, 1986). Another interesting Orthodox approach is taken by J. Simcha Cohen in his book *Intermarriage and Conversion: A Halakhic Solution* (Ktav, 1987). Rabbi Cohen believes that converting all youngsters at or near birth will alleviate the current conversion dilemma.

The history of conversion in Judaism is discussed in *Proselytism in the Talmudic Period* by Bernard J. Bamberger (Ktav, 1968), *Jewish Proselyting In the First Five Centuries of the Common Era* by William G. Braude (Brown University, 1940), *Conversion to Judaism: A History and Analysis* by David Max Eichhorn (Ktav, 1965), *Conversion to Judaism: From the Biblical Period to the Present* by Joseph R. Rosenbloom (Hebrew Union College Press, 1978), and other works.

There are also many valuable autobiographies by and biographies of converts to Judaism. One is *So Strange My Path* by Abraham Carmel (Bloch, 1964) about a priest who converted. A contemporary volume also about a priest's conversion is *Ordained to Be a Jew* by John David Scalamonti (Ktav, 1992). Julius Lester's *Lovesong: Becoming a Jew* (Henry Holt, 1988) is a beautifully written memoir of a black man's turn to Judaism. One very moving autobiography is by Devorah Wigoder and is titled *Hope Is My House* (Prentice-Hall, 1966). This is a very readable and inspiring book.

Unfortunately, there is not a lot of material for children on this subject. Luckily, there is one excellent book: *Mommy Never Went to Hebrew School* by Mindy Avra Portnoy (Kar-Ben Copies, 1989). Rabbi Portnoy has written a humorous, sensitive book that adults will learn from as well. The publisher of this book has many available children's titles.

A good deal of the writing about conversion is sandwiched in chapters or books on intermarriage. There are many valuable and important books that discuss these subjects, and if you are interested, see especially *Mixed Blessings: Marriage between Jews and Christians* by Paul Cowan with Rachel Cowan (Doubleday, 1987). This excellent, insightful book details some of the "time bombs" that go off in marital relationships when unresolved religious questions remain. The best-known scholar on intermarriage is Egon Mayer. His book *Love & Tradition* (Plenum, 1985) discusses research in the field up to the date of the book's publication. Dr. Mayer has published many important pamphlets and articles on intermarriage and conversion for such places as the American Jewish Committee. Dr. Mayer also directs the Jewish Outreach Institute, which publishes his and other scholarly publications. For information contact the Center for Jewish Studies, CUNY Graduate School, 33 West 42nd Street, New York, NY 10036. Another important book on intermarriage is *Intermarriage* by Susan Weidman Schneider (Free Press, 1989).

Appendix B
A Brief Guide to Jewish Films

With the advent of the videocassette player, Jewish films are finally available for wide viewing. Although most Jewish content in American films is peripheral to the main story, and many Jewish characters are minor or stereotypical, there have been a large number of outstanding films that enhance an understanding of Jewish life. Here are a very few of the feature films available. It should be noted that there are also many excellent documentaries available through the different movements and ordinary video distribution channels.

Avalon is a lush remembrance of immigrant life in Baltimore. Its Jewish content is muted but unmistakable.

Cast a Giant Shadow tells the exciting story of Mickey Marcus, an American who helped Israel. Although flawed as a movie, the film is exciting and informative.

The Chosen, based on Chaim Potok's book, tells the story of how traditional Jews deal with modern American life. The film offers valuable insights into chasidic life and the internal intellectual struggles many traditionalist Jews undergo.

Conspiracy of Hearts tells the story of how nuns in a convent hide Jews in wartime Italy. The film is excellent and deeply moving.

Counsellor-at-Law, made in 1933, is a fast-moving story about a Jewish attorney (played by John Barrymore).

The Diary of Anne Frank (1959 version) is a deeply moving film based on the famous Jewish teenager whose record of courage and maturity provides an ennobling role model for all young Jews.

Exodus, based on the best-seller by Leon Uris, is a sweeping epic about the birth of Israel.

Fiddler on the Roof, based on the musical, describes Russian-Jewish life at the end of the nineteenth century. The music is outstanding.

The Fixer, based on Bernard Malamud's novel, tells the story of a Russian Jew imprisoned for a ritual crime against a Christian child. Based on a true story, this film plays down the Jewishness of the main character.

The Frisco Kid is an extremely funny movie about a rabbi from Poland who joins up with an American Western outlaw. There are many insights about the difficulties of living Jewishly in America in this film.

Garden of the Finzi-Continis describes the Holocaust in Italy.

Gentleman's Agreement is a famous movie about anti-Semitism in America during the 1940s. The film stars Gregory Peck as a journalist who pretends to be Jewish to see how people will react.

· *Hester Street* is a wonderful movie about life on the Lower East Side at the turn of the century. There are excellent portraits of Jewish immigrant life.

The House of Rothschild, nominated in 1934 for an Academy Award for best picture, is a biographical account of the famous Jewish family. It provides insights into the methods Jews used to survive during difficult times.

The Jazz Singer stars Al Jolson as a cantor's son who wants to perform popular music. The film, which introduced sound in 1927, is also important for its theme of a Jewish–Gentile relationship.

Judgment at Nurenberg is an outstanding film about the trials of Nazi war criminals. The horrors of the Holocaust are made vivid in this film.

The Juggler, starring Kirk Douglas, is a moving story of a Jewish immigrant's difficult adjustment to Israeli life after the Holocaust. This is an excellent film.

Lies My Father Told Me is a warm, telling glimpse of Jewish family life. It is an outstanding film.

Me and the Colonel is an hilarious story starring Danny Kaye as a Jewish refugee who must join up with a Polish aristocratic anti-Semite so that they can escape the Nazis.

The Pawnbroker is a powerful movie about a Jewish pawnbroker's painful memories of the Holocaust and his life in urban America after the war. Painful to watch at times, this film is extremely interesting in its use of symbols.

The Story of Ruth, an important film for those who have become Jewish, is not necessarily an excellent film in a cinematic context.

Symphony of Six Million was made in 1932, so the title refers not to the Holocaust but to the inhabitants of New York. This is the story of a Jewish doctor who assimilates and then has second thoughts.

Yentl is Barbra Streisand's loving rendition of the work by Isaac Bashevis Singer about a Jewish girl who lives at a time when women are not allowed to study Jewish holy texts.

Appendix C
Additional Resources

Jewish Converts and Interfaith Network
Lena Romanoff, Director
1112 Hagysford Road
Penn Valley, PA 19072
(215) 664-8112

The Center for Conversion to Judaism
Rabbi Stephen C. Lerner, Director
752 Stelton Street
Teaneck, NJ 07666
(201) 837-7552

Jewish Ties
Margo Sue Bittner, Editor and Publisher
1091 Quaker Road
Barker, NY 14012
(716) 795-3709
   Jewish Ties is a newsletter for "interfaith couples, Jews by Choice, Jews by Birth, and their families."

Dovetail
Joan C. Hawxhurst, Editor
3014A Folsom Street
Boulder, CO 80304
(303) 444-8713

    Dovetail is "a newsletter by and for Jewish-Christian families." Although it is aimed at intermarried couples, it includes articles about conversion.

Jewish Music Council
15 East 26th Street
New York, NY 10010
Contact the Council for resources in Jewish music. Local Jewish bookstores and synagogue shops often have a selection of Jewish music as well.

Appendix D
Table of Acronyms

American Jewish life is filled with an alphabet soup of organizations. Here is an attempt to list the best-known acronyms in an attempt to provide a guide to Jewish organizational life. For a fuller discussion of organizations, including all addresses and phones, see the most current *American Jewish Year Book*.

ADL   the Anti-Defamation League of B'nai B'rith, which combats anti-Semitism.

AIPAC   the American Israel Public Affairs Committee, a pro-Israel lobbying group.

AJC   the American Jewish Committee, which promotes Jewish rights.

AJCongress   the American Jewish Congress, which seeks to promote Jewish rights. Sometimes, AJC is used for the abbreviation, but because the American Jewish Committee is older, the designation is usually reserved for the Committee.

ARZA   Association of Reform Zionists of America.

BBYO   B'nai B'rith Youth Organization.

CAJE   Coalition for the Advancement of Jewish Education.

CAMERA   Committee for Accuracy in Middle East Reporting in America.

CCAR   Central Conference of American Rabbis.

CJF   the Council of Jewish Federations, which raises money.

CLAL National Jewish Center for Learning and Leadership.

FJMC Federation of Jewish Men's Clubs.

HIAS Hebrew Immigrant Aid Society.

IDF Israel Defense Forces.

JCC Jewish Community Center.

JDC American Jewish Joint Distribution Committee, which provides assistance to Jewish communities. Also known as the Joint.

JDL Jewish Defense League.

JESNA Jewish Education Service of North America.

JINSA Jewish Institute for National Security Affairs.

JNF Jewish National Fund.

JPS Jewish Publication Society.

JTA Jewish Telegraphic Agency.

JTS Jewish Theological Seminary.

JWF Jewish Welfare Fund.

NATPAC The National Political Action Committee.

NFTB National Federation of Temple Brotherhoods.

NJCRAC (pronounced Nack-rack) the National Jewish Community Relations Advisory Council, a coordinating body for community relations agencies.

ORT Organization for Rehabilitation Through Training, which provides vocational education for Jews worldwide.

RA Rabbinical Assembly.

RCA Rabbinical Council of America.

SCA Synagogue Council of America, an umbrella group.

UAHC Union of American Hebrew Congregations.

UJA United Jewish Appeal, which raises funds.

UOJCA Union of Orthodox Jewish Congregations of America.

USCJ United Synagogue of Conservative Judaism, formerly the United Synagogue of America.

WZO World Zionist Organization.

YM-YWHA Young Men's–Young Women's Hebrew Association.

YU Yeshiva University.

ZOA Zionist Organization of America, which fosters United States–Israeli cooperation.

Appendix E
Glossary of Jewish Terms

Here is an index to some of the terms used in Jewish life. This index, however, is very abbreviated, but should get you started. If you like to work with a glossary, see *A Glossary of Jewish Life* by Rabbi Kerry M. Olitzky and Rabbi Ronald H. Isaacs, published by Jason Aronson Inc.

aggadah   all nonlegal literature such as theology, folklore, ethics, and other writing.

aliyah   (plural *aliyot*) literally means ascending or going up and refers to going up on the *bimah* to say the blessings over the Torah. The word *aliyah* also refers to immigrating to Israel.

Amidah   refers to the nineteen prayers making up a main part of the Jewish daily prayer service. The *Amidah* is also known as the *Shemoneh Esrei* or *Tefillah*.

Ashkenazi   (plural Ashkenazim) Jews who trace their ancestors to medieval Germany.

bar mitzvah or **bat mitzvah**   ceremonies at which young men and women accept the obligation to obey the commandments of Jewish life.

B.C.E.   Before the Common Era (to replace B.C.).

Bet Din   a court of law for such occasions as conversion to Judaism.

bikkur cholim   refers to visiting and taking care of the ill.

bimah   the raised platform from which the service is conducted.

Birkat Ha-mazon   the blessing for food, also known as the Grace After Meals.

brit milah   circumcision ceremony by which a Jewish male enters the covenant, or agreement between God and the Jewish people.

C.E.   Common Era (to replace A.D.).

chazzan   cantor.

chesed   showing kindness.

Chumash   the Five Books of Moses, also known as the Pentateuch (and, in a narrow sense, the Torah), or any book containing the five books.

chuppah   a marriage canopy.

chutzpah   Yiddish for having a lot of nerve.

cohen/kohen   a Jewish priest.

devar Torah   a discussion of the weekly Torah portion. (Also, such a discussion is called a *derashah*.)

Diaspora   living outside the land of Israel.

fleishig   Yiddish for food made from meat, which is not supposed to be mixed with milk products according to kosher rules.

gelt   Yiddish for money.

Gemara   completion of, or commentaries on the Mishnah.

ger   (plural *gerim*) originally "stranger," but by the Talmud the term referred to those who had become Jewish.

get   a bill of divorce.

gonif   Yiddish for a thief, or a tricky character.

goy   (plural *goyim*) means any Gentile. Although the term is neutral it is sometimes used in a disparaging way.

Haftarah   the portion from the Prophets read on a given Sabbath.

heimish   Yiddish for warm and comforting.

halachah   Jewish law.

Hatafat Dam Brit   a drop of blood drawn when circumcision has already been done or is not possible.

Havdalah   the religious ceremony concluding the Sabbath.

Kabbalah   the Jewish mystical tradition.

kaddish   a prayer associated with mourning.

kashrut   the laws of keeping kosher.

kibbutz   a collective settlement in Israel.

kosher   fit for eating according to Jewish law. Used very loosely to refer to something that is legitimate.

Magen David   the shield of David, a six-pointed star.

mensch   Yiddish for a real man, that is to say mature, helping others, and performing kindly deeds.

meshugah   Yiddish for crazy.

mezuzah   a parchment containing the first two paragraphs of the *Shema*, rolled, put in a case, and attached to doorposts in a Jewish home.

midrash   an interpretation of a biblical verse undertaken by rabbis in the postbiblical period.

mikveh   a ritual bath or immersion.

milchig   Yiddish for foods made from milk, which should not be mixed with meat products according to kosher rules.

Minchah   the afternoon prayer service.

minyan   the number of people needed for a prayer service; consists of ten.

Mishnah   the code of Jewish law completed in 200 C.E. by Judah Ha-Nasi. The *Mishnah* plus the *Gemara* constitutes the Talmud.

mishpachah (Sephardic), **mishpocheh** (Ashkenazic)   family.

mitzvah   a Jewish ritual obligation. Also, *mitzvah* is used more loosely to refer to any good deed.

mohel   the person trained to perform ritual circumcisions.

parashah   the weekly Torah portion.

seder   the order of the Passover home service.

Sephardi   (plural Sephardim) people descended from Spanish countries.

shalom   peace.

sheigetz   a non-Jewish man, sometimes used in a derogatory way.

shiksa   a non-Jewish woman, sometimes used in a derogatory way.

Shema   the statement of the unity of God.

Shulchan Aruch   an important code of Jewish law compiled by Joseph Caro in the sixteenth century and still regarded as authoritative by Orthodox Jews.

tallit   prayer shawl.

Talmud   Literally, Talmud means "learning" and refers to those commentaries (one in Babylonia and one in Jerusalem) made on the Mishnah. It is generally used to refer to the Mishnah plus all the commentaries (*Gemara*) on the Mishnah.

Tanach   an acronym for Torah, *Nevi'im* (the Prophets), and *Ketuvim* (the Writings), the major sections of the Bible. Thus, *Tanach* refers to the whole Bible.

tefillah   Jewish praying.

tefillin   phylacteries for prayer service.

tevillah   immersion, a part of the mandatory conversion process in Orthodox and Conservative Judaism, and optional in Reform Judaism.

Torah   literally means "teaching," or "the way," or "direction." Narrowly, the term *Torah* refers to the first five books of the Bible. More broadly, the term *Torah* can be used to refer to all the sacred literature and learning within Judaism, and, most broadly, to all of Judaism itself.

tzedakah   giving charity, which is a *mitzvah*.

Zionism   movement to restore a Jewish nation in the land of Israel.

Zohar   medieval book of *Kabbalah*.

Appendix F

Guidelines for Conversion by the Various Movements in Judaism

REFORM GUIDELINES

Divre Gerut: Guidelines Concerning Proselytism

(Prepared by the Committee on Gerut of the Central Conference of American Rabbis.)

[Note: This guideline was prepared by the CCAR Committee on Gerut in 1980 and endorsed for circulation by the Executive Board in April, 1981. This revised version incorporates the final report of the Committee on the Status of Children of Mixed Marriages as it was adopted by the CCAR national convention, March, 1983.]

INTRODUCTION

The Central Conference of American Rabbis represents a diversity of views on theology and ritual observance; thus, these guidelines and suggested procedures seek to establish a working consensus of practice within the Reform Rabbinate rather than a set of standardized requirements, in matters concerning *gerim*.

[Note: This document uses the Hebrew terms: *ger/gioret/gerim* (a male/female proselyte(s); *gerut* (the process of becoming a Jew); *giur* (the actual ceremony through which one formalizes the acceptance of the *ger/gioret* as a Jew). These terms are found to be more appropriate and less potentially stigmatizing than the usage of such intrinsically non-Jewish terms as convert and conversion.] The Conference publishes these guidelines as a reaffirmation of its long-standing position on the full acceptance as Jews of those individuals who of their own free will wish to accept the joys and responsibilities of the Jewish faith and people. This document underscores the inherent freedom of Reform Judaism, and draws from the vast literature of the tradition in confronting an issue fundamental to *Am Yisrael*.

THE STATUS AND ACCEPTANCE OF GERIM

The status of those individuals who become Jews through formal *giur* has long been established in Judaism as fully equal to those born as Jews. The *Tanach* and rabbinic literature are replete with statements regarding the meritorious status, respectively, of the *Ger* and the *Ger Zedek*, the righteous stranger who chooses to become a member of the Jewish people and faith. Thus, it is incumbent upon our colleagues and congregations to accept fully, as equals, in all areas of participation, those who complete *giur*. To that end, we emphasize that once an individual has gone through the requirements of *giur*, he/she is fully Jewish. The warmth and vigor with which we accept these Jews and integrate them into our communities and activities are among our highest priorities and obligations.

CHAVEIRUT

The entire issue of the status of those born as Jews who may have become estranged from Judaism and wish to reaffirm their Jewish identities must be dealt with on an individual basis. A process or ceremony of *chaveirut* (affiliation) would be appropriate in actualizing such a reaffirmation. The CCAR Committee on Gerut has prepared such a ceremony.

MARRIAGE AND GIUR

We are aware that each individual has his/her own unique and complex motivation in making the final decision to become a Jew. We recognize the issue of mixed marriage as a critical area of concern. The CCAR has long held the position that the initial motivation of marriage is a wholesome and appropriate stimulus in seeking Jewish identity.[1] Thus, as the problem of mixed marriage continues to concern the Jewish community, the Conference once again reaffirms its stand: the individual who seeks Judaism because of his/her desire to establish a Jewish marriage, Jewish home and *shelom bayit* is to be encouraged in all matters of *giur*. Further, the Conference urges its members to implement more actively point two of the third paragraph of its 1973 Resolution on mixed marriage: "To provide (for those already mixed married) the opportunity for *giur* of the non-Jewish spouse."

An individual involved in *giur* should be sensitized that the gravity of any decision and the necessary exposure to Judaism have higher priority than the social pressures of a wedding date. The rabbi, whenever possible, should work closely with the potential *ger/gioret* and the mate or future mate as well as the respective families. It is important whenever possible that the mate or future mate be encouraged to attend the classes in Judaism with the *ger/gioret*. The rabbi, congregation, and community should provide these individuals with opportunities to share the experiences, learning, and feelings attendant to *giur* with Jews who came to Judaism through *gerut*.

CHILDREN AND GIUR

The CCAR reaffirms its current practices and standards regarding children and the question of *giur*. Such cases involve: (a) An adopted child, (b) A child born of a mixed marriage.[2]

For the adopted child, the practices of Reform Judaism which pertain to any natural child are recognized as appropriate. (See Solomon B. Freehof, CCAR *Yearbook*, vol. LXV, 1956, pp. 107–110; *Gates of Mitzvah*, CCAR, p. 18).

The current position of the Reform Movement regarding the status of a child born of a mixed marriage was established in 1983:

The Central Conference of American Rabbis declares that the child of one Jewish parent is under the presumption of Jewish descent. This presumption of the Jewish status of the offspring of any mixed marriage is to be established through appropriate and timely public and formal acts of identification with the Jewish faith and people. The performance of these mitzvot serves to commit those who participate in them, both parent and child, to Jewish life.

Depending on circumstances, mitzvot leading toward a positive and exclusive Jewish identity will include entry into the covenant, acquisition of a Hebrew name, Torah study, bar/bat mitzvah and Kabbalat Torah (Confirmation).[3] For those beyond childhood claiming Jewish identity, other public acts or declarations may be added or substituted after consultation with their rabbi.

The above position may be found in the new edition of *The Rabbi's Manual*.

GERUT—THE PROCESS OF BECOMING A JEW

Gerut involves a complex set of variables for each individual. Each person brings his/her own emotional, familial, spiritual, and intellectual needs and background into *gerut*. It is beyond the scope of these guidelines to define any *specifics* regarding how long each process should take or the course of study for it. We offer a consensus of opinion and practice, knowing that the rabbi and prospective *ger/gioret* will ultimately have to define such terms within each given situation. The time required for *giur* will vary depending upon the rabbi and the community's educational program, whether it is a group course or private tutorial, and the prospective *ger/gioret* and his/her specific background in Judaism. With all these variables considered, the least amount of time recommended for *gerut* should be four months, with an average of six to nine months and some situations extended to a full year.

The fundamentals of Judaism which should be taught encompass ritual observances of Shabbat, holy days, festivals, and life cycle *mitzvot* in the home and the synagogue; basic theology and values; Jewish history; liturgy, and Hebrew language. These areas provide the basis of the educational process of *gerut*. The particulars of any course are relative to the community and rabbi. It should be carefully noted to the *ger/gioret* that any course of study is by definition only an introduction to Judaism. Rabbinic involvement in *gerut* beyond an educational level is essential; mere sponsorship in a community course without regular tutorials and meetings is not appropriate. Individuals will undoubtedly require advice, counseling, and encouragement during and *after* their decision-making process.

Since *gerut* involves more than just cognitive leaning, the *ger/gioret* should be encouraged to experience Jewish life by attending Sabbath services regularly and participating in holy day and festival observances and other Jewish communal activities. Opportunities for exposure to Jewish home observance of the Sabbath and festivals should be made available. Finally, the importance of synagogue affiliation and a Jew's communal responsibility should be discussed and emphasized so that the *giur* will be a statement of a communal as well as religious commitment.

GIUR—THE CEREMONY OF WELCOMING

The CCAR requires that the *ger/gioret* declare acceptance of the Jewish faith and people before three adult witnesses made up of no less than one rabbi and two associates or lay people. Such a group might be considered, for those so inclined, as a *bet-din* and function in such a capacity. Some suggest that the use of the *witnesses/bet din* as a part of *giur* is also of great value, for it provides the opportunity to discuss and evaluate with the *ger/gioret* the process of becoming a Jew. This should not take on a critical or defensive tone, for the rabbi should already be aware of the *ger/gioret's* knowledge and commitment.

The traditional *halachic* ritual requirements of *berit milah*, *hatafat dam-berit*, and *tevilah* have not been required practices by most Reform rabbis. There is a long-standing CCAR position which obviates

the necessity for these traditional *halachic* prescriptions.[4] Today, the
spectrum of belief, interpretation and practice within Reform Judaism is broad and diverse. Thus, many members of the Conference now
". . . recognize that there are social, psychological and religious values associated with the traditional rituals and it is recommended that
the rabbi acquaint prospective *gerim* with the *halachic* background and
rationale for *berit milah*, *hatafat dam-berit* and *tevilah* and offer them
the opportunity, if they so desire, to observe these additional rites."[5]

The actual ceremony leading to *gerut* may vary in place, time
and format depending on the rabbi, community, and *ger/gioret*. However, any ceremony should include the rabbi's asking the *ger/gioret*
the following six questions,[6] or using the affirmation which follows:

1. Do you choose to enter the eternal covenant between God
   and the people Israel and to become a Jew of your own free
   will?
2. Do you accept Judaism to the exclusion of all other religious
   faiths and practices?
3. Do you pledge your loyalty to Judaism and to the Jewish
   people under all circumstances?
4. Do you promise to establish a Jewish home and to participate actively in the life of the synagogue and of the Jewish
   community?
5. Do you commit yourself to the pursuit of Torah and Jewish
   knowledge?
6. If you should be blessed with children do you promise to rear
   them as Jews?

Affirmation: I make this affirmation as I enter the eternal covenant
between God and the people of Israel: I choose to become a Jew of
my own free will. I accept Judaism to the exclusion of all other religions, faiths and practices and now pledge my loyalty to Judaism and
the Jewish people under all circumstances. I promise to establish a
Jewish home and participate actively in the life of the synagogue and
the Jewish community. I commit myself to the pursuit of Torah and

Jewish knowledge. If I am blessed with children, I will rear them as Jews.

The ceremony may include appropriate liturgical passages as well as readings dealing with *gerut*, such as Ruth 1:16–17. The rabbi may then choose to speak to the *ger/gioret* welcoming him/her into *Am Yisrael*. As a symbol of the newly acquired Jewish identity, the *ger/gioret* is given a Hebrew name. The Hebrew name should be chosen by the proselyte, and is added to the traditional phrase *ben/bat Avraham Avinu Vesarah Imeinu*.[7] After conferring the name, the ceremony concludes with the *Birkat Kohanim*.

A certificate, *te-udat gerut*, is presented with the appropriate signatures of the rabbi and other witnesses. Three additional copies of the *te-udat gerut* should be kept, one for the synagogue's archives, one for the rabbi's records, and the other for the American Jewish Archives in Cincinnati, Ohio.

Whenever possible and appropriate one should take into consideration the *ger/gioret*'s family and friends. Their presence at the *giur* can be a very positive and supportive act. The rabbi might take the opportunity before or after the ceremony to speak with them to further their understanding and clarify their questions. The relationship developed with the rabbi and *ger/giroet* should continue beyond the ceremony of *giur*.

NOTES

1. *CCAR Yearbook*, 1947, p. 158ff, Solomon Freehof's Report on Mixed Marriage.

2. In reference to the above-stated practice in Reform Judaism, it is essential to explain carefully to parents the variants of this issue as practiced by other branches of Judaism. This is suggested in order to insure a fully sensitized understanding by the parents and, when appropriate, the child.

3. A full description of these and other *mitzvot* can be found in *Gates of Mitzvah* (CCAR, 1979).

4. See *Rabbi's Manual*, 1928 ed., pp. 153–154; *CCAR Yearbook*, vol. I, (1891–1892), p. 36.

5. Statement of the CCAR Committee on *Gerut*, 1978, published in *Gates of Mitzvah*, CCAR, pp. 146–147.

6. These have been suggested as the questions to be used in the new edition of the *Rabbi's Manual*.

7. While the traditional phrase is only *Avraham Avinu*, it is well within the mood of the Movement to be more broadly inclusive. *Berachot* 16b provides us with the generalized terms of patriarch and matriarch:

"*Ein korin avot ela leshelosha ve-ein korin imahot ela le-arba.*"

"The term 'patriarch' is applied only to three and the term 'matriarchs' only to four." Therefore, references to both patriarchal and matriarchal names are appropriate.

ORTHODOX GUIDELINES

CONVERSION GUIDELINES FOR THE RABBI DRAFTED BY THE RCA COMMISSION ON GERUT

I. The Interview

A. Three Steps
1. Discussion covering the following areas:
   a. Religious and educational background
   b. Familial relationships
   c. Motivations, e.g., marriage, friends, search for spiritual meaning
   d. Economic and occupational situation
2. General outlines of Jewish concepts and practices
   a. Concept and role of G-d
   b. Shabbat, Kashrut, Tefillah, Taharat hamishpacha
   c. Ethical values
   d. Bible and Talmud: Sources of Halakha
3. Outlining a program of studies and religious and cultural experiences

B. One preliminary interview will most likely be inadequate. The interviewing rabbi requires additional time for probing and for digesting both the information and the impressions made by the candidate. And furthermore, the prospective candidate may not be relaxed during the first session, and in order to do him or her justice, more than one session would be in order. It may also be necessary for the interviewing rabbi to consult a colleague, Bet Din or a special committee for their Chavas Daas. This point will be taken up later in the memorandum.

II. Required Schedule of Studies and Religious Experiences

A. The candidate must undertake a formal program of studies. He/she should enroll in the synagogue's adult education program and if it is inadequate or unavailable, he/she should enroll in an institute of Jewish studies.

1. In areas where such formal studies are non-existent, a private tutor should be engaged.

2. Should the sponsoring rabbi be the tutor in an area where other options for formal instruction are available? Most members of the commission are of the opinion that it is preferable for the rabbi to undertake the task. In this way, the rabbi becomes the spiritual mentor of the candidate and the relationship will continue after the conversion process is completed as well as after it, for the convert will require continued guidance and encouragement until he/she is fully acclimated to the new situation.

The other view is that the sponsoring rabbi should not be the private tutor. The two roles, namely that of a formal tutor and that of a spiritual mentor should not be confused. The rabbi should, however, schedule periodic meetings at which time he will assess the candidate's progress, discuss any questions he may have and clarify points in an informal atmosphere. The spiritual relationship can be forged in the same manner as a rabbi does with congregants in general.

B. The following is a minimum schedule of skills and topics to be covered:

    1. Hebrew reading—a moderate fluency is required

    2. Basic Tefillot, e.g. Shema, Shemoneh Esrai, Berachot, Birkat Hamazon, Kiddush

    3. Selections from the Torah, e.g., Parashat Hashavua with commentary: Nach—a bird's-eye view in the vernacular.

    4. Fundamental Halakhot—Shabbat, Kashrut, Taharat Hamishpacha, Tzedakah, Yomim Tovim, Mitzvot Bein Adam L'Chavera.

    5. A cursory reading on Jewish history

C. Outline of religious concepts

    1. Nature of G-d

    2. Reward and Punishment

    3. Mashiach

    4. Torah Min Hashamayim

    5. Torah She B'Al Peh

    6. Ethical and moral principles

    7. Peoplehood of Israel

    8. Eretz Israel

D. The following experiences are recommended:

    1. Weekly Shabbat morning shul attendance and weekday morning shul attendance (at least once a week).

    2. Monthly invitation for a Shabbat at a religious home

    3. Three Yom Tov invitations

E. A minimum of one year of study and experiences are recommended

    1. At mid-point the candidate should meet with a committee of three rabbanim to determine the level of knowledge and the seriousness of the motivation. It may also be necessary to decide whether additional requirements are advisable.

III. Procedures for the Conversion Act

A. A Bet Din of three rabbanim should make a thorough investigation of the attitudes of the candidate and the materials studied.

A written list of questions should be prepared in advance of the meeting.

B. Commitments should be made regarding the following: Shabbat, Kashrut, Taharat Hamishpachah, Tefillah, Tzedaka, Yeshiva education for their children and future children.

    1. Additional commitments: Membership in an orthodox shul, and residing within walking distance of a shul.

    2. Both an oral and a written commitment should be made.

IV. Bet Din, etc.

A. The RCA Bet Din or a specially appointed commission on Gerut procedures should serve as the formal consultation body for Halakhic questions on Gerut for RCA members.

B. It is recommended that the already existing Batei Din in the several cities across the country shall be asked to serve as regional Batei Din. In those regions where formal Batei Din are absent, regional Batei Din shall be established under the guidance of the national office.

    1. The function of these regional Batei Din shall be twofold: First, they or their designees shall supervise conversion procedures.

Second, they shall advise the regional rabbanim on Halakha and L'Fi R'os Eyney Ha Bet Din guide them in cases requiring special Halakhic application.

C. The Conversion Bet Din should consist solely of rabbanim.

D. The commission recommends that fees should not be received for conversions.

E. If one adopting parent is non-Jewish and is not intending to convert, the adopted child should not be converted.

F. Minimum Halakhic standard for RCA acceptance of conversion of adopted children should be as follows:

    1. Kashrus.

    2. Encourage Shabbat observance.

    3. Membership in an Orthodox shul within walking distance.

4. Yeshiva education for the child.
It is suggested that the parents should be urged to accept Shmirat Shabbat.

V. Purpose of Guidelines

The approval of the Guidelines will be an important step in establishing minimum Halakhic guidelines for Gerut. The Guidelines incorporate both Halakhic positions and supplementary conditions to enhance and strengthen the meaning and procedure of Gerut. In special situations the national or regional bodies will rule in accordance to the principle of L'Fi R'os Eyney Ha Bet Din. Conversions which conform to the Guidelines will receive the imprimatur of the national office.

RECONSTRUCTIONIST GUIDELINES

These Guidelines were prepared by the Reconstructionist Rabbinical Association and were approved at its Annual Convention in Philadelphia on January 16, 1979/17 Tevet 5739.

I. Introduction

We understand conversion to be a process, the goal of which is a wholehearted and informed acceptance of Judaism for its own sake. We consider the formal adoption of Judaism by a person who has been born a non-Jew to be a decision which is to be accorded respect and a process to be invested with seriousness of purpose and dignity.

The preparation, counselling and final ceremonies should give expression to the fact that even though conversion to Judaism is primarily a religious act, its dimensions and consequences are more encompassing. A person seeking to become a Jew should be sensitized to the realization and manifest an awareness that there is involved also an act of incorporation into a people whose civilizational values are now entrusted to him/her to internalize and express in attitude and practice.

We deem it the responsibility of Jewish congregations and of the Jewish community at large to welcome warmly into their midst, and involve in all their activities, persons who have converted to Judaism.

II. Conversion for the Sake of Marriage

We recognize that the decision to convert is in each case unique and involves a multitude of feelings, influences, motivations, and purposes. We deem marriage to a Jewish partner to be a justifiable and commendable initial reason for conversion. It must be, of course, evident that the candidate, after proper instruction and counselling, freely chooses to become a Jew. Conversions for the sake of marriage may serve to strengthen the marital relationship (*Shelom Bayit*) and can also serve to enrich Judaism and enlarge the Jewish people. A significant number of converts, through marriage, have become truly dedicated Jews (*Gerei Tzedek*).

III. Outreach to Converts

Every possible outreach effort should be made to incorporate warmly into the Jewish community those people interested in conversion to Judaism, especially non-Jewish spouses of Jews.

IV. Process of Preparation

1. The duration of the process of preparing a candidate for conversion will be at the sponsoring rabbi's discretion. It is suggested that it last between six months and a year, affording the candidate the opportunity of both theoretical Jewish learning and the personal experience of a major portion of the Jewish calendar cycle.

2. The learning process should include both group instruction (where possible) and individual tutorials and counselling. Additional

participation in adult education programs should be encouraged, as well as attendance at services and participation in other areas of Jewish communal, religious and cultural life.

3. When the prospective convert is married to or contemplating marriage to a Jew, the Jewish partner should also participate in the preparation process.

4. The role of the rabbi in the conversion process should not be limited to the transmission of information, but should take into account the varied emotional needs on the part of the convert and his/her Jewish spouse or friend and their respective family relations.

V. Procedural Guidelines

1. We endorse *T'vilah* (ritual immersion) as an initiatory rite, for both men and women proselytes.

2. Non-circumcised male proselytes should be circumcised *L'ot B'rit* if there is no extraordinary physical or emotional hazard.

3. The practice of *Hatafat Dam B'rit* (symbolic circumcision on already circumcised males) will be at the discretion of the sponsoring rabbi.

4. The proselyte should be encouraged to make a *tzedakah* offering to a Jewish cause, in keeping with an ancient Jewish custom (cf. *Gerim* 2:5).

5. The *Beit Din* should consist of three adult Jews, of which at least one should be a rabbi. Male and female alike may serve in a Reconstructionist *Beit Din*.

6. The function of the *Beit Din* will not be primarily to put the candidate through a "dissertation defense" type of examination, but to elicit from him/her thoughts and feelings, to discuss areas of concern and interest, offer encouragement and counsel, and reiterate the responsibilities of involvement with the Jewish people and Judaism. The *Beit Din* experience should be warm and memorable.

7. A religious ceremony of acceptance of Judaism should be celebrated following the completion of ritual requirements and the *Beit Din* session. These have been usually private ceremonies, but

some may wish to consider a group and/or public ceremony of conversion. Such a religious service would emphasize the covenantal link established mutually between the convert and the Jewish people, and it would have the additional positive function of sensitizing the community to the need to welcome and support the convert (*Hakhnasat Hager*). Certain holidays such as Hanukkah, Shavuot, Simhat Torah lend themselves particularly to such a ceremony.

8. The ceremony should include a "Declaration of Acceptance of Judaism" on the part of the convert. The ritual may be enriched with appropriate selections from classic or contemporary Jewish sources. The rabbi or a member of the congregation may wish to address the candidate, who, in turn, might want to make a personal statement.

9. A Hebrew name is to be selected by the convert, followed by the expression: "ben/bat Avraham avinu v'Sarah imenu."

10. A document, signed by the three members of the *Beit Din*, officially certifying the conversion should be given to the convert, and copies kept in congregational and the Movement's records. It is suggested that copies be also kept in the personal records of the rabbi.

VI. General Remarks

1. The convert is to be considered a full Jew, with all the privileges and responsibilities this identity entails.

2. Since Reconstructionism does not consider applicable the division of Jews into the categories of Kohen, Levi and Yisrael, laws pertaining to prohibited marriages between converts and the priestly class are not binding.

3. In the spirit of *K'lal Yisrael*, the Reconstructionist Movement recognizes conversions performed under the sponsorship of bona fide rabbis or movements within the Jewish community, whether or not similar conditions as those upheld by the Reconstructionist rabbi or Movement were recognized.

4. If one parent is Jewish, either mother or father, the offspring is to be regarded as Jewish and should undergo the rites prescribed

by our tradition (*B'rit Milah* for boys, or a covenantal naming ceremony for girls); but no special conversion procedure is required.

CONSERVATIVE GUIDELINES

Inquiries about conversion guidelines by the Conservative movement should be addressed to the Secretary of the Committee on Jewish Law and Standards, c/o The Rabbinical Assembly, 3080 Broadway, New York, NY 10027.

Index

About the Author

Lawrence J. Epstein is a professor of English at Suffolk Community College in Selden, New York. The author of *Samuel Goldwyn* (1981), *Zion's Call* (1984), *A Treasury of Jewish Anecdotes* (1989), *The Theory and Practice of Welcoming Converts to Judaism* (1992), and *A Treasury of Jewish Inspirational Stories* (1993), he has also written more than 100 articles, stories, and reviews on Jewish life that have been published in major Jewish periodicals. Dr. Epstein served as Middle East advisor to a United States congressman from 1981 to 1986 and currently lives in New York State, with his wife, Sharon, and their four children.